THE **KEEPER** OF **FAMILIES**

Jean Heringman Willacy's
Afghan Diaries

SUE HERINGMAN

authorHOUSE®

AuthorHouse™ UK
1663 Liberty Drive
Bloomington, IN 47403 USA
www.authorhouse.co.uk
Phone: 0800.197.4150

Published by AuthorHouse 01/17/2019

ISBN: 978-1-7283-8064-3 (sc)
ISBN: 978-1-7283-8063-6 (hc)
ISBN: 978-1-7283-8065-0 (e)

Contents

Disclaimer ix

Foreword xiii

Preface xv

Acknowledgements xix

Endorsement xxi

Prologue: Who Is Jean? xxiii

Jean's Photographic Timeline xxvii

Map of Afghanistan xxix

PART 1
Before the Russians

Jean the Businesswoman... 1

   Of Hippy Coats and Liquorice Root 1

   Karakul in Kunduz 3

   German Furriers Visit Afghanistan 24

   A Fashion Show in Kabul 25

   Trip to the Northwest Frontier.............................. 26

Jean Sallies Forth 42

   A Misadventure or Two... 42

   From the Streets of Kabul 46

PART 2
The Communist Coup

"And So the Stage Was Set ..." 99

I Am an Eyewitness 104

Life in the New Soviet Puppet State of Afghanistan.............................. 115
Young, Modern, and Afghan 130

PART 3
The Soviet Invasion

Am I Too Old? 165
Map of Refugee Camps in Pakistan 192
Into the Camps... 193

PART 4
Torn Apart

Habiba: "We Are Always Afraid!" 227
Seeta: A Widow's Struggle 246
Ghulam: "We are Being Deported!" 251
Soraya: The Forgotten "Red-Tape Refugees" 264

PART 5
Memories of Home, Dreams of Homecoming

An Exhibition in Paris 287
The Artwork of War by Afghan Refugee Children 290
The Drawings 291
The Children 299

PART 6
Battling the Bureaucrats

The Afghan Relief Programme in Pakistan by Nancy Hatch Dupree ... 307
Dialogues with Officialdom 311
Jean's Challenge to the Aid Agencies 318

PART 7
Epilogue

Self-Discovery 325

APPENDICES

Jean's Afghan Timeline 329
Glossary 331
Index..335

Disclaimer

Whilst all the stories in this book are true, to protect the anonymity and privacy of the people who figure in them, I have changed some names, dates, places of residence, occupations, and other identifying details.

I have also taken the artistic license of completing two of the refugees' stories from Jean's notes. To aid the reader, I have added an approximate timeline that corresponds to the current events mentioned.

This is a work of memoir and love. The opinions expressed in this book are solely those of my mother and those people whom she quotes or to whom she refers.

—Sue Heringman

For Lain, my son.
For my sisters, Anne and Kay.
And for all Afghan refugees
with whom we share
in loving memory
the remarkable woman who was
Our Mom, Mère, Nana,
and
Our dear, "deariest" Mother.

Foreword

Known as the "Grandmother of Afghanistan", the late Nancy Hatch Dupree (1929–2017) was an internationally acclaimed American scholar, author, and authority on Afghan history and culture. She founded both the Afghanistan Center at Kabul University and its partner, the Louis and Nancy Hatch Dupree Foundation. She and Jean met in Kabul, and again in Peshawar during the Afghan-Soviet war years. When dealing with the refugee crisis in Pakistan, they shared many of the same concerns and frustrations. Nancy was an important influence on Jean and her work, and, at my invitation, very graciously agreed to write this foreword.—S.H.

It is a pleasure to welcome this account of life in Afghan refugee camps by an observer dedicated to easing as well as reporting the traumas of exile and the hardships of making do in crowded, alien environments. Over the long years when this displaced Afghan population gained unhappy repute for being the world's largest concentration of refugees from a single country, a profusion of critiques, official reports, and analyses were written. None focuses so dramatically on the emotional human dimension as do these on-the-spot diary notes of Jean Heringman Willacy. *The Keeper of Families* is a notable addition to the study of displacement which, sadly, continues to be a major human issue of growing proportions.

The refugee saga began with the 27 April 1978 Saur Revolution, staged by left-oriented urban intellectuals in Kabul. Their heavy-handed attempts to impose reforms on a closely knit, kin-related, rural population met with early dissent that soon flared into an open conflict that prompted the Soviet Union to invade in December 1979. Systematic ground and air offensives by the Soviets and their Afghan surrogates flattened villages and deliberately destroyed the agrarian infrastructure by decimating livestock and depopulating rural areas. The entire socio-economic framework of the country was imperilled.

At its peak, between January to June 1981, 4,500 Afghans crossed the Pakistan border daily. Another 1.5 million went to Iran; others scattered to havens around the world. All told, one-third of Afghanistan's pre-war population of approximately 15 million resided in host countries outside their homeland.

Jean went to Pakistan following the many close, valued friends she had made from the time when she founded her own export company, JW Enterprises, in Kabul. These days, the world moves from crisis to crisis with such rapidity that one is overshadowed by the next before it can be fully understood. Jean's perspectives on the human dimension of displacement will make sombre reading for those now dealing with the current manifestation of exile posed by those anxiously leaving Afghanistan by their own choice. The refugees in former days had faith that the jihad would dispatch the invaders; most fully expected to return. Those who leave today, however, are selling all their properties and making a permanent break, as they leave nothing to return to. Yet, the fields that beckon are not always green. New Jean-type reporting is needed to deal with this serious new crisis.

Nancy Hatch Dupree
Executive Coordinator
Afghanistan Center at Kabul University
Kabul, Afghanistan
14 January 2017

Preface

When my mother died, at the age of eighty-four, she left her family an unusual legacy: a book in waiting. *The Keeper of Families: Jean Heringman Willacy's Afghan Diaries* documents the latter, most incongruous part of Jean's life, first as an unlikely businesswoman in Afghanistan before the Soviet invasion (1967–1980) and afterwards as an independent benefactor inside the Afghan refugee camps of Pakistan and in those Western cities granting asylum (1980–1993). More than just diaries, they comprise a unique collection of rare eye-witness accounts; notebooks; war bulletins; personal letters; spontaneous, on-the-street tape recordings; formal interviews; children's wartime drawings; and innumerable photographs. Together, they vividly capture daily life in a range of times and places and give singular insight into this turbulent period of history.

The diary entries abound with Jean's impassioned politics, shrewd observations, and self-deprecating humour. Notes for meetings with senior government officials are followed by homely reminders to polish her shoes. Often there is an entry in unfamiliar handwriting which conjures up a picture of her thrusting her notebook at her "source" and encouraging the person to write down his or her details, sketch a map, or record a recipe. She compiled an astounding database of business cards that reflects not only the prodigious number of people she met but also the wide range of her interests and efforts. Jean was a "fixer", a natural facilitator with the knack of connecting the right people to each other to try to accomplish whatever was needed. Her to-do (aka *can-do*) lists were legendary, a testimony to her seemingly boundless energy and perseverance.

When her adventurous life in Afghanistan ended in the horrors of the military coup that led to the Soviet invasion, she suddenly found herself plunged headlong into the Afghan refugee crisis. Compelled by the despair and compassion she felt for her many Afghan friends, Jean resolutely dedicated herself, for no less than the next twenty years, to the ever-growing number of war refugees seeking her help. What emerges is the story of their struggle and how, in trying to overcome the ravages of loss and exile, their lives came to be inextricably bound together with a love as strong as any family tie.

On visits to my mother at her cottage in Dorset, I met many of the Afghans whom she sponsored and, sadly, heard the plight of many others. Every morning over breakfast, she would read their letters aloud: "Please! I have lost everything. I feel so alone in this large world." Such were the pleas Jean received daily, pleas that never went unanswered. She could be a formidable foe when fighting the tyranny of bureaucracy but was a staunch ally to all whom she befriended. At times, she could also be headstrong; sometimes her good intentions failed. Yet, she never gave up.

I helped to edit and attended some of Jean's talks that captivated her audiences. She made me part of her work, and I like to think that I helped to support her in it. Tragically, so much of what she experienced and witnessed is still relevant today. Before she died she said, "I have a lifetime of memories and experiences during my years in Afghanistan and would deeply love seeing something rewarding from those days."

I felt I owed it to Jean and to her adoptive family to make every effort to transcribe all the diary material and publish her compelling narrative with everything she had so lovingly preserved of their lives. In this way, they could live on and touch other people's lives with their stories, even if under the different names and guises that Jean gave them in order to protect their identities. This book is a tribute to the voices of those Afghan refugees as much as it is to Jean's.

The illustrations are but a small selection from Jean's extensive slide collection and an 'artwork of war' project she devised for Afghan refugee children. Due to the ongoing conflicts, Jean was never able to fulfil her dream of returning to Afghanistan. However, I have donated 3,000 of her slides and copies of all the children's wartime drawings to the Nancy and Louis Hatch Dupree Foundation at Kabul University where they can be displayed, appreciated, and preserved. Nancy Hatch Dupree was the first person to encourage Jean in her work, so, in some poetic way, Jean has come full circle and returned to the land that she so loved and where she was so happy.

In today's troubled world, when we ask ourselves what we can do, Jean with her indomitable spirit stands as a source of inspiration for how one individual can make a difference and, no matter how unlikely, become an ambassador for humanity. At the best of times, she did effect life-transforming changes and, at the very least, she gave desperate people hope. Small wonder that Jean was considered by the people she championed as "Our Dear Mother, The Keeper of Families".

Sue Heringman
Dorset, 2017

Acknowledgements

Compiling and transcribing my mother's Afghan diaries, together with all the related Afghan material discovered after her death, has been a labour of love of many years. In pursuit of this project, I have been very fortunate to have had the full support, and patience—bordering on endurance—of my husband, Richard Inverne, senior lecturer in Performing Arts at Solent University Southampton. His judicious advice, keen editorial eye, and figurative red pen have been as invaluable as his care of me throughout this endeavour.

Whenever in need of confidence-boosting or memory-checking, I could always rely on my son and my sisters, for which I will always be grateful. Thank you, Kay, for your artistic input and for selecting the best of the slides, and you, Anne, for being an invaluable sounding board and expert in-house proofreader. Lain, I especially want to thank you for choosing to follow, like your grandmother, the "road less travelled" to reach out to others.

I am deeply indebted to the late Nancy Hatch Dupree, known as the "Grandmother of Afghanistan", for her encouragement and steadfast belief in the value of the diaries. She herself made several attempts on my behalf to find a publisher. Her own contribution to the book regarding the non-governmental organizations in Pakistan greatly enhances Jean's description of their work in the Afghan refugee camps. Her recent death is a huge loss, and my great regret is that she will not be able to see the book in its final form.

One of the highlights of embarking on this project has been making the acquaintance of the wonderful Duggie Dupree Gill, discovering shared concerns and her own deep compassion for refugees. Granting me publishing permission at the eleventh hour, together with her personal endorsement of the value of the book, was a boon of the highest order.

It has been a pleasure to correspond with Mr Abdul Rahman, director of the Louis and Nancy Hatch Dupree Foundation at the Afghanistan Center at Kabul University. He kindly translated the writing on the children's drawings and provided me with much needed information. I will always be grateful to him for giving Jean's's slide collection its rightful place in Afghanistan and for digitizing much of it to make it readily accessible.

My warmest thanks must also be extended to Afghanaid and the International Medical Corps for granting permission for the publication of refugee-related letters written to Jean.

At AuthorHouse I have been most fortunate to have had Dorothy Lee as my CIC/Publishing Service Associate. No question or problem was ever too much trouble, and Dorothy was nothing less than patience itself. I owe her a debt of gratitude for making the book look even better than how I envisioned it.

To Will Bartola, Senior Marketing Consultant and also of AuthorHouse, I give heartfelt thanks for his taking Jean's life and work to heart, and for working so hard to ensure that her story will have as wide a readership as possible.

This book would not have been possible in its present form without the inestimable aid and encouragement of Cynthia Wolfe, my editorial associate at AuthorHouse. Working with her has been a thoroughly enjoyable and edifying experience. In addition to her professional expertise, it was Cynthia's understanding of Jean's character that enabled us to bring together all the strands of a rich, multi-layered life, and render a complicated text into a cohesive narrative.

The greatest thanks of all go to my mother herself, for all I learned from her and hope to have passed on.

Endorsement

"Over the long years when the displaced Afghan population gained unhappy repute for being the world's largest concentration of refugees from a single country, a profusion of critiques, official reports and analyses were written. None focuses so dramatically on the emotional human dimension as do these on-the-spot diary notes of Jean Heringman Willacy. *The Keeper of Families* is a notable addition to the study of displacement which, sadly, continues to be a major human issue of growing proportions. New Jean-type reporting is needed."

Nancy Hatch Dupree (1929–2017), founder of the Afghanistan Centre at Kabul University and acclaimed historian known as the 'Grandmother of Afghanistan.'

Prologue: Who Is Jean?

It is the 1960s, and Jean Heringman, a middle-aged American housewife, finds herself divorced and alone. How does she end up conducting business in Afghanistan? What is she doing in Kabul on the very day of a bloody military coup? What does she experience in the new Soviet puppet state? And how is she caught up in the terrible exodus of refugees following the Russian invasion of Afghanistan? Meet Jean.

Born in Chicago in 1919, Jean grew up, the elder of two sisters, in a comfortable middle-class family. A tall, striking beauty with two years of finishing school behind her, she enjoyed a busy and fashionable social life. As a hobby, she helped out at a photographic studio where she found she had a natural talent for photography.

Yet, she yearned for a life of travel and adventure. She would later describe how she marked her dreamed-of destinations on a world globe until it bristled with coloured pins. The closest she got at the time was working as ground crew for American Airlines during World War II. Her job was overseeing consignments of munitions and medical supplies being airlifted to troops overseas and, when necessary, fearlessly bumping off any passenger from a flight—once, even the first lady, Mrs Eleanor Roosevelt.

Forgoing the obvious career as a travel photographer, she married an up-and-coming young surgeon, Craig Heringman, with whom she raised three daughters. The family lived in Los Angeles where Jean's interest in world affairs led her to serve as an active member on many boards and committees of international organizations for cultural, educational, and charitable causes. A gracious hostess, her home was always open, especially to foreign guests, some of whom were seeking political asylum.

Following her divorce and much soul-searching, Jean reinvented herself as a modern version of the Victorian lady traveller. Paintbox and sketchbook gave way to camera bag and modest little tape recorder. Armed with these and an immense curiosity, she embarked upon what would become the adventure of a lifetime and the very antithesis of her previous lifestyle. Her passion to be a self-styled roving reporter led her to document everything and everyone she encountered through tape recordings, photographs, handwritten notes, and letters.

Enthralled by mountains, Jean journeyed dauntlessly through the countries spanned by the Himalayas. She met her kismet in Kabul, falling headlong in love with the wild, rugged landscape and the colourful vitality of the Afghan people. There she also met and became the lifetime partner of Englishman Henry Willacy, adding his surname to hers. At that time, Henry was in charge of overseeing the *karakul[1]* wool trade in Afghanistan for Hudson's Bay Fur Company. Jean Heringman Willacy's Afghan diaries began.

In order to remain in Afghanistan, Jean boldly began her own business venture. Through JW Enterprises, she imported cosmetics and English-language books from the US and the UK and exported liquorice root and *postinchas*, the colourful, fur-trimmed Afghan coats that were then so popular in those two countries. Despite her lack of experience and the predominantly male Afghan business world, her company was a resounding success—so much so that it enabled her to set up an embroidery cottage industry for the impoverished widows she was meeting on Henry's business trips to the remote karakul sheep districts. When she and Henry were nearing retirement age, they relocated to a cottage in Dorset, England, but continued to work and travel in Afghanistan.

These carefree and happiest of years came brutally to an end in April 1978 with the bloody communist coup that led to the Soviet invasion. Caught up in the maelstrom of friends suddenly becoming refugees, Jean's compassion and despair led her from the role of businesswoman to that of self-appointed benefactor. Despite much anguished self-doubt over being "too old" or "unqualified", Jean spent the next twenty years of her life befriending, sponsoring, and recording the lives of the stateless and the persecuted. An angry witness to the sometimes impersonal and

---

[1] . A breed of sheep highly prized for its curly grey and unusually soft, silky fleece. (*Where Jean uses terms in Pashto, Farsi or Urdu, her spelling and definitions have been respected.*)

ineffective side of aid programmes, she dedicated herself not to a cause, but to desperate individuals, helping them to rebuild their lives with dignity and to realize their dreams and aspirations. She became "The Keeper of Families".

As incongruous as it may seem for one lone, Western woman in her sixties, Jean embraced this commitment. Undaunted, she did not shy away from sharing the squalid living conditions of the refugee camps in Pakistan or, even at risk to herself, from smuggling precious identity papers over the border. She generously used her own funds and ingenuity to help improve the welfare of Afghan refugees, including those living in exile, and never tired of trying to find them new homes abroad.

Especially concerned about the plight of Afghan refugee women and children, Jean also put her talents as a photographer to good use for numerous successful fundraising projects. The most ambitious was a Paris exhibition, organized with Médécins du Monde, that featured her slides and a collection of Afghan children's wartime drawings.

In 1990, Jean suffered a near fatal car accident and was in hospital for several months. Determined as ever, she made a remarkable recovery and continued to keep in touch with her extended Afghan family and to do battle with the bureaucrats. For the next decade, she ceaselessly telephoned, made visits, wrote letters, and shuttled back and forth among head offices in Peshawar, London, and Washington to challenge the aid agencies and fiercely harangue government officials over immigration quotas, sponsorships, and red tape.

When no longer able to explore the world as before, Jean spent the last few years of her life at her home in Dorset. Her great heart gave out on 17 August 2004.

Jean's Photographic Timeline

Jean in the 1950s

Jean at 48 in Kabul

Jean at 56 in Kabul

Jean at 68 in Peshawar

Jean at 75, Visiting Friends and Family in California

Jean at 80,
Dorset, England

Map of Afghanistan

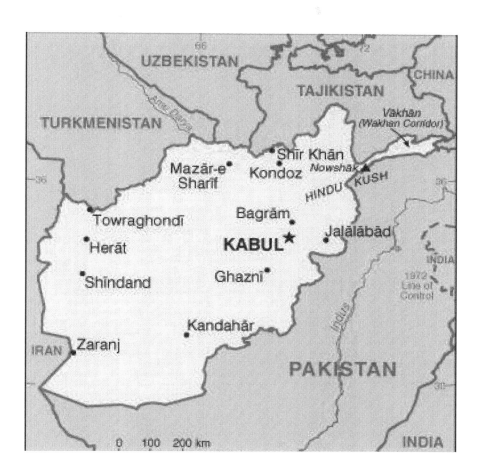

"I have a lifetime of memories and experiences during my years in Afghanistan and would deeply love seeing something rewarding from those days." —J. H. W.

PART 1

Before the Russians

Jean the Businesswoman

OF HIPPY COATS AND LIQUORICE ROOT

Beginning with a handshake in Kabul, Jean describes the novelty of running her first and only business venture, JW Enterprises.

Between 1967 and 1980, I lived in Afghanistan. I was captivated by this incredible mountainous country from my first glimpse of it and felt an urge to see and learn more of its beautiful and isolated landscape, its culture, its history, and its people. I felt I had to find a way to stay there and to support myself.

In this, I was very lucky to meet Azad, an Afghan merchant who owned two of what he called "departmental stores". His stock consisted of men's and ladies' clothing, which he bought from London wholesalers, Marks and Spencer, and from suppliers in Germany and Japan. The difficulty was getting the goods to Kabul within a reasonable time. His "battle" was moving his purchases through the complex custom procedures and onto the infrequent flights to Kabul.

We talked at some length about our two problems, and finally, he offered a solution which satisfied us both. "I'll help you," he said, "if you'll help me." He suggested that I start a business exporting the postincha, the Afghan winter coat made of colourful, hand-embroidered sheepskin on the outside and lined with soft, karakul lambswool on the inside. I was shown samples, thought this a good idea, and asked what would be required of me in return. He asked if I would agree to supervise the purchasing of his articles and get them through customs and onto the next available plane.

1

In return, he would hire tailors to make the coats and arrange for the embroidery, and he would see them packed and shipped off to England. We opened a joint bank account, each putting in £50. We shook hands solemnly and declared ourselves in business. I named my company JW Enterprises—J for me and W for Henry.[2]

Working with "tailors" who didn't understand that both sleeves had to be the same length, that hems must be even, and that English ladies were not all the same size was both frustrating and funny, not to mention what to do about the very strong sheepskin smells which the London experts knew how to eliminate (at too expensive a price) but the Afghan tailors did not. In the end, I switched from exporting the coats to England and did rather well in San Francisco where the hippies loved them. At the same time, I was able to juggle buying trips for Azad, and both of us were very pleased. We remained friends for years, and I came to know his family very well.

Through a mutual friend, I also began to export liquorice root to the UK, learning about glycerine content, pharmaceutical and confectionary uses, impurities, market prices, and shipping methods. The best quality came from the northern town of Maimana and the central highlands of Hazarajat and could be procured at the end of July or the beginning of August. My first deal was for a shipment to Japan at $800 per ton. I arranged for the goods to travel from Afghanistan by land route to Karachi.

By 1977, I was also importing various goods to Afghanistan, especially cosmetics such as Elizabeth Arden and Max Factor. Other business propositions included Persian/Pashto typewriters, bicycles, and English-language books and tapes. Most amusingly, I would sometimes be approached with unusual requests such as introducing the artificial insemination of thoroughbred riding horses or researching ways to ship good breeds of milking cows!

What I most enjoyed were the trips to the remote karakul sheep districts, as they enabled me to create employment for widows who helped with the embroidery work on the coats. One of the projects that grew out of this links our UK Women's Institute (WI) with its Afghan equivalent, the Democratic Organization of Afghan Women. The idea is to share our English ways of daily, rural life, following the cycle of the year, telling

---

[2] . Henry Willacy, Jean's lifetime partner.

2

what we do and how and giving advice. Whereas governments become entangled politically and strangled by their individual bureaucratic systems, thus unable to implement their programmes, we can perhaps accomplish specific things by cutting right across the red tape—women, women!

KARAKUL IN KUNDUZ

In this unique travelogue on tape, the excitement heard in Jean's voice reveals as much about her thrill of discovery as her curiosity to learn all she could about her brave new world.

Jean: *(into the microphone)* This is my first karakul business trip with Henry and Azad, and we are driving to the northern town of Kunduz. As an expert in the fur trade for Hudson's Bay Fur Company here, it's Henry's job to visit the local furriers, inspect the tanneries and the flocks of sheep, and, hopefully, of course, close any deals to secure a ready supply of the silky, soft lambswool fleeces and tanned hides. Of course, I'm taking my trusty little tape recorder with us.

At the Kabul Bazaar. Horns honking. Noise of crowd.

Jean: This is how one bargains Afghan style. In this case, Azad is buying knives.

Azad: I actually don't bargain with these people.

Jean: *(surprised)* No?

Azad: No, because I want to encourage them. Otherwise, usually for the big business, I do.

Henry: Yes, exactly.

Jean: But for this, you take the set price.

Azad: Yes, I take.

Conversation between Azad and vendor in Farsi.

Jean: And we are also buying cucumbers. So, the knives will cut the cucumbers and we'll have a delicious feast as soon as we get into a cool place.

Azad: (*to the vendor*) *Namaq.* Namaq means sold.

Vendor: Namaq.

Rustle of notes being exchanged.

Azad: That's better.

Jean: How much were the six cucumbers?

Azad: Each cucumber was one afghani.

Henry: Sounds very cheap.

Jean: (*with a mouthful*) Umm, they're marvellous cucumbers! Now we're on our way again: up to the Salang Pass![3]

Azad: We usually on the big journey using the cucumbers as if water, because there are many places where not enough water, so in the hot season we are using them. Good for the thirsty.

Henry: It's a great idea.

---

[3] . A spectacular high mountain pass in the Hindu Kush Range, 12,723 feet above sea level.

4

Jean: Oh, it's marvellous! They're so juicy and not sweet; quenches the thirst wonderfully. Mmmm!

Horns honking. They stop at a vendor's stall. Azad and vendor converse.

Azad: Cheese.

Jean: Hmm?

Azad: Very good cheese. Is hard and stay very long time. Is very good.

Jean: Now we've stopped. What sort of a place do you call this, Azad? It's like a picnic ground.

Azad: This is the beginning of the Salang Road. The people, they stop here to get refreshing and water and tea or something.

Jean: And we're sitting at a wooden table under the mulberry trees in the lovely cool shade, and Azad has just ordered some food for us before we go on up into the Salang Pass. We've already entered a little bit of the gorge, and the water is on the left-hand side, running very fast and cascading down from the melting snow. It makes the surrounding area very fertile. And it zigzags as it comes down. I imagine the road will be very twisty and winding and very high. A little girl has just come along offering us some mulberries, which are very popular here. She has on pretty pink plastic shoes and a very pretty smile.

Sound of running water.

Azad: After the food we will have, what do you call them?

Jean: Mulberries.

Azad: Mulberries. And then, if you like, we will have tea, and then we start to climbing up the Salang.

Jean: So, we have just completed a most marvellous lunch with the most delicious rice I've had in Afghanistan. It's very white and very dry, fluffy, and light in texture, and we had several different kinds of kebabs with lovely golden simmered onions and fruit and tea, and the yoghurt … well, I passed by. And now we are about to take off for the Salang Pass. I see on my right a most brilliantly coloured bus, and I'm going over to take a photograph of it.

Sound of mountain rapids.

Jean: (*breathless*) We're standing on a rock jutting out into this rushing torrent of water in the Salang Pass area, and in the distance I can see the snow-covered mountains and a beautiful, lush green valley on either side of the gorge which the riverbed cuts through. The water is icy, icy cold, and the air is cool from the spray. The sun is bright and warm; it's the most beautiful of days!

We're back in the car now, and to try to describe the scenery that we are travelling through is a very difficult task because it's so magnificent, so grand, so rugged and wild and beautiful. Leaving Kabul, we drove through broad, flat valleys of wheat and rice fields, many vineyards and fruit orchards, the entire area ringed by low mountains in the distance. It seems to take forever to reach them. They're all snow-capped and remain snow-capped for the entire year.

Having left Kabul, which this morning had a temperature of ninety-two degrees, we are now travelling through a very narrow gorge formed by the river, and on either side of us are large swathes of snow. As we start a very steep ascent, we leave the farmland part of the gorge behind and the terrain becomes much more rocky and barren as we go higher.

We are now travelling through the Salang Tunnel, just beneath the mountain pass itself. It is situated at the highest point of any tunnel in the world, some eleven to twelve thousand feet. It's a magnificent piece of engineering, done by the Russians with the Afghans supplying most of the labour. It must have cost a great deal of money and took some seven or eight years to build, finishing in 1964.

Azad: This pass is one only north-south connection in the country and is all the year long open.

Jean: The snow lies on top of the tunnel and, as we go around a curve, I can see it there. As it melts, it falls off down the mountain slopes forming trickles of water which collect and gather force and momentum until they become the rushing torrent at the bottom of the pass. *Inshallah*—God willing—no avalanches today!

This portion of the tunnel is open on the side, and I can see across to the other side of the gorge, but now we're entering a closed-in section that has been engineered this way because of the heavy snowfalls. It's very cold and very black in this part of the tunnel. There's so much snow in this portion that there's even snow inside the tunnel here. People stop and collect it to take back to their villages for the purpose of keeping cool and making ice cream.

The next portion of the tunnel has electric lights, and that in itself is an incredible feat of engineering—to have electricity up this high. And there's nothing higher anywhere in the world where one can travel in a vehicle. One feels as if one's on the roof of the world!

We've now emerged onto the other side of the tunnel, and everything is snow covered. The very tiptop of the mountain juts up above the snow in craggy, barren, rocky masses. You can hear the sound of the water as it melts from the snow directly over our heads. Ahead of us is another tunnel with snow that spills off its sides and plunges down this immense chasm into the gorge below where it forms a swiftly flowing river. The water seems to run in two directions at the very peak of the mountains, going towards Kabul on one side and towards Kunduz on the other.

Well, we've just come down into the valley on our way to Kunduz, and we've stopped at a roadside teahouse known as a *chaikhana* right next to a little stream, a tributary of the big one. Here in the shade we're going to have some mulberries that are being washed in this clear mountain stream, and we shall say "inshallah" so that we don't get sick from tasting them.

Sound of water splashing and conversations.

We're situated under a tree at this very lovely rest house. There's a *charpoy*—that's a traditional Indian-style low bed strung with ropes—and seated on it are perhaps thirty men and children listening to Radio Afghanistan, which is now playing a national Afghan dance—what beautiful music! I wish they'd actually start dancing. They look like they'd almost like to. Most of the people are very shy and don't want to talk, but here's someone who's offering to do just that.

A boy speaks in Farsi, then sings a slow, sad song.

Jean: *Tashakor,* thank you. Very good!

Azad: This is poem this boy made up his self about the Salang Pass and this place. It is very beautiful and poetic; also, very correct grammar.

Jean: We've just finished our three-hour rest; actually, we're waiting for the heat of the day to disappear. And now we've left again and are passing through very fertile, green, yellow-green valleys which have beautiful rice paddies. Rising from the sides of this valley are steep, barren, brown hills. Many of the farmers are cutting their wheat, which they do by hand, gathering it in, even as early as spring. There's a man down there up to his waist in water, planting rice—little rice plants. There are little girls and boys threshing the wheat by throwing it up into the air and catching it in their baskets.

We arrived in Kunduz just at sunset and drove directly to our hotel where Azad and Henry checked the rooms and made arrangements. While the driver took Azad to where he would be staying, we settled in our room, had a wash, and went into the dining room for dinner. Just as we started to eat, the room began to rock and shake. Well, it was very apparent that it was an earthquake! As we sat there with our forks poised en route to our mouths, a waiter came dashing up and escorted all us diners into the garden at the back of the hotel. Here we were out in the open and quite safe in the event that the quake became so violent that any debris might fall.

We stood there and watched an iron pole, set in concrete, rocking back and forth, but fortunately, nothing happened to us. It was at this point that I turned around to look at Henry, and there he stood, amidst all this furore, calmly eating his hors d'oeuvre! In true English fashion, just as we were leaving the dining room, he had, with great aplomb, picked up his hard-boiled egg and stood outside in the garden calmly eating it. Everyone went into absolute gales of laughter!

Henry: Then we went back to the dining room and finished our meal. I ate the other two hard-boiled eggs.

Jean: While we were sitting at our table, chatting and trying to cool off, we talked about the trip we'd just had up through the beautiful Salang Pass.

Henry: *(laughing)* Mostly, we were listening to the conversations of the other couples sitting around us, trying to determine what nationalities they were.

Jean: Yes, it is fun. Then we noticed an Afghan gentleman approaching us, looking about sort of questioningly. He came up to us and, with great difficulty, we finally decided that he was trying to locate "Jean and Henry". He escorted us into a beautiful 1970s white Mercedes and took us to pick up Azad, and then we were all taken to the home of one of Azad's uncles. This is the man Henry's come up to Kunduz to see about the karakul sheep.

We were taken into a huge room which was furnished in typical Afghan fashion: gorgeous, priceless rugs on the floor and miserable

9

furniture lining the walls which were bare of any adornment. We were seated and, of course, there were dozens of men in the room and I was the only woman. We were told that it was our host's pleasure for us to stay at his home. "Plenty rooms," he assured us, and he was really quite put out because Azad had taken us first to the hotel. After much conversation back and forth, it was decided that we would change our accommodation this very night. So, back we went in the Mercedes to get our things and return to the house to be his guests for a day or two.

At about 11:30 in the evening, after conversation and watching one of our host's two television sets and listening to Radio Moscow, we were invited into the dining room where an elaborate feast was spread out for us. Lamb prepared in six different ways, chicken prepared in about four different ways, mounds of rice, all sorts of cucumbers and tomatoes, onions, and radishes and *naan.*[4] It was an enormous spread, and I had to sit at the head of it. This repast was followed by all sorts of sweet desserts and yoghurt and bowls of fruit, and then we were escorted into the lounge where we had tea and sweets. By this time, Henry and I were so full of food, having first feasted ourselves on those eggs, that we were absolutely miserable. Fortunately, throughout the day we had taken plenty of Entero-Vioform,[5] so we felt quite safe in sampling all the food.

At about 12:30 a.m., we thought that we ought to hit the hay because the following day would begin rather early, so we were escorted to our bedroom where we are now. It has two very uncomfortable beds, each covered with a sort of Indian sari, the most exquisite mauve and gold cloth that I have ever seen. We have a big electric fan and two miserable flies, which I am sure will keep us awake all night. Next door to us, however, we're very lucky because there is a beautiful modern *tashnab*, a bathroom, and instead of being tiled, the walls and floor are covered in beautiful plum-coloured marble, and the fixtures are all very, very modern. The floors in the bedroom are covered in beautiful red Afghan carpeting and the walls painted a dark, very attractive grey, which is rather unusual in

---

[4] . Traditional flat bread baked in a clay oven.

[5] . Medication used at the time to treat travellers' diarrhoea.

Afghan houses. Usually they're just whitewashed. The ceiling is carved wood in true Afghan fashion.

We've all been up early. I've been up since 4 a.m. and written twenty postcards. The rest of the household is slowly getting moving, and we've sat around having endless pots and pots and yet more pots of tea. Although the breakfast that was served was very elaborate, no one seemed to want it because it's so terribly hot out. I think it's a hundred and twenty degrees Fahrenheit.

Sound of vehicle driving over bumpy road.

Jean: Now, at about 10:30 a.m., we're wending our way along a rutty road through the estate that belongs to our host. The property belongs to him as far as the eye can see. The dust rising in thick clouds surrounds us as we bump along in this Land Rover, which I saw one of the servants washing this morning. Ahead of us are some Kuchi[6] children who shyly turn their faces to the wall as we pass by. The road meanders through the lanes that are walled on either side with this dusty, dun-coloured mud and clay. Every once in a while, there is a wooden door or a carved gate in the wall that hides an orchard. Oh, there are some lovely little children skinny-dipping in some cooling water. Behind the wall on our left, I can see a man threshing wheat.

We have now arrived at the gathering place, the *ashkana,* literally driving over animal skins. We are seated on charpoys ranged round the outside and along the edge, facing all the men who work here. They are seated or standing in a semicircle. One man is tuning up a very crude-looking wooden instrument that resembles a banjo. I'm sure that he's made it himself.

---

6 . Northern nomadic tribe of Afghan Pashtun people.

Man singing to the accompaniment of a plucked string instrument and drumming. Applause.

Everyone is sitting around having a marvellous time with these home-made instruments. This string instrument is unbelievably crude, and the tapping noise—the rhythm part—comes from an old aluminium bucket. Now they're urging one of the men to come forward and sing. Well, instead, they've sent for another boy from one of the far corners of the ashkana, and they want him to perform a dance, and they're clearing a space for him. (*Music resumes.*) This young man is extremely graceful. He's draped a shawl over his head, but his hands and feet are flying about with tremendous grace. Now he's got sort of dizzy and he's kneeling on the ground here, swaying from side to side. (*Applause.*)

We've left the ashkana and are driving back to the house by the same route we came. Azad has told us that this family numbers approximately 5,000 people. They are so strongly interwoven and intermarried and work together with such unity that they actually represent a considerable force. They consider themselves to be and are like a nation and, actually, are almost in competition with other such tribal groups within the country. This kind of system is an advantage for the family because they can wield great power, but it doesn't exactly appear to me to make for unity in terms of what is best for the entire country.

We return to the house covered with layers of dust. It is so thick and powdery that I doubt if we shall ever really get free and clear of it. It's in our nostrils and our ears and everywhere about us. And we smell of dust. It has a very dry, acrid odour, not unpleasant, but sort of powdery.

Noise of clinking and conversation.

Jean: For about another hour till noon, we've sat about, drinking Cokes and orange Fantas until lunch is announced. Again, we enter the enormous dining room with its long table and all the men assembled. Opposite me, at the other end of the table, or rather, on it and eating from a plate, sits one of the youngest children, cross-legged in Indian yogi style. I was told earlier that this little boy is too small to sit at the side of the table.

In the centre of the table are enormous bowls of *pulao* rice,[7] and underneath it I can see thick hunks of legs of lamb that have been roasted. There are plates of another kind of lamb dish, swimming in a very tomatoey, oily sort of substance. There are platters of fried fish and roasted chicken and huge trays of cucumbers, thinly sliced, and tomatoes and onions cut up very finely into a sort of a salad. First, we are served a bowl of soup which is made with noodles and a sort of chickpea and is very tasty and, actually, a Bukhara[8] speciality. Then we just plunge into the rice and the various other things. I notice that all the men pack the rice very tightly into a solid ball in their right hands and then, with a very deft and graceful motion, just toss the rice into their mouths without their fingers ever touching their lips.

During a meal, there is not one word of conversation spoken. It is as if everybody is on his or her own and drawn into his or her own thoughts while eating the delicious food. At the end of it, everybody rises and individually goes to a corner of the room where there is an exposed wash basin, plenty of towels, and a bar of soap to wash one's hands before retiring from the dining room into the lounge. There, seating is on one of the many banquettes along the sides of the room, and one awaits tea, which is brought into the room very quickly. I should think they must make thousands and thousands of gallons of tea each day; the samovar must be boiling constantly.

After we have tea, we eat a sweet and we take our leave of the room to rest for a couple of hours. It's much, much too hot to be outside at this time of the day. At about 4 or 5 p.m., we will assemble again. I don't know by what sort of signal, but I do know that we will be taken through the

---

[7] . Basmati rice cooked in broth seasoned with herbs and spices until fluffy and golden.

[8] . Province of Uzbekistan.

bazaars, which are almost entirely owned by our host. We will also be taken to see some of the *serais*[9] and other properties that he has.

Sounds of clinking bottles.

Jean: Azad and I are taking off in the big van for a sightseeing tour of Kunduz. In the back of the van is one of the house boys who's loaded up four cases of empty Coca-Cola bottles and a great big tray with some of the Fanta orange drink bottles. I suppose he's going to take them and replace them with fresh ones. In the meantime, on these rutted roads, they make an incredible racket.

Although there's a good plastics factory in Kabul that makes containers for water, some of the more primitive methods are still used. On the left side of the road here there is a pump and a girl filling a huge goatskin with water.

Kunduz appears to be an extremely prosperous-looking town with people who are largely descendants of the Turkmen[10] people. They are well dressed and have a very happy appearance. Most of them have jobs either in the agricultural or … Oh, we just passed a *gari!*[11] As I was saying earlier, the streets in Kunduz are neat and clean in comparison to the ones in Kabul. I think primarily it's because the streets are wider and tree lined and there are fewer cars. It's a much more rural looking community. By and large, the people are employed in agriculture, which abounds around here, and there are many textile and cotton and rice and wheat factories in the area too. So, most people have jobs.

Azad: Also, the best karakul skins in all of Afghanistan come from here this area.

Sounds of traffic, people talking, bells.

---

[9] . Literally a palace or great house.
[10] . Turkic people from the state of Turkmenistan in Central Asia.
[11] . Horse-drawn cart.

Jean: The centre of Kunduz has a huge circular area, similar to an English roundabout design. It leads to four streets, each with its separate bazaar; it's very beautiful, tree lined, and very shady. That tinkling sound is the bells on the gari as it goes down these lovely dirt-covered streets. On this street corner, there are many kinds of eating bazaars: a lot of bread is being sold, different coloured drinks, great big cucumbers, apricots. *(Sharp, scratching sounds.)* That scraping noise is the knife-grinder who's here at the corner with his wheel, working it with his foot and sharpening the knives.

We've gone into the bazaar to purchase some lovely wooden Bukhara spoons, which are painted and lacquered in bright colours and can be used for soup. Azad has found a friend and has arranged for the price, and at the conclusion of the business arrangement, we have been sitting down here in the shade having a glass of tea from a beautiful Russian pot. It's green tea, which is quite bitter, so it's served with a sweet, which you place in your mouth and suck as you drink the tea.

Azad: Here in this sports field, we make football and wrestling and also to bring that dog which are sometime fighting and sometime special bird that is much bigger and they train it for a very, very long time until they are ready to make fight. There is usual game. In the cooler times, they have horse race and horse *buzkashi*[12], which they have a goat and try to catch it from the ground. They have a hundred horse that come together on the centre and they want to fetch it from the earth. Who is the catcher, he run away about a mile. The other horse follow to catch from him until they bring it to the circle, to special place. He throw it down, he's the winner.

Jean: Azad has just been describing the famous game of buzkashi, which originated in Kunduz. The horses in this area are the most famous in all of Afghanistan. This game takes place in the cooler season of the year, but right now, on this very same sports field, there are many, many

---

[12] . The fast and furious national sport of Afghanistan, akin to polo. Two teams of horsemen battle fiercely at full gallop to take possession of a goat's carcass in a test of cunning, courage, and strength.

people gathered, men in a large circle watching some wrestling. Over in the distance, on the other side of the field, I can see some younger men playing football and, scattered throughout the entire area, are sheep and cows mingling amongst the people and grazing very peacefully.

We are standing next to one of the brothers of our host, and I understand that he is a very famous buzkashi rider. *Assalamu alaikum.*[13] This gentleman is wearing a cloak of pure silk draped gracefully over his shoulders, in the most beautiful shades of raspberry, plum, gold, dark green, and all in lovely wide stripes, and on his head he has, at a rakish angle, the most exquisite karakul hat. He stands with great arrogance, arms crossed. He must look marvellous on his steed when he rides at the buzkashi.

Here we are in a compound where we've come to see some buzkashi horses, and in this area is a little baby deer. It's only about eighteen inches high. *(to stable lad)* How old is it?

Stable lad: One month.

Jean: One month! And it's walking about on four spindly little legs. It's the sweetest little thing! Two dogs lying here are paying no attention to it at all. And there it goes out the gate! In a corner, there's a good-looking young man with some grain spread out in front of him which he's about to grind, and that will be food for the horses. And over here in a cage is a bird raised for fighting. It's a lovely mauve colour with black-and-white striped wings.

I've just walked through a gate into another compound, which is an enormous area with two beautiful horses, a great big charpoy with lovely Afghan carpets spread on it, and lots of good-looking men around. Azad is describing where the horses come from.

Azad: Actually, is from Turkmen. This is not like Arabic horse. Arabic horse is much weaker and more broken in and good looking. But this one

---

[13] . Traditional greeting among Muslims meaning "May peace be upon you".

16

is extremely, very powerful. It is bred only for the game. You would be surprised how it jump to catch the ball.

Jean: I saw the buzkashi.

Azad: *(surprised)* You saw?

Jean: Yes, a couple of years ago. It's an extremely skilful game. The skill is not only in securing the goat and carrying it, but in doing this in combat against a team of men on horseback, and both the use of knives and whipping are allowed, so it's a very dangerous game indeed. And these horses around here are beautiful and very costly to buy in the first place and to maintain in the second. The owner of this farm and the horses we are looking at has just brought the whips that are used by the buzkashi riders. What are they made of?

Azad: They are special, very strong. This is leather and also a wooden handle.

Jean: They're fierce-looking weapons and very, very hard wood. I should imagine that if a man is beaten with it, the wounds would be very, very severe.

Azad: This one, which is made of wood, which is the length, is about two feet. This one, the leather, which is mixed with several other things, is also about two feet. They both have special affection because the oldest is around three hundred years old. It is not ordinary wood which has for result they keep them clean without any dirt or something not touching them at all. They has special purity to cure sometimes if a horse gets a wounded or something is cutting. They touch it with this and by rubbing this, there it gets cured very quickly and stops infection.

Jean: And they are decorated very beautifully with brass and silver carvings at either end. Now, we shall enjoy the Afghan custom of having tea, *chai*.

Azad: It doesn't cost very much, but it is the custom of our society, talking and getting together. It's very, very important.

Jean: I'm standing in the garden in the house in Kunduz. It's our last evening. People are sitting around waiting for dinner and trying to cool off after this incredibly hot day. The air is still very warm and dry, but a breeze is beginning to blow and everyone is breathing a sigh of relief. The temperature rose to almost a hundred fourteen degrees and, what with all the dust swirling and blowing about, it was really very uncomfortable.

Over in the back part of the compound here is a little fire glistening, and the smoke is drifting from it as the kebabs are prepared for our dinner. The smell is delicious, and I'm sure that inside somewhere there is a big pot of rice being prepared. The menu never seems to vary, and though I love the fruits and vegetables and the fluffy, golden pulao rice and the *chelou*[14] rice with its crispy crust, it does get a bit boring, for Western taste anyway. At least, after being assured by Azad that the yoghurt was made from boiled milk that has been boiled "really hard", I've been able to have a very nice portion of it on top of my freshly sliced cucumbers and tomatoes, and I've relished them very much. Dessert last night was very soupy, melted red, green, and yellow Jell-O, which didn't come off very well because we couldn't scoop it up onto our plates, but it was the only variation in the meals which we have enjoyed so far.

Since we've been here, I've met six of our host's several brothers. The youngest one, I think, is aged twenty-one. He has spent some time in Holland, and he is quite adamant in being anti-Communist[15], anti-Afghanistan, and against all the religious customs he's grown up with. He wants to go back as quickly as he can and get a job there as he's been trained as a mechanic, having attended school in Lahore. He also wants to

---

14 . Persian rice dish flavoured with saffron and cumin, especially favoured for its crunchy crust.

15 . When writing, Jean's visceral hatred of communism was such that she unconsciously personified it as a malevolent force, always capitalizing the initial letter, like Sloth or Greed, whether correct or not.

marry a European girl. He's very definite in his departure from an Afghan way of life.

Thus far, we have not seen a single woman in this vast and enormous compound with its complexity of buildings. Actually, we've only stayed in the guest house, and the cooking, the cleaning—everything—is done by the menservants.

We had a good night's sleep, although I was up at 4:30 in the morning to record the bird calls. Following a slight delay for the water to be pumped into the tanks for washing up, everything went along smoothly. We had a nice breakfast—tea, naan, and some apple jam. Then I had a picture-taking session with the patriarch of the family, a handsome old gentleman with a white beard. Now we have taken our leave with many goodbyes and greetings for a future meeting, and we're en route back to Kabul.

We're passing through the outskirts of Kunduz, and the hills are rich with the wheat crops. We've just gone by a little school where the children are all sitting in the shade. It must be insufferably hot inside the building, so they're taking their lessons under an awning outside.

Sound of a car crunching over gravel, murmured conversation, and music.

Jean: We've climbed back up into the mountains and have stopped at a chai house beside a little stream in this village halfway up to the Salang Pass. We'll have some tea and break the journey. I'm listening now to this lovely music.

Azad: Music Indian. Is Indian music.

Jean: Yes. Very melodic. The water here is beautiful and clear and very pure, and we're refreshing ourselves again with some mulberries. Ah, they're good. (*to Azad in surprise*) You're not on your second portion, are you? Your second plate?

Azad: That my second plate. I eat like this even if I'm not hungry. I could eat at least six of this. This is the bigger plate—dinner plate, not the small.

Jean: They're so, so good!

Azad: We eat about a pound I think. I have done once.

Jean: You're going to turn into a mulberry! (*They laugh.*) I've got some sultanas. You like them?

Azad: Yes.

Sound of torrent.

Jean: We've gone deeper into the Salang Pass now and are stopping for lunch at this roadside place. We're having lamb, pulao rice, chai, and naan bread. We're sitting by the side of the rushing mountain stream, and we can hear how thunderous the noise is; the current is fierce.

As I look across the stream to the other side, I see a group of four people leading a goat down the side of the cliff ... and ... oh, yes, they're killing it. Yes, it's dead now. They're skinning it. Hanging from the branch of a tree is a scale. Oh, there are two goats, a black and a brown one. They've taken the black one, and it's hanging by the hind feet from the limb of the tree while two other men continue skinning the brown one. I've just had my kebabs and don't feel very well. And still the slaughter goes on. The men have now killed three sheep, three goats, and are continuing to skin them and do all the necessary things. I think it will be a very long time before I have any kebabs again!

The climb up to the Salang Pass on this northern Kunduz side is a much longer and slower ascent than on the southern Kabul side. It's very, very hard on the cars, and the lorries can only travel at a rate of about five miles per hour. From here I can see up the length of the valley, created by the water from the melting snows, for a distance of perhaps thirty miles.

We've just come onto an accident here. A small crowd of people has gathered, and there are some lorries parked on the side of the road. Oh, my goodness! One of the great big lorries has just gone right over on its side.

Azad: It is one of the big lorries that carrying the petrol. It was too high the road, and he couldn't climb up and slowly come down, so the lorry went over on its side. Nobody was hurt. Only was upside down.

Jean: But it looked terrible.

Sound of wind as car moves on.

Jean: We're now going through the Salang Tunnel at the top of the pass. The temperature is very cold, about two degrees below zero, and as we emerge from the tunnel, we can see that the water has changed its course and is now flowing from north to south. The Afghan Tour Company has built a ski lodge and restroom here but, as Henry says, it looks more like a coal bunker than a lodge.

The rest of the trip home was uneventful, apart from a severe storm which caused flooding and is a bit unusual at this time of the year. It did create two beautiful rainbows. We watched the complete second arch for a distance of about twenty miles, and just as we came into Kabul, we seemed to go almost underneath it. It was one of the brightest that I've ever seen.

And that's the end of our trip to Kunduz, which we thoroughly enjoyed and hope produced good results.

Jean and the Goats

The Mulberries

The Salang Pass Highway

GERMAN FURRIERS VISIT AFGHANISTAN

There is no year written for any of the entries in Jean's short, unfinished account of what was one of many business trips she helped organize for her partner, Henry Willacy, who was an expert in the karakul wool trade. However, by matching the dates with historical calendars, it is likely to have taken place around 1975. This was when Jean was exporting the colourfully embroidered Afghan coats called postinchas, made of the distinctly pungent karakul sheepskins. The main purpose of these fact-finding missions was to visit the tanneries, inspect the flocks of sheep, and broker any deals.

Jean had become the Afghan Karakul Institute's unofficial tour guide; in this case, for a group of German furriers to northern Afghanistan. She also would arrange the entertainment, which could be weddings, wrestling matches, or fish barbecues. For this particular group, she organized a fashion show featuring the postinchas and traditional Afghan costumes to help promote her own export business.

Moreover, sensitive by now to the treatment of women in Afghanistan, she artfully persuaded local Kabul businessmen to contribute samples of their different wares for a fundraising bazaar to be held alongside the fashion show. The businessmen would receive free publicity whilst she arranged for the proceeds to go to the Afghan Women's Organisation (AWO). Stapled three or four to a page are dozens and dozens of business cards from export-import merchants, jewellers, tailors, boutiques, bazaar shops, carpet shops, clothing manufacturers, and the like, whom Jean would have visited personally and cajoled into contributing to her cause.

The diary entries very much reflect the bold, single-minded way in which Jean would launch herself into a project. Any experience deemed necessary for such a venture was simply swept aside by her extraordinary energy, entrepreneurial acumen, and personal charm.

A FASHION SHOW IN KABUL

Go to Intercontinental Hotel:

1. See ballroom—Check with PR man or lady.
2. Decorations and flowers for ballroom at shop in hotel—Intercontinental providing!
3. Note stage and entry for walkway—mark where to stand with chalk. Intro by Mr Sajadi, our Afghan host, with commentary in German.
4. Emcee—English/Farsi commentators from Radio Afghanistan!

Scripts must include thanks to each contributor as means of advertising.
Girls' names to be announced, followed by: "… wearing [costume or postincha coat] compliments of [name of shop owner]."

5. Basheer[16] to do music—tape recorder? Get long cable from hotel.
6. Send invitations to contributors for "fundraising bazaar."
7. Exhibition of lapis lazuli[17] and goldsmith work/other merchandise.
8. Arrange make-up.
9. Refreshments at interval between costumes and fur coats.
10. Lottery at end.
11. Get money for flowers and film.
12. Rehearsals on Wednesday at Intercontinental at 2:30 p.m.
13. Arrange publicity.
14. Three hours for whole event.

Meet president of the Afghan Women's Organisation (AWO):
Arrangements made with shops in hotel lobby to offer goods for sale with 50 per cent of the profit for AWO! Elizabeth Arden products will be sold with a 40 per cent discount.

Models:

---

[16] . Son of Jean's business partner who ran a music shop.
[17] . A semi-precious gemstone highly prized for its rich, deep blue colour, used since antiquity for jewellery and mined primarily in northern Afghanistan.

1. Free ticket for each girl's mother.
2. Order of costumes and any help with changing.
3. Slips of paper to be handed to the announcer with each girl's name, a description of the garment worn, and with "from whom" in English and Farsi.
4. Transport for models to hotel at 5 p.m. from AWO. Bus there and back?
5. Get film about AWO from their office.

Programme: ninety-minute fashion show

1. Introductions—Mr Sajadi (five minutes).
2. Credits.
3. National costumes—fourteen girls; fourteen outfits (thirty minutes).
4. Interval and refreshments.
5. Lottery tickets (eighteen tickets for models and their families).
6. Fur fashions—models and coats (thirty minutes).
7. Draws and gifts (thirty minutes).

TRIP TO THE NORTHWEST FRONTIER

Day One: Arrival

Saturday, 28 June

The German furriers arrive at the airport about two hours late owing to delayed departures en route. Two bags are lost or at least not on board. While waiting, we sit in the airport dining room with all the ministers, officials, and dignitaries who have come to see Naim Khan, brother of President Daoud.[18] He is the minister of foreign affairs and deputy

---

[18] . Mohammed Daoud, president of Afghanistan from 1973 to 1978.

prime minister, no less, who is leaving with four delegates on a mission to Bucharest. Much kissing, bowing, and salaaming.

Also crowding the lounge are several hundred people (mostly women in black dresses and white scarves) awaiting the arrival of the body of a dearly beloved relative and friend, wife of the former ambassador to Yugoslavia, who died in Paris. Everyone I run into seems to be related to her.

Into our minibus and off to Intercontinental Hotel with Mr Sajadi, our Afghan organizer, with the two German passengers following us later by taxi as they must fill in the forms for the missing luggage. En route, I point out various places of interest.

Group checks into this truly luxurious, Western-style hotel, its appointments and décor as remote from the reality of Afghanistan as its physical position in the outskirts of the city. Guests go for a swim, have lunch, and I go to the city to attend to some matters for the fashion show, returning at 2 p.m.

Sightseeing of Kabul, including a walk in the bazaar, visits to fur shops, and looking at karakul bazaars near the river. Guests are exhausted, so return to hotel for a rest and swim before 7:30 dinner at Sitara Restaurant. Dinner is well received, as is Afghan music.

Day Two: The Show

Sunday, 29 June

Mr Sajadi hosts the group as I am fully involved with plans for the style show. They visit some representative from the minister of commerce office, see Kabul Museum, and shop a little before lunch in Little Lantern in Shar-i-Nan (Karakul Institute hosts). In the afternoon, they visit the sorting house and return early to hotel for a swim, a rest, and to film the "model mannequins" in the sheepskin fur coats.

"Story of my day" filled with aggravations and frustrations of presenting this fashion show. Everything, of course, is late, and no one minds but the foreigners. Instead of 7 p.m., it's 8:45 when we begin, and then only because I advise the ladies that they have reserved the room for a mere three hours and time's awasting!

Excellent results for the show. Costumes gorgeous, and the girls outdo themselves. Much well-deserved praise, and a long day ends about midnight.

Day Three: To the Northwest Frontier

Monday, 30 June

I wait at hotel for 5:10 a.m. pickup, and of course, driver is late. He says he was looking for a tarpaulin for the luggage, but I think he overslept. At the hotel, we load up ice chests and drinks from the bazaar and leave one hour late! A precedent I'm afraid. Very Afghan and very un-German!

Through the Salang Pass, a gorgeous drive, and the scenery and countryside look marvellous to me. At the summit, the clouds thicken and darken as rain and mist close us in, and the descent is a bit dangerous. We stop in the northeastern town of Pul-i-Khumri for lunch, which no one likes and which is too expensive (complaint to Sajadi, especially for overcharge of drink).

One furrier, whom I have dubbed "Mein Herr", is impatient and very German. His kind, smiling face belies his drive for regimentation and perfection, and I can tell immediately that he will be upset at the too-loose plans. Mr Sajadi has said, "This is the programme!" But it is not so far. Although correspondence has taken place since December, nothing has been confirmed, and it's up to Mr Sajadi and me to organize as we go, for nineteen people. Especially in Afghanistan, this is a monumental undertaking, for here everything takes much time and much talking.

However, we continue, and the weather brightens as we reach Mazar-i-Sharif[19] after a long, hard, nine-hour drive. Outside the city, a reception awaits us, for Mr Qayum has driven to welcome us. The Ballkh Nights Hotel is an old "friend" of mine, but the Germans are unimpressed. It's hard for them, for they have had no preparation or briefing.

---

[19] . Second largest city in northern Afghanistan, renowned for its holy shrines and Blue Mosque.

The purpose of this trip is twofold: 1) to show the karakul buyers the difficult problems and primitive conditions that exist in this industry at its source, and 2) to make a ciné film about the karakul sheep and the shepherds who tend them, developing the strong healthy flocks that make the karakul industry one of the largest earners of foreign currency in Afghanistan.

First, we go to film the work done with the sheepskins at the curing/sorting house. The younger brother of Mr Nawabi[20] is there, and we greet a lot. Here, the group sees the wet karakul skins being skilfully sorted before being sent to the ashkana—gathering place—on the outskirts of Mazar, which is our next port of call. The large area is dotted as far as the eye can see with outdoor pools where the skins are given a further wash. We're shown the vats made of the stomachs of camels or horses where the skins are then soaked in a mixture called *quassing* that forms the white backing of the skins.

After being turned several times in the vats, they are laid out on the hard-baked ground to dry in the sun where they stiffen and become easy to handle for loading. The entire process takes about three weeks. The group film the colourful lumbering lorries which transport the skins about three hundred miles southward over the towering, snow-clad Hindu Kush mountains, through the Khyber Pass, and on to the sorting house on the outskirts of Kabul. From there, the final assortment is made, and skins are baled and shipped by air to the auctions in far-off London.

We walk back for filming at the crowded karakul bazaar. Even in this last stage, the group remarks on the absence of mechanization they've seen throughout the karakul industry here, for it remains a labour of human hands by trained and skilled men who, year after year, produce the beautiful and highly valued skins. The tour ends with a quick look round Mazar, including its magnificent and famous Blue Mosque.

At the hotel, each room has been scrubbed, made up with fresh linen, *and* flowers and fruit arranged. No first-class hotel could produce more effort. A wash and the long drive to the guest house near the town of Aqcha. Carpets and chairs are laid out on the veranda, and nothing is spared: hard drinks, wine, whisky, brandy, champagne, vodka, gin, sherry from Moscow, nuts, fruits, raisins, sweets, and of course chai. Then,

---

[20] . One of Henry's business friends.

delicious kebabs as an appetizer and then, the banquet! The usual chicken pulao, creamy chicken *korma*[21], chicken and chips, salads, yogurt, and puddings. Too, too much. Back to hotel and bed.

Day Four: The Flocks

Tuesday, 1 July

Can't sleep; go walking at 5 a.m. Wake the group at 6 a.m. to hear complaints of no water, no fans, no fresh towels, etc. Breakfast is brought at 7 a.m. by Mr Zayum with special china and service for all. What a thoughtful person he is.

We are one hour late leaving for the town of Aqcha because of one couple sleeping late. Too bad because that means no visit to see karakul in the nearby town of Balkh. In Aqcha, our troubles begin. Mein Herr wants to get to the flocks *immediately*, but *nothing* has really been arranged! We try in vain to get out of our lunch appointment with our host, Mr Shahnawaz, but, again, I'm embarrassed because I know the hospitality drill. So many men and more keep coming to prepare the meal. We are promised okay, no lunch. Instead, only chai, naan, and sweets. But we see the preparations taking place and, in the end, Mr Shahnawaz has his way—and we have another banquet!

Meanwhile, the police have arrived. They wish to know who we are and what we want and why! The palaver is endless, and Mein Herr is beside himself. Finally, after an enormous meal, we leave for the next town of Shiberghan, having had no time for carpet shops, weaving, or arranging the Turkman wedding! We are told we must go to the governor's in Shibarghan for "investigation", and this we do. But he is out with his flocks somewhere, so our escort Jeep, led by Mr Shahnawaz, takes us to the chief of police.

There, after many phone calls, arrangements are made, and now we go to the hotel where we rendezvous with two Jeeps and two lorry trucks and many Afghan flock owners plus Mr Shahnawaz. Who rides with whom is a matter of strict protocol, with Mr Shahnawaz and Mein Herr leading.

---

[21] . Mild curry sauce.

30

Our drive is now to Dasht-i-Layli, the vast barren plateau in the northern desert area bordering on Russia where the Amu Darya River separates the two countries. It is not a well-defined border; if flocks cross either side, they are scurried back.

There is no road when we cut off from the dirt one just outside of Shibarghan—just flat, sometimes rolling, wasteland sparsely covered with vegetation, yet somehow beautiful with only an occasional shepherd and his flocks of black-and-grey karakul sheep and the sound of flute-like music from afar. There are huge numbers of flocks in this hot, barren desert. Under the scorching sun in the clear, dry air, the shepherds carefully tend their sheep, seeing that they have sufficient food and water each day, watching over them like parents over their children

We drive over the dunes for about two to two and a half hours, seeing only puffs of sand swirling above the vehicles and guided only by the knowledge of the kindly sheep owners who help us reach the watering and grazing places of these scattered, hardy flocks. It's a solitary, lonely, beautiful place—this heart of karakul land, surrounded by the vast silence of the mighty Hindu Kush, here in far off Central Asia.

In the Heart of Central Asia

Karakul Sheep

Afghanistan's Prized Export

Tanning the Skins

Washing the Skins

Dressing the Skins with 'Quassing'

Laying Out the Dressed Skins

Karakul Skins Drying in the Sun

Henry Assessing the Quality of the Wool

Stacking the Dried Skins for Shipping

Spinning the Wool

Yarn Dying

Preparing the Skeins of Yarn

Designing Embroidery on a Postincha Coat

The Finished Product

Jean Sallies Forth

A MISADVENTURE OR TWO

Taken from one of Jean's letters to her sister, Peggy. Jean's two travelling companions were Henry and her middle daughter, Anne. The trip took place in April 1973.

Naturally, I have saved the juiciest tale for the last, but seriously, it was the most frightening experience of my life. Even so, such are the trials and tribulations of travel, and I wouldn't trade, believe me. We had begun by planning an eight-day trip to the northern province of Badakshan right on the Russian-Chinese border and once a stopover on the ancient Silk Road. I'd never been there and knew only that it was very wild and primitive and that was where much of Henry's fur buying was accomplished. His mission this time was to find foxes, martens, and spotted mountain cats. We purchased bath towels, soap, Kleenex, Entero-Vioform, four pounds of biscuits, and bags of oranges. And matches!

Early in the morning we flew in a tiny, twin-engine Russian Yak to Kunduz. Flying just barely above the massive, snow-covered Hindu Kush mountains was thrilling. In Kunduz we had to change planes, and there was a delay owing to bad weather. We were within an eyelash of cancelling our plans because we could have stayed over there with an Afghan family friend, but at the last moment there was a flurry and a pushing and shoving, and suddenly we were off, this time in a tiny twin-engine Canadian Otter.

We had a gorgeous, dramatic approach down through a mountain pass, and since we were sitting right behind the pilot and could see the runway zooming up at us, it was a super landing. But it was in a field with no asphalted runway, just a levelled strip! And surrounded by these mountains! Now we were in the province of Badakshan and heading for the main village of Fayzabad. A sort of a bus (or rather, a bus of sorts) took us, eight passengers in all, on a long ride into the village, and even that was scary, for the road was just dirt, filled with ruts and boulders, and we had to cross several washes!

The village is a collection of typical bazaar shops. No women to be seen at all, but lots of colourfully clothed men and beautiful horses, for this is a part of the country where horses are the only means of transport. Our "hotel", the only one there, was a joke and indescribably crude. We nearly died over the "one-holer"[22] but had to make the best of what was there. *For there was no turning back!* We had arrived on a Saturday afternoon, and the first plane scheduled out was not until Tuesday.

Meanwhile, as Henry checked out his chores, we began scouting around. We contacted some Peace Corps kids and made some tentative enquiries about hiring a Jeep to drive out before Tuesday. No dice, no Jeeps! And no food! This area was one which had been stricken by the famine and drought, so no rice. All we had were kebabs and the food we had brought with us and tea.

By Sunday afternoon, Henry had finished his business, but the weather had taken a turn for the worse. A check of the air schedule revealed that the plane might not even arrive owing to storms and bad conditions on that landing strip, but we had a chance that we could get out on it since it was scheduled to operate on Tuesday, Wednesday, Thursday, Friday, and Saturday. We learned that there was a local bus operating from Fayzabad to Khanabad, *if* the road was open, but it was listed as unimproved for a start. If we could get that far, then we could catch another vehicle to the safety of Kunduz.

The Peace Corps kids scared the hell out of us about the conditions of that road, but they were a queer lot, and in the final analysis, it was a very tough decision to make, for we knew we risked a lot: either taking the chance that the plane would make it, which seemed increasingly doubtful from estimating the weather, or taking the chance on getting

---

[22] . Literally, a hole in the ground for a toilet.

stuck somewhere in the wilderness on the bus. We jawed over the pros and cons, finally took a vote, and unanimously agreed on the "bus".

We convened at six o'clock in the morning at a muddy intersection and, for two and a half hours, had to hold our seats as we'd been advised to sit in the first row behind the driver. Do you know what Afghan buses are like? This one was ancient to begin with. It had about ten rows of seats, and we were squeezed in, six in a row. The men wore heavy *chapans*[23] and blanket-like robes, so comfort was *out*. Meanwhile, the "conductor" kept up his cry of "Khanabad, Khanabad, Khanabad!" And all the while the belongings kept piling up on top: bedrolls, metal trunks, sheep, chickens, and more passengers. There was a sort of ladder at the rear of the bus, and the two helpers hung on there. They must have the most horrendous ride! By now the weather looked threatening and had turned very cold, and soon we were off!

I can't begin to describe the dangerous and tortuous journey this turned into, but it was a miracle that we finally got through. Every inch of the way was oozing mud as we snaked up precipices with the mountain streams thousands of feet below us. Sometimes we had to get out and walk; sometimes the two helpers had to build a road where the spring torrents had washed it away entirely; and sometimes they had to push huge boulders over the sides of the cliffs! It became a real test of our strength and courage, and we all were trying to conceal our raw fear. Our driver was one helluva man, and after each ordeal he would take a pinch of the green *naswar*[24] tobacco, which is sort of like chewing tobacco, and then we'd know we were okay for a little while. But truly there was not one minute when we could relax.

By nightfall, we were travelling along the bottom of a riverbed on sheer rock, and how the driver could see a path, we don't know. The mist came down, and through it we saw a light. I was reminded of a children's story and knew it would be a haven of some sort. It was a lone chaikhana, and there we stopped for the night! An adobe building with one wood stove for heat and warmth and some charpoys. We had a nibble of our food, some tea, and don't ask how Anne and I (the only women) went to the john!

---

[23] . A heavy, embroidered winter coat for men.

[24] . A moist, smokeless, powdered tobacco that is taken like snuff, or stuffed into the mouth or cheek for lengthy periods of time.

The men were very kind to us. First one gave us a blanket, then another a jacket and so on until we were able to settle down, all squeezed into a tiny corner on a charpoy for the night.

We slept from exhaustion and the sheer relief that we were still alive, and by morning we felt better. Until we looked out to a steady driving rain and a sea of mud! For over an hour, we all just sat in silence, huddled in our chapans and watching the driver who never took his eyes off the lone door, which was open to the miserable weather. Suddenly, he put on his shoes and, as though that was the signal, we all shuffled out to the bus, loaded up, and set off once again.

Within minutes we knew that this day would be far worse than the previous one, and so it was. The strain was grim, and the perils of the road so incredibly bad that I just can't describe it. Neither would I even want to. We held our breath round every bend, and always it was worse than we could imagine. Sometimes there was just no road; it would disappear under a gushing torrent of water. Then the two helpers would jog ahead of the bus to test the area, splashing into water sometimes hip high. Then out would come the oh, so primitive spades to build a passage for the bus. Sometimes we would have to walk on boulders to relieve the weight in the bus, and all this in the pouring rain!

Well, enough. We made it to Khanabad, and that's the happy ending to this story. We found a truck going from Khanabad to Kunduz and wound up at our friend's after all. God, how we needed baths! We stayed there two days and then drove on one of the few asphalted roads in Afghanistan to Mazar-i-Sharif.

I leave tomorrow for home and am quite looking forward to some civilization, some gardening, and even a bit of spring house cleaning. Perhaps the weather will be better in England, but everywhere on the continent it's been very cold. Lots of rain and not much sign of spring, which is tantalizing for me to consider the jungle paradise of Thailand and Malaysia.

No more now except to add lots and lots of love and that it will be good to be in closer touch once again.

FROM THE STREETS OF KABUL

Whenever Jean was out and about, she loved to tape-record daily life. From certain events mentioned, these exchanges are most likely to have taken place in the spring of 1972.

Day One: "Bye-bye, Baby!"

Jean: I'm standing at one of the main intersections in Kabul, Afghanistan. It's like the noisy intersections of most street corners in most big cities. The only difference is that, here, the traffic is controlled by the beeping of horns. There are no policemen in sight, no streetlights or laws that govern the movement of the cars, and right here at this intersection, there are plenty! One's life is very much at risk just trying to cross the street.

In front of me now there is a young boy about ten years old with a bucket of water, throwing the water onto the street to dampen down the dust. (*Woman's voice singing in the background with noise of traffic.*) Today is bright and sunny, quite windy. The air is very dry.

If I could read the bus signs, I'd hop on a bus to go to the Russian Embassy where I want to make some enquiries about air travel to Russia and London, but they're all in the Farsi language[25], so I can't do that. I'm going to try and get a taxi, and off we'll go. Oh, here's a lovely blue one with a red band around the centre. *Assalamu alaikum. (Asks in Farsi to be taken to the Russian embassy.)* Thank you. Tashakor. Thank you.

Only a movie camera can do justice to the sights. We're passing a flock of goats being driven by a very tattered-looking shepherd. Now a cart loaded down with huge logs being drawn by a very old man. Bicycles scooting in and out everywhere. Donkeys laden with tins and bladders of water. A few old lorries carrying petrol. There's a bicycle almost hidden from view because of the big load of green onions that is strapped to the peddler's back. And everywhere there are little carts piled high with all different kinds of fruits. Seated on top of them are the vendors. They curl up into a teeny, weeny space, their legs tucked underneath them, and perch like so many birds hovering over their goods.

---

[25] . Afghan Persian also known as Dari.

Taxi Driver: Fifty afghani.

Jean: Fifty afghani! No! *Ne, ne, ne!*

They haggle and agree on a price.

Jean: And off goes the taxi driver into the distance. Here I am, in this lovely quiet area where the Russian Embassy is situated, on the outskirts of Kabul. It cost me about seventy-five cents to get here, and that included the tip or *baksheesh.*[26]

As I approach the door of the embassy, there are six Afghan boys standing here with their school books. They are chattering in Farsi. (*to the boys*) Do you speak English?

Boy: Yes, I speak English.

Jean: Do you want to hear how you sound?

Boy: Yes.

Jean plays the tape back for him. Laughter.

Jean: You are boys who go to school?

Boy: Yes.

Jean: How old are you?

Boy: I am sixteen.

Jean: No, you are not more than fourteen!

All laugh.

Boy: Yes! Look, English Hungary book.

---

[26] . Tip or bribe.

Jean: English book or Hungarian?

Boy: Hungary.

Jean: You got this book from the library? I see.

The boys have evidently been to the library here where, surprisingly, they have books which are being translated from Hungarian into English. And now, in just these few minutes, quite a crowd's gathered. As I look around me, there are nine, twelve, fifteen boys and also two men with fierce-looking faces and turbans on their heads, very graceful in their carriage and bearing. (*to the boys*) I'm going into the embassy now. Say goodbye in Farsi.

Boy: *Khoda hafez.* Goodbye, see you tomorrow.

Jean: (*laughing*) Khoda hafez. See you tomorrow. Tashakor!

When Jean comes back outside, the boys have been waiting for her.

Boy: Where you want to go?

Jean: (*speaking slowly*) I'm going to the Intourist office now to get travel information.

Boy: Where their house?

Jean: Around the corner.

Boy: Please to have lunch with us?

Jean: (*laughs in surprise*) Please to have lunch with you?

Boy: Yes.

Jean: Oh, that's very kind of you, a lovely invitation. I really don't know what to say. Thank you, but no thank you. Ne tashakor.

The boys are still following me, although I'm quite some distance ahead of them now. As I walk around the corner of this beautiful compound, I can smell the orange blossoms on the other side of the fence. Two Afghans are busily whitewashing it. The modern building is absolutely lovely. It sparkles in the bright sunshine.

Boy: Mostration.

Jean: What? A demonstration?

Boy: Yes. Demonstration.

Jean: At your school?

Boy: Ne, ne. At that school. At yellow school.

Jean: I'm not quite sure, but evidently, across the street in one of the schools, although I don't think it's his school, there is some sort of a demonstration. Maybe I will go there after I go to the Intourist office.

Boy: My brothers and I went to that school.

Jean: I see.

Boy: What time is it?

Jean: I don't know. Hmm, let's see …(*She speaks in Farsi; laughter.*) I got my numbers a bit confused there, so no wonder they didn't understand what I was saying because I was saying half past twenty instead of half past ten!

Jean is leaving the Intourist office.

Jean: Well, now I know a little bit more of about how to get to Russia and I've had my first sort of setback. So now I'm going to go to the

Afghan-Swiss Tourist Office in another district, on the other side of town, and see if I can find out something about a better fare.

Walking toward me are three, four ladies, each clad in a *chadri,* known here as the "Afghan *burqa*". It is a loose, full-length outer garment worn by Muslim women when in public to keep them respectfully and completely covered. It is draped over the head and body with a small mesh net or grille to hide the eyes, but which they can see out through. Traditionally the chadri is sky blue in Kabul. Here they come with one, two, oh God, eight children, all of them giggling at me because I've got the tape recorder out. I don't think they know exactly what I'm about.

I've just come up to the corner of the main street, Darlaman. I'll either have to hire a taxi or see if I can navigate a bus. Under a great big beautiful tree here, there is a woven sort of a bed called a charpoy, and on it is sitting a young Afghan boy surrounded by his baskets of nuts, raisins, plums, and great big cucumbers. Next to that there's a table with a display of green and puce-coloured drinks, which I'm sure he's prepared himself because they are in Coca-Cola bottles, and only Coca-Cola is supposed to be in those bottles. He's offering me this beverage, which I shall politely refuse. Here is a group of men I can ask.

Jean: Bus? You know bus?

Men: Bus, yes. Stop here.

Jean: Tashakor. To centre Kabul? *Chand*? How much?

Man: Thirteen, Darlaman bus.

Jean: Bus thirteen? Or thirteen afs?[27]

Man: Thirteen.

Jean: Thirteen afs, or number thirteen bus?

Man: Number thirteen bus!

---

[27] . Short for afghani, the Afghan currency.

Jean: *Baleh*—okay. Chand?

Man: Chand what?

All laugh.

Jean: Now that I've established that it is the number thirteen bus, which I shan't be able to read anyway, I'm trying to enquire about the fare, but it's hopeless. *(to the man, laughing)* I may as well walk! Tashakor. *(Sound of traffic. She changes her mind and calls out.)* Taxi!

The driver and I have established the price first this time, and it's ten afs less than the trip out, and it's, oh, just three or four minutes beyond where I was dropped off. *(gasping)* God, what a sight! The entire road is blocked by sheep being driven across it by a little boy with a twig. There must be hundreds of them, and we have to wait until he gets them across.

We're driving along a street now, which is packed on every side with little bazaars and carts where vendors are selling their wares. This is the beginning of the fruit season in Afghanistan, and the carts are loaded with mounds of apricots, cherries, courgettes, eggplants, and peaches.

I'm trying to find our way through the maze of streets here, as I don't know this tourist office location too well. The driver doesn't understand what I'm talking about. So now I've missed one turning. Certain keywords are very helpful. Right, left and ... oh, there it is! *Roo b'raah*, straight ahead. Now we'll start with the bargaining again as custom demands.

Jean: Chand?

Taxi Driver: Forty afs.

Jean: Tashakor! We haven't actually had to do any bargaining because he's stuck to his original price, which is quite unusual. He's fascinated by the tape recorder. You talk.

Taxi Driver: I used to be take lessons.

Jean: That is English! I no speak Farsi! *(Both laugh.)* Tashakor!

Taxi Driver: Tashakor. Thank you. Excuse me.

Jean: You speak very well. Khoda hafez. Goodbye.

Jean: I've just been talking to Mr Bakshi. Is that correct? Did I say it right?

Mr Bakshi: Yes.

Jean: It doesn't seem to be possible to go to Russia on the cheap fare from here, so I've been talking with Mr Bakshi about going to Kashmir instead. It's a beautiful time of the year to go there, and I think we've worked out a better arrangement. Henry and I will fly to Amritsar for a few days and then go on to Srinagar and spend some time on a houseboat on beautiful Dal Lake, known as the jewel in the crown of Kashmir, isn't that so? And the houseboats are called "floating palaces", are they not?

Mr Bakshi: Yes, that is true.

Jean: Could you describe the plan for me?

Mr Bakshi: Every Friday and Sunday, there are flights from Kabul to Amritsar. You have sightseeing of Amritsar, Golden Temple[28] and Jallianwala Bagh[29] and stay one night. A double room, air-conditioned, will cost around fourteen dollars. Next day, you fly to Srinagar by Indian Airlines. The houseboat man will receive you at the airport and take you to deluxe-class houseboat on Dal Lake, which will be exclusively for two people. The houseboat, including three meals and the *shikara*[30], that is boat crossing the lake, will cost around seventeen dollars for two people per day. There is a special fare from Kabul to Kashmir and back, a hundred ten dollars and sixty cents.

Jean: It sounds very lovely and certainly reasonable to me. Is the price of the sightseeing in Amritsar included or is that extra?

---

[28] . Holiest Sikh shrine.

[29] . A public garden with a memorial to the pilgrims and civilians killed by British forces in the Amritsar massacre of 1919.

[30] .Wooden, often canopy-covered, brightly coloured taxi-boats used on Dal Lake.

Mr Bakshi: No, that is extra.

Jean: Would you know about how much that is?

Mr Bakshi: Going to the Golden Temple and Jallianwala Bagh by taxi for three to four hours will cost about two or three dollars.

Jean: Does one make an arrangement with just any taxi driver or a special one through your company?

Mr Bakshi: The owner of the hotel is a good friend of mine. I will give a personal letter in his name, and he will hire you the taxi because, otherwise, you will have the problem of the language.

Jean: What is the language there?

Mr Bakshi: Amritsar is in the Punjab part of India, so people speak Punjabi, and also Hindi and Urdu.

Jean: All right. Thank you very much. I'll say cheerio. You know in England we say cheerio?

Mr Bakshi: Yes, I know this word because I am Indian, and at the time when I was studying, the Britishers were ruling India. We were studying English, and sometimes these words used to come up, so we are familiar with them.

Jean: So you don't say cheerio. What do you say?

Mr Bakshi: *(laughing)* You see, actually I stopped, because I have worked for about ten years with the Americans and I am more familiar with American words than the English words because I am not working with any Englishman.

Jean: I see, I see. What is your native language though? What part of India are you from?

Mr Bakshi: Actually, I am from Rawalpindi area in Pakistan. In 1947, I migrated to India.

Jean: So what language is your native tongue?

Mr Bakshi: I speak Punjabi. I speak Hindi. I speak Urdu, English.

Jean: English. And Farsi?

Mr Bakshi: Farsi.

Jean: Pashto?[31]

Mr Bakshi: No. I'm sorry. I can understand few words of Pashto, but I can't speak it. I know figures like *yaw, dwa, drai, salor*[32] because I spent four years in Frontier Province. I knew Pashto at that time, but I have forgotten it as I was out of touch for fourteen years by living in India and, when I came to Afghanistan, I never paid any attention to this language.

Jean: But all the rest you do very well. That's a lot of languages. So, now what do you say when I say cheerio to you?

Mr Bakshi: I'll say … Bye-bye, baby!

Jean: That's your American!

Both laugh heartily.

Jean: I've just left the travel agency, and I'm now walking along the street, which is a rather busy one. I'm going to go to see Basheer, Azad's eldest son, to take some photos of his very interesting music shop where he sells hi-fi equipment and does tape recordings. Right now, I'm walking over

---

[31] . One of the two official languages of Afghanistan, spoken by the Pashtun (Pathan) people.
[32] . Numbers one through four in Pashto.

some very beautiful Afghan rugs that are spread on the pavement for the purpose of being walked on. It seems that the more they're used and the older they look, the better the price is for them.

I'm just coming to a little row of shops. The first one has a charcoal brazier in front and is used for making kebabs. Across the street, there is a local cinema. There's another little stall with a great big jar filled with carrots, which are very popular. And here's a tea shop and a meat shop, absolutely swarming with flies. Two young children are sitting on the doorstep in front of a sort of an appliance or plumbing appliances shop.

Little boy: Fanta?

Jean: Ne, ne, tashakor.

The little boy is offering me a bottle of Fanta which is an orange drink. (*Music with man singing, horns honking.*) Here's a little stationery shop and a sort of a repair shop. It's a little hole in the wall. I'll ask these men standing in front of the shop.

Jean: Do you speak in Farsi?

Man: No. Bicycles.

Jean: Umm?

Man: He's a bicycle.

Jean: A bicycle shop?

Man: No. He's a maker.

Jean: Oh, he makes bicycles! And *chand* bicycle? How much?

They're trying to describe to me how he makes a bicycle, including everything, all the nails, bolts, nuts, and grease. It comes to *sad* afghanis, which I think is a hundred. I don't know.

Man: One hundred afghanis.

Jean: One hundred afs, and they're eighty-four to the dollar. Oh, there's the sound of the bicycle bell! Tashakor, tashakor …

A little farther on is a tiny tailor shop, and all the help in the shop are, of course, men and little boys. Most of them are sitting on top of the tables, squatting and sewing away. They have German and Japanese sewing machines … Now, this is an interesting shop. They're making chairs with beautiful woven rush bottoms, sort of crude backs, not very clever designs, but they look quite sturdy. *(to the carpenter)* Salaam alaikum.

Carpenter: Salaam alaikum.

Jean: You are sawing wood?

Carpenter: Yes. What you want?

Jean: I want to watch you.

Carpenter: Yes. Making box and furniture and everything.

Jean: It is amazing the number of people speaking English, broken as it may be, but the increase is huge. Everywhere we can see more signs written in English, as well as hearing it spoken. The carpenter's showing me how he's planing the wood. A lovely smell of wood in this shop. Tashakor … Next door is a workshop with lots of copper wire and motors in the window and the sign under the Farsi writing says:

We rare motors, water pumps, and electrical equipment.

Walking down the street, chattering away, are five young schoolgirls in their navy-blue uniforms, long black stockings, and white scarves on their heads. *(to the girls)* You speak English? No English? Farsi?

Girls: Farsi! Salaam alaikum.

Jean: Pashto?

Girls: No, no!

Jean and Girls: Khoda hafez. Goodbye.

Music is playing in the background.

Jean: Now, here I am in Basheer's music shop. I'm looking around, but I don't see him anywhere … Oh, so nice to see you, Najibah! Salaam alaikum. Najibah is Azad's next-to-the-youngest daughter, aren't you? Say hello!

Najibah: (*giggling*) Salaam alaikum. Hello. Basheer's in the office.

Jean: Is he? Oh, very good. Thank you very much.

Basheer: Salaam alaikum.

Jean: This is my friend, Basheer, who helped me so much with the paperwork and customs when I was here before. We're going to listen to a demonstration tape which Basheer is playing on his stereophonic equipment. Afghan people love their own music, but they have a very keen taste for all sorts of foreign music. They especially like English. Oh, now Basheer's playing the Beatles' song "Hey Jude"…Oh, hello Azad. Salaam alaikum. How are you?

Azad: Salaam alaikum. Thank you, fine. How are you?

Jean: Very well, thank you.

Azad: You staying in Kabul a good time?

Jean: Oh, it's very good, thank you, and thanks to Basheer, my tape recorder's now working.

Azad: It's fine?

Jean: Yes. It's working very well. He said it would cost five afghanis. I can't complain at that price. Oh, here's Henry.

Henry: I have a suspicion that she was taping something this morning about four o'clock. Is this right or not?

Jean: I did. I woke up this morning and I heard the *muezzin*[33] calling. I tried to put it on the tape but it was too far away.

Henry: What time would that be?

Azad: That's about half past four.

Jean: Yes, I was up taping at that time. (*They all laugh.*) Basheer, you were married about two weeks ago, weren't you?

Azad: Yes, has been married. Was very big celebration. In spite we could have invited about seven hundred people, we obliged to cut the people due to the small space. The biggest hotel in Kabul, they accepted four hundred fifty invitations. We have done it in spite we didn't invite the whole my family completely, and also we didn't invite all of our friends. We didn't invite the business people, the Rotary Club or the Chamber of Commerce. We owe them, some way we have to cover for this.

Both laugh.

Jean: So this was mostly family and friends.

Azad: Yes.

Jean: How many people were there?

Azad: Two hundred fifty from two sides.

Jean: (*gasping*) Two hundred fifty people!

---

[33] .The cleric who calls Muslims to prayer from the minaret of a mosque.

Azad: Yes, from bride side and from our side.

Jean: How many lambs did you have at the feast?

Azad: We had four complete big sheep roasted in four sides of the dining room.

Jean: I'm looking at a colour picture of the table, almost two hundred metres long, and absolutely staggering to see as it's loaded down with all sorts of good food. *(to Azad)* I'm terribly sorry we missed it. Maybe we can arrange to be at the feast where you are making it up to your business friends!

Jean and Azad chuckle.

Henry: Jean and I want to invite you, Basheer and Najibah, to be our guests for lunch. We can make up for repairing the tape recorder this way. Please let us do it.

Azad: No, better is when we come to London, we will come to your house to have some food.

Jean: *(whispering)* This is an English class. My friend, Zahra, is teaching the boys from a blackboard. She repeats each word three times and they repeat it after her.

Zahra: Listen to me. Minute. Now repeat.

Class: Minute.

Zahra: Now, quarter.

Class: Quarter.

Zahra drills the class together several more times, then asks each individual student.

Student: Time, o'clock, past, half, hour, minute, quarter.

Zahra: *Haf.* The *l* is silent. (*She continues with the drill.*)

Jean: Zahra says there is no English department in this school, and I can well believe it, as it's very basic. This is an adobe room with whitewashed walls. The ceiling has tree beams that are covered with smaller twigs and straw, I suppose to keep out the rain. The wooden desks are very primitive, and the room is very small and close. It is heavy with the stench of the students, who all look very washed and clean, but, because of the lack of air, can't help the circumstances. There's a great deal of politeness evident between the boys and the teacher.

Student: Past, hour, minute, half, quarter.

Zahra: What time is it?

Student: It's one o'clock.

Zahra: The numbers.

Jean: *Yek, do, se, chahâr, panj.*[34]

They laugh.

Student: My name is Shapoor. My father's name is Sohail.

Jean: Good.

Student: My name is Ahmad. My father's name is Jamal.

Jean: You can say anything. Do you like school?

---

[34] . Numbers one through five in Farsi.

60

Ahmad: Yes. I have a car. I like Afghan music. I like American music.

Jean: Do you like to dance?

Ahmad: Yes.

Another student: I like school and Afghan music and American music.

Another student: I'm going to be an engineer.

Jean: Will you go to university?

Student: Yes.

Jean: Do you like to play football?

Student: Yes!

Another student: Me also.

Jean: Do you play cricket?

Another student: No. I am interesting the English.

Jean: The boys want *me* to sing a song. But I'm absolutely hopeless in this department, so I'm trying to get them to sing for me.

A student sings. Applause.

Jean: Zahra and I are sitting outside in the courtyard now, absolutely surrounded by bicycles that belong to the boys. The boys are gathering closely. They want to see what I'm doing here with the tape recorder and are chattering in excitement. Farsi? There are about fifty boys here. And here's the principal. *(to principal)* Salaam aleikum. I have taken photographs of the boys.

Principal: All the boys?

Jean: Yes, the boys in Zahra's class. I will send them pictures, all right?

Principal: All right.

Jean: Then you can have them for your school.

Principal: Thank you.

Jean: What is your name?

Principal: Mr Ziya.

Jean: How many students are in your school?

Principal: There's about sixty-five.

Jean: They're very nice boys.

Principal: Yes. I was wondering if you come sometimes to classes, because the boys don't have good pronunciations and they need it.

Jean: Thank you very much. I will be most happy to.

He leaves.

Jean: Zahra and I are now sitting in what is sort of a reception room, and we're waiting for her next class to begin. How many are in your class?

Zahra: There are twenty-five. The school has two groups, one morning period and one afternoon period, so more children can attend the school. They all come for four hours a day only.

Jean: Here come the students. (*to the students*) This is a tape recorder. I will tape your voices as you speak your lessons and then play them back so you can hear how you sound. All right?

Students: *(enthusiastically)* All right! Yes!

Jean: This is another adobe type building with whitewashed walls, the same kind of thatched roof covering the beams, but this room is a little bit larger and has a lovely big door, making it nice and airy. The students look between fifteen to seventeen years old. Zahra's taking the roll now.

Zahra: Jean, please pronounce the word. If the students have some problem, they can ask you?

Jean: Yes, of course. *(whispering)* I don't know how the boys study in the winter because there are two little windows with no glass, no covering on them at all. The blackboard is difficult to read because it's been used so very often that sitting where I am at the back of the class, I can't even see what Zahra's writing. I know the lesson is going to be about telling time.

Now, she's coming to the word *hour*, and that's where they run into trouble because of the *h*. She's telling them that the *h* is silent but having difficulty pronouncing the word herself. She drills the boys over and over. They're very good, because the other class hadn't mastered it quite as well.

Zahra: Now the boys are going to sing a song for you.

Singing.

Jean: That was lovely. I liked how you boys used your desks as drums!
Now, one boy in particular is very brave and is going to sing in Farsi.

Boy sings.

Jean: Bravo! To me it sounded just as good as any of the Afghan records I have heard.

This boy is very shy and kept his eyes cast down the entire time he was singing, but the quality of his voice and the music, I think are very nice indeed. *(to the boy)* Tashakor, tashakor.

Day Two: "You speak. Farsi. Into the microphone."

Noise of busy intersection near the bazaar.

Jean: I think the traffic here is really incompatible. The number of automobiles in Kabul and the number of donkeys and camels carrying heavy loads present problems for each other, don't they?

Henry: Yes.

Jean: Then, there are these huge, two-wheeled carts that the men carry the fruit and vegetables on.

Henry: Maybe in a few years' time, they'll ban all these.

Jean: This could well be.

There's a cart with huge watermelons, another with potatoes and eggplants in baskets straddling a teeny, weeny donkey, which you can hardly see for the load that it's carrying on its back. The man weighing the watermelons is selling them in great big pink slices. They look good, but I wouldn't dare try one without my Entero-Viroform.

At this early hour, all the little shops are open. In front of me is a great big samovar steaming away. Lots of people are sitting on the cupboard doors used to make a sort of bed and having a cup of tea and a slice of naan. Never have I seen so many flies! But, here, the nuts and raisins at least have a kind of mosquito netting over them to protect them from the flies. There's a sizzling kebab fire over there. Men and women are walking along carrying immense loads on their heads, and they're so graceful! Afghan people have a beautiful way of walking and marvellous posture. They never drop anything, but turn and move with great ease.

Henry and I are on a local bus, the first one we've been on since we got to Kabul. It's pretty good. We got on near the end stop, near the museum we just visited, and it was rather empty, so we've got a front seat. The conductor is sort of cranking it up on the outside. But, now the driver's starting off without him! Oh my, the conductor's just got on at the end with a flying leap.

Now it's more crowded. I don't know how people manage to stay on. We're surrounded by ladies, almost every one wearing a chadri, and it's an astonishing sight to see these mounds of cloth sitting on the seats. They don't look like anything human, do they?

Henry: No. Not at all.

Jean: Most of them have babies underneath the blue cloth and are pregnant besides. I don't know how the conductor will know how much to charge us. How can he remember where everybody gets on? I don't see him issuing any tickets.

Henry: It's probably a flat rate.

Jean: Yes, it's possible. Now the conductor is collecting our money. What did he charge you?

Henry: It's cost us three afs.

Jean: Imagine, just three afs to go back on the bus when it cost us sixty afs to get out to the museum!

Now, we're at the police barracks to try and arrange for our re-entry permits for when we return from Kashmir. What do you bet that we've been directed to the wrong office and we wind up back here?

So, it turns out to be even more of a ridiculous situation than we had anticipated. We didn't get sent back to the original office, but we were told instead that we must go to the official Afghan tourist office, which will give us a letter that we must then bring back to the police, who will then issue a re-entry visa. Now, all this back and forth and extra trips for us, which involve time and effort, could have been avoided if the man who issued the tickets to us in the first place had said, "Now you must go to the Afghan tourist office to get a letter, and then go to the police." Actually, he didn't even tell us that we needed a re-entry permit. We just luckily knew that!

Noise of bustling crowd.

We're now walking to the bazaar. A woman is singing in the distance. Here is a vendor in front of his stall. You talking, please?

Vendor: Baksheesh.

Henry: You speak. Farsi. Into the microphone.

Jean: He wants some money. *(to vendor)* Ne, ne, ne. No baksheesh.

We're walking down the street now and passing a lot of little bazaar shops, and all the charcoal glaziers are glowing with hot, hot coals, and the smoke is billowing in clouds. You can hardly see the man behind the smoke as he fans the flames to get good, glowing embers. The smell is divine. Oh, I'm so hungry.

Vendor: Kebab? Four kebab?

Jean: Baleh—okay. Tashakor.

Vendor: Pancake. Onion.

Jean: Yes, please.

This vendor's got a little wood fire on which he has a large metal tray piled high with pancakes, which are cooked with onion. Oh, they look marvellous.

Henry: *(to vendor)* I would like a pancake.

Jean: Tashakor. What is *qabli* pulao?

Vendor: Pulao is rice. This kind you say is rice with raisins and carrots, chopped up. You put these things in rice.

Jean: What is *shinwari* kebab?[35]

Vendor: *Shinwari* kebab is, you know, lamb chops?

Jean: Yes.

Vendor: Exactly like this, because you put on the spit here and you cook by the charcoal.

Jean: Can I have some shinwari kebab and some pulao? Is all right?

Vendor: Yes.

Jean: With qabli pulao?

Vendor: Yes, sure.

Jean: Tashakor.

Now, we're going over to Basheer's music centre because he wants me to draft some letters for him. I'll let his typist do the actual typing. Henry and I are in a taxi, as it's just too hot to walk. It only takes fifteen to twenty minutes to walk there, but it's very hot, even though it's after five o'clock in the afternoon. No shade to speak of on the way. The air is very dry and dusty by this time of the day.

---

[35] . Rib of lamb made into kebabs and named after one of the large Pashtun tribes.

Henry: As the sun goes down, the wind gets up and it stays windy until evening, until it gets dusk.

Taxi Driver: We're here, yes?

Jean: Yes. Tashakor.

We've come from Basheer's to this restaurant for dinner and are admiring these marble-topped tables.

Henry: Yes, they're exactly as when the first piece of rock was hewn out of the ground. Yesterday, I watched as they were making these table tops by standing a huge piece of marble on its end and sawing through it at various widths. Water was being dowsed on it from a sort of shower. I must have watched for about twenty minutes and saw no impression. I came back again after about half an hour, then one hour, and they had cut through about only two inches.

Jean: So, it's very difficult to saw through.

Henry: Yes, without splitting.

Jean: Did you notice how these marble slabs are set on tree stumps?

Henry: Yes.

Jean: Or, like this one in front of us, set on two tree stumps because it's a double table, but over there, are some free-form logs that are big enough to be table height.

The banquettes are beautiful with Afghan cushions and pillows at the back in lovely striped material, and the magnificent old chairs are carved in lovely black wood and decorated with all sorts of Afghan yarn hangings, like streamers, at the sides. The walls are draped with beautiful pieces of Afghan carpet, and there are separate little rooms, sort of like caves, which are dark behind the beautiful silken cloths at the entrances to them. Huge water ewers and urns stand in the corners, and it's air conditioned!

Henry: The outside really doesn't do the inside justice.

Jean: No, not at all. The lights are nice and dim. What did you say those fixtures were made of?

Henry: I think that the sides of the lamp are stretched goatskin.

Jean: Makes a kind of indirect lighting scheme.

I've just been served this absolutely beautiful, huge plate. There's a sword on it, under which are skewered three lamb chops which have been barbecued over the coals. The pulao has raisins and carrots in it, and there is a little salad. And I think all of this cost sixty afs, which is … well, less than a dollar!

We've just come back to our hotel to find a wedding party going on in the big room here. Lots of music and laughter. Everybody's invited to weddings. The bride and groom haven't made their appearance yet and won't until midnight. I don't think I can last that long. I'm surrounded by children, all very good looking. The women are all decked out in rayon, silk, and lots of glittery things. They seem to sit around for about six hours—that's the custom—listening to music and chatting, sort of playing musical chairs.

The handsome little children are very shy. The mother of the children has come over because she thinks they are bothering me. (*to the woman*) No, that's quite all right. Really, thank you. No, it's fine. I've taken a tape recording of the music. It's very lovely.

Day Three: "Do not attack or suffocate the person in front of you or clerk."

Jean: We're at the travel agent's trying to plan a trip.

Henry: How often does Bakhtiar Airline go to Bamiyan?[36]

Agent: I think about four or five times a week.

Henry: Do you know what day?

Agent: No, I don't know exactly because the day changing all the time.

Jean: Where can we find out?

Agent: At their home office in the corner of Kabul Hotel. It is better to go personally. They have an office in the Intercontinental Hotel but never the man is there.

Henry: In the Kabul Hotel did you say?

Agent: Yes.

Jean: And how have you been?

Agent: *(surprised)* Me?

Jean: Yes, you. You have been well?

Agent: Yes. There were some ladyships which I take to Mazaar-i-Sharif and Bamiyan.

Jean: Really? To Mazar?

Agent: I came yesterday Bamiyan.

---

[36] . Largest town in Hazarjat, in the central highlands of Afghanistan, famous for the enormous statues of Buddha carved into the rock face, destroyed since by the Taliban.

Jean: And you are back already?

Agent: Yes.

Jean: That was very fast!

Agent: Five days trip.

Jean: Five days trip! Tired?

Agent: Yes!

Jean: We're on our way to the post office now, and we're passing by the Kabul River in the centre of the city. It's a muddy, yellowy-tan colour because of all the mud and silt that has been washed down by the rain we had yesterday. Against a brick wall here, there are some birdcages, and all the birds are singing. I don't know if they sell them or use them to attract customers. The man sitting beneath the birdcages is selling prayer rugs. Here's a little boy selling pens. *(to the boy)* How much are your pens?

Boy: Ten afs. How many?

Jean: Five afs.

Boy: Six afs.

Jean: Five afs

Boy: Okay. How many pens?

Jean: That's okay, just one. I think this little boy must be probably seven years old. He's very polite.

Boy: You want envelope?

Jean: No, just pen. Thank you.

Boy: Thank you.

Jean: Now we're at the main post office, at the Poste Restante,[37] checking our mail, which is no longer held at the embassy for us. It seems that the embassy was inundated with visitors' mail and couldn't cope, so it's all sent over in a bag every few days. Here it's sorted according to alphabetical letter, together with mail from other embassies and, in effect, all the mail that comes in. First we have to produce our passports. They are quite strict here, which is a comforting thought.

Jean: We are looking for the letter *W.*

Clerk: Yes, it's right over there. Passports? I'm just checking you identify.

Jean: Yes. When is the next mail due?

Clerk: Nearly at four o'clock this afternoon.

Jean: And tomorrow?

Clerk: Maybe about ten o'clock or ten thirty.

Jean: Tashakor. Thank you.

Posted on a sign next to the window here are some instructions in French, German, and English with regard to picking up mail. There's a five-afghani charge for every letter one receives here. At the bottom of the English sign, it says "Enjoy your post office" with little flowers decorating it on either side. Under that it says:

---

[37] . Post office service where mail is kept until the recipient comes and collects it in person, often used when travelling and there is no permanent address.

Patience is a virtue. Do not attack or suffocate the person in front of you or clerk. These rules are for your protection. When you do not receive mail, do not imagine that we have eaten your letters.

Now we're going to get some airmail stamps for postcards we've written, and I'm also getting some beautiful ones for my daughter, Sue, in Spain. They're gorgeous, aren't they? I wonder if the clerk's going to want anything extra for them. *(to the clerk)* How much are the airmail stamps for Spain?

Clerk: Twenty-one afs. For letter?

Jean: Yes. How much do I owe you?

Clerk: Wait a minute. I count. All postcards is thirty afs.

Jean: Yes. But, you have not charged for these.

Clerk: Never mind.

Jean: No, you give me special stamps.

Clerk: It's okay.

Jean: Thank you very much.

Clerk: Thank you. Every time you bring your letter here, I put for you very beautiful stamps.

Jean: Who designs the stamps?

Clerk: I do.

Jean: You do! My, my. Tashakor.

Clerk: Tashakor.

Jean: Outside now and these little boys are brushing my shoes.

Boy: Okay. Now very good polish.

Jean: No, no, ne polish, just brush.

Boy: Yes, okay.

Sound of bells tinkling.

Jean: That's the noise of a *gari* or horse-drawn cart going by, and the road is absolutely smothered with cars and taxis.

Jean: We're in luck as the airline office is open.

Agent: Flights are except for on Saturdays and Tuesdays, then we don't have a flight.

Henry: Except Saturdays and Tuesdays.

Agent: Yes. From Kabul to Bamiyan.

Jean: Even on *Jumma*[38], on Friday, there's a flight?

Agent: Yes, but on Sundays, our departure time is at six in the morning and we turn it back at four in the afternoon.

Jean: Is there time to go from Bamiyan to Band-e Amir?[39]

---

[38] . Friday or Friday prayers for Muslims.
[39] . Afghanistan's first national park high in the Hindu Kush Mountains, renowned for its six beautiful, sapphire-blue lakes.

Agent: No. It is better to make contact with tourist office. It's about five or six hours' drive.

Jean: That far? Really?

Agent: The road is very bad.

Jean: We've just made the enquiry about the schedule from Kabul to Bamiyan and Band-e Amir and determined that the round-trip flight will cost $18 per person, which is more than to fly from London to Paris! Obviously, it's because there's so little business around. I think we'll probably go Sunday week and stay overnight and then go to Band-e Amir and return the following Monday.

I'm standing now in front of a little book stall, stacked with paperback books—oh, 99 per cent of them are in English. I can just imagine that they have been collected in America and in England, the used copies that is, and sent over here for re-using.

We're walking by the main taxi stand now and most of the taxi drivers are busy washing their cars. Oh, there's a chap right inside the motor, cleaning it out! Taxis are marked with red stripes on either side, and at night they have a little blue light in the windscreen. All cars that are bought are old because, when a car is five years old, it comes in with a very low duty. Otherwise, the duty runs up to 167 per cent. Only people like the king and the extremely wealthy can afford to buy new cars.

Here's a chap sitting on a little stool at his stall holding lovely yellow mangoes, but he's admiring himself in a mirror, absolutely ignoring the customers clamouring for mangoes.

We've come over to have our first look at a new department store that's been built. It's about three stories high. Lots of Afghan people are standing outside the door, but nobody seems to be going in. Ah, there we are. The entrance is very nice with lace curtains and pots of geraniums on the marble floor. A kind of fairground music is playing. The display area on this first floor seems to be mostly for household goods, some fans, some Thermos bottles, knife sharpeners, squeezers of juices, copper jelly moulds, plastic butter dishes, covered salt and pepper shakers, some transistor radios, kitchen equipment, cups and saucers, yarn for knitting, some ladies' purses. I should think this is the only store in Afghanistan where there are lady salesgirls.

Salesgirl: Yes, it is, about a hundred of them.

Jean: This must be the first time that young girls are being employed in a public way. There are one or two scattered in the tourist offices, perhaps one or two at Radio Afghanistan, but this is a new experience for the ladies of Kabul. This counter has mounds of Lux soaps, hair sprays. Oh, that's good because I need some! *(to the salesgirl)* This one is German?

Salesgirl: Yes.

Jean: And this one?

Salesgirl: Also German. Schwarzkopf.

Jean: That's incredible! Two hundred afs for a big tin of hairspray is about only two pounds! I'll try and pick some up in one of the bazaar shops to see if I can get it for less money.

We're walking up the stairs now to the clothing section. Again, there are young Afghan girls working as salesgirls. There are very lovely sweaters here, beautifully displayed really. A salesgirl has just come and approached me in a very nice way. There are scarves and nightgowns and blue jeans and short pants, long pants, baby clothes, towels, um ... shirts. The sections are mixed for men and women, and I find that a bit strange. There are people walking around, buying hats, socks, and underwear. There are Venetian blinds at the windows and very nice indirect lighting fixtures. And of course, the lovely marble floors everywhere. Someone over a loudspeaker is announcing some sort of a bargain, and here's a knit suit quite the equal to any I would see in England. At the far end of the floor, there is nice lightweight kind of luggage, and here's a very attractive young girl selling handbags. *(to the salesgirl)* Farsi? Handbag?

She's a very bashful girl and doesn't want to translate handbag into Farsi for me. The girls think I want to know the price of the articles, all of which are quite plainly marked.

Now we're on the next floor up. I got a bit of a scolding for recording the girls on the floor below. Here are all sorts of cookers, electric fans, little refrigerators, all sorts of lighting fixtures, and many more girls being employed than are necessary. It's very attractively laid out, I must say. There are some very good-looking vacuum cleaners and another large display of coffee pots, household goods mostly. Here's another announcement for a special bargain. There are even some toasters here, paraffin heaters. Ah, here are some tape recorders. Against the wall are neatly stacked electric light bulbs. The little vacuum cleaner that Henry has checked on costs twenty-five pounds. The tax—the import duty here—is just exorbitant. It's no wonder people can't afford to buy these things.

The department store has opened only recently because up here, on the very top floor, they are still working to build what will be an outdoor restaurant. I can see the iron framework for the awning. They're planing wood to make the tables. Inside are all sorts of children's toys, even tricycles and shoes. It really is beautifully laid out.

Now we're in a little bazaar shop trying to bargain with a vendor.

Vendor: Six hundred fifty.

Henry: No.

Vendor: Six hundred.

Henry: No.

Vendor: Five hundred forty-five.

Henry: Five hundred thirty-five.

Vendor: Five hundred forty.

Jean: And so it goes, with five afghani variations on either side and both men are smiling and having the best of times. The vendor's showing us a very beautiful hand-carved knife that looks like it's been made from the hoof of an animal, banded around with silver. It's very primitive looking. He's already come down from eight afs to six afs, but it's a good shop. One would prefer to deal with one man rather than go around and bargain with a lot of shops.

We're walking along the streets of the bazaar, and there's a donkey laden with beautiful green grapes, the first ones I've seen. He's absolutely reeling underneath the burden on his back. Behind him there's a stall with some cantaloupes, and there's a man with beautiful flowers. Mangoes are in season. Listen! *(Music.)* That twanging noise is a little boy with a carrot scraper. Now he's playing, very loudly, what looks like a little flute. He has the most beautiful lapis ring, one of the prettiest I've seen. I think this exquisite blue gemstone is mined mostly in northern Afghanistan, and one can see it used everywhere in Afghan jewellery.

Boy: One thousand afs! Okay?

Jean: Not okay.

Another vendor: I have better one than this one. And I say for you, one hundred afs.

Jean: Ne, tashakor.

We are now on the Street of Chickens where there are many bazaar shops. We've just bought two pairs of earrings and are being pursued by the little boy who wants to sell Henry the ring. He's obviously pinched it from some shop, because every time we go near one, he disappears. Now, here he is again because we're not near a shop.

Henry: *(to the boy)* No! Ne, ne!

Jean: It's no fun having to stand here on the corner waiting to be picked up by Henry's friend, Len Hadley, because of the terrible wind. It's fierce. The sun is going down, and I hope the wind will die down a bit after that. In the meantime, Mr Hadley is supposed to pick us up and take us out to the USAID staff house where we're going to have a drink. Then, Henry and he will disappear discreetly around a corner and have a little business chat.

In the background, you can hear the noise of the traffic as people wend their way home. Just in front of me, a man's pulling a wooden cart loaded with crates of onions, some of the red Spanish variety, others of the green spring variety. Oh, there's Mr Hadley, right on time. Nice little blue car.

Henry: Hello there!

Jean: Hello, Len! How are you?

Henry: Hello. Meet Jean.

Len: I know Jean. How are you? Get in.

Jean: Nice to see you. Thank you.

Len: Well, have your old friends come back here?

Henry: They always return to the scene of the crime. Yet, I don't see as many as I expected to see.

Jean: Yes, there are far, far fewer tourists here this year, and the country, particularly Kabul, is feeling the loss of the tourist business very severely. Walking about the streets, we can see almost no tourists at all. We can count them actually, they are so few. We went to the Intercontinental Hotel the other night for dinner and were told that they have only twenty-seven guests. That's disastrous for a hotel built especially for the purpose of accommodating tourists.

Len: That's because of the Indo-Pakistani war.

Jean and Henry: Oh?

Len: Because of the border.[40] You know, the dope run used to go through here to Pakistan, India, or Nepal. They'd get their hash here and there and some would spend the winter in Goa.

Jean: I see, following or prior to coming to Afghanistan.

Len: But with the border closed, they don't come. Not so many. In fact, our workshop's down about 20 per cent on the repairs for travellers who used to come around driving.

Jean: Really?

Len: Yes, a lot of our business was from these people driving around the world in Land Rovers and Volkswagens.

Henry: Well, we noticed that, you know. Around the post office and places like that, there's not half the numbers we saw three years or so ago.

Len: As I say, last year it was really something. Of course, the government hates those kinds of tourists.

Jean: Len, do you notice any other changes here? I mean, you live here all the time.

Len: Well, that's just it. You don't notice them when you live here.

Henry: No.

Len: Of course, most of them are superficial. The people are still the same.

Henry: Exactly.

---

[40] . The 1971 conflict between India and Pakistan affected trade and tourism in Afghanistan until a peace treaty was signed in July of 1972.

Len: Doing business here is still the same. I had a very, very busy year last year.

Henry: Although we find that there are a lot more cars, there are also a lot more people who stop you in the street and are begging.

Len: Yes, well, they had a drought for three years.

Jean: Oh, that accounts for it!

Len: Yes, these people have come in from the provinces.

Jean: Because before, begging was one of the big differences between here and India.

Len and Henry: Yes. That's right.

Horns honking.

Len: Boy, these bicycles and pedestrians are driving me crazy. A good snowfall next winter will help somewhat. It's going to take some time to recover. We've been getting wheat from people all around the world, free you know. But, you know the Arghandab Dam ran dry.

Henry: Really?

Len: Yep. Dry as a bone. It was about, oh, two feet from the arch.

Jean: Oh, my. The drought must have been terribly severe then.

Henry: I thought it was filling up from the snow now.

Len: No, it filled long ago and it's dropping again. Well, here we are.

Day Four: "The meat cleaver swishes, and there go the bones."

Jean: It's another beautiful day. The weather is absolutely gorgeous—warm, very dry, and sunny. It's not too hot at all with a nice little breeze. The air is so clear that, in the distance, I can see a big beautiful mountain, but bare and brown as can be. Shahid, the family driver, is taking Najibah and me down a street right near the king's palace.

Shahid: King, king!

Jean: Shahid is looking more at me and the tape recorder than where he is going! Everyone is happy with my leaving it just running, and they love to hear the tape played back to them.

Yesterday, we were walking down this street that runs along the Kabul River, and Henry had his wallet pinched. We're just going past the scene of the crime now. This is one of the toughest parts of Kabul, so jam-packed with people, you can't get through. And so many donkeys! To my left, there's one loaded down with a basket of tomatoes, another with sacks of potatoes. Over there, another staggering under a load of red onions, yet another with beautiful purple eggplants.

Najibah and I are going to the Street of Chickens to see what kind of garments we may be able to purchase for me to take back to England. Then, perhaps, you and I, Najibah, can have a little business. We've made an arrangement whereby she'll do some buying for me here, and her brother, Basheer, will get the things through customs and shipped to London. I'll sell them in the boutique shops in and around where we live in Dorset, and we'll hope to have a little profit.

We're back in Basheer's shop, and I would like to introduce a friend of the family and a very good friend of Basheer's. Can you say your name for me please?

Abdul: My name is Abdul, and in near future, I will leave Kabul for London for six months.

Jean: This young man has won a United Nations Fellowship to go to London and study postal telecommunications. Then he will return and be a teacher here and show what he has learned while he has been abroad. *(to Abdul)* Are you afraid of going?

Abdul: Yes, because this is the first time I leave my country for a country that I've just heard about. I've not seen it so far.

Jean: Well, I don't think you'll have any trouble with the language. You speak English very well.

Abdul: Yes, but I don't think my English is sufficient. But, anyway, I'll go to try to improve it. Also to learn something about what I'll teach here in the future.

Jean: Well, I certainly wish you all the best of luck.

Abdul: Thank you very much. I do appreciate it.

Jean: Thank you and goodbye.

I am now sitting in the restaurant-bar-lounge-café-information centre of our very ritzy-sounding but not so ritzy hotel named The Plaza. Henry hasn't come back yet, so I decided to come in and have a cup of tea. I ordered two pots of tea by mistake, thinking he would be here. I shall probably have to drown myself in tea. Afghan tea comes in two varieties. The more popular one is black Indian tea, which is very tasty, and green tea which is Chinese tea. It's very bitter and has to be drunk with a sweet in the mouth. Oh, good. Here's Henry.

Men's voices haggling.

Henry and I are at a plastic shoe bazaar trying to buy a pair of shoes for him so that he can get into the shower without putting his feet on the floor. Those look good.

Henry: Sturdy.

Jean: Now Henry's trying to bargain the seller down, but he says no bargains. He wants thirty afs for them. How much did you get them for?

Henry: For twenty-eight. Yes, after having said *no deal!*

Jean: We're just passing a little ice cream shop with its huge block of snow standing in front. That's how you can tell there's ice cream inside. Little birds are singing in cages hung on a stand nearby.

Vendor: Five afghanis.

Jean: Would you say three afghanis?

Vendor: Okay, three afghanis.

Henry: The ice cream looked clean, didn't it?

Jean: Yes, it did. Ummm!

After picking me up again from my hotel, Shahid has brought the three of us—Halimah *[Azad's wife]* and their daughter, Nurah, and I—here in their little French Citroen car. I know this meat bazaar to be one of the most expensive in Kabul. We're standing in front of a stall and Halimah's going to buy some lamb. In the back of this bazaar is a tree trunk standing on end. It's about four feet high and used as a chopping block. The butcher is cutting some meat, but first he has to brush all the flies away. Then he will put it on a scale and weigh it. Shahid's overseeing the entire job and has a basket into which he'll put all the things that Halimah buys.

That's lamb chops they're going to have. I can tell by the way the butcher is cutting all the meat away from the bone. I wonder if they wash it before they eat it. It's not going to be lamb chops after all. It's for kebabs.

The meat cleaver swishes, and there go the bones. The meat does look awfully good, I must say, but Halimah's not satisfied with one little piece, so she's changing it for another one. I can see that she's being very, very particular indeed about the quality of meat she's buying.

Halimah's wearing trousers with beautiful lace edging on the bottom, black patent shoes, and what looks like an English raincoat on top. Thrown over her head is a chiffon scarf. Her daughter carries her handbag, the servant carries the shopping bag, and all she does is look, feel, and point, and they do all the rest.

In the next meat stall is a little bird cheeping in its cage. There's a little boy who's tempting it with some food. That's why it's chirping so. It's a blue bird with a white breast. I suspect that when no one is looking, it reaches out and pecks a piece of meat because its cage is hanging right in front of it.

While Halimah is pinching and squeezing the meat in another stall and having an argument about it, this young boy is trying to sell me a pound of lamb, and it does look nice.

Boy Vendor: Twenty afs for you, for one pound lamb.

Jean: Is good lamb?

Boy Vendor: Yes, is good.

Jean: Let's see, that's twenty-five cents a pound. Yes, *tashakor,* thank you.

This young boy speaks very good English and is very attractive. He's got smiling eyes and beautiful white teeth. I think he's perhaps fifteen or sixteen years old, and he's cutting the meat, which is now on a hook, with the skill of long years of practice. He really is beautiful to watch with graceful motions as he cuts and chops. Here too, as his chopping block, is a great big tree stump.

In front of the bazaar are stalls with beautiful flowers. This is the time of the year in Afghanistan when, because of all the rains, flowers are brought to market. They are absolutely gorgeous: yellow, purples, reds, oranges, whites. They have anemones, carnations, some sort of tiger lily, beautiful daisies, lovely flowers.

Well, this is the way to shop. Everybody is sitting in the car but Shahid. He's gone into what's like a little grocery store to buy some cooking oil, and Halimah directs the whole procedure from the seat of the car. Now they are haggling over the price. He's also buying what I think is salt. There's nothing on the box except Farsi, so I can't be sure.

Nurah is Azad's and Halimah's youngest daughter. She's just turned eighteen and is very pretty. She speaks English fairly well, but her comprehension is not so good. She wants to learn and practice, so I try to give her every opportunity. The other day when I was at the school in Zahra's class, the principal said he was going to contact the minister of education to see if he could get special permission for me to come and teach "pro-noun-ciation".

Now, Nurah is staying in the car, I suppose to guard it, and I've come out with Halimah. She's getting *more* meat! A man at a table is grinding meat into what looks like mince. God, the profusion of the vegetables all laid out here on the hard-packed dirt walkway! Every kind of fruit and vegetable you can imagine! Needless to say, all swarming with flies, but nevertheless, looking very beautiful. I think the family use potassium permanganate[41] to clean things before they eat them. I hope so because we've been invited there for a meal!

We're standing in front of another mound of potatoes. Halimah didn't like the first one. The vendor's showing us the different varieties of potatoes. Shahid's trying to tell me how much they are. The array of food stacked here is staggering! Things seem to have come into the market early this year. Everywhere, as far as I can see, are mounds of lettuces, radishes, carrots, spinach, green and yellow wax beans, courgettes, eggplants, red onions, lovely little cucumbers, great big white onions, tomatoes, melons. An incredible sight of colour. Everything's arranged in straw baskets with lovely mint decorating the edges, beautifully and artistically displayed.

All the vegetables look bright and glistening, but they've been washed with water from the river here, which is as dirty as I've ever seen. There's a boy

---

[41] . Used as a general disinfectant and for purifying water.

about twelve years old with a bucket of water and a tin that he's made into a crude cup. He's calling out, trying to sell his pitiful little supply of water.

Shahid's putting fresh peas into a paper bag now. They don't trust the stallholders, so he's doing all the weighing and measuring himself. I notice something different this year: the introduction of polythene bags. A lot of young boys are selling them now, and some vendors are starting to use them to put the vegetables and fruits in.

All the fruit and vegetables are brought from the countryside to a main sort of depot, and from there they're dispersed to the various bazaars throughout the city. There's no big delivery by lorry; it's all done by men, either by loading the produce onto donkeys or pulling carts for great distances. Man or beast, they strain at the loads they're so heavy.

A very rude chadri-dressed lady is pushing her way past Halimah, but she's having none of it. In front of me is a woman who looks like one of the Afghan nomadic tribal people. She's pregnant and carrying a baby with two children following her. She must have come in from the provinces where the drought has created a great deal of poverty and resulted in a lot more begging on the streets of Kabul.

Day Five: "We sitting talking and talking for two, four hours, then we eat."

At Azad's home. Music playing softly.

Jean: Salaam alaikum. Good afternoon, Basheer. How are you?

Basheer: Fine, thank you.

Jean: Ooh, you're looking very, very … what shall I say? Debonair. Pink shirt, beautiful pink, and tan tie.

Basheer: *(laughing)* Thank you, thank you. Hello, Henry, how are you?

Henry: Hello. Fine. How are you?

Basheer: I'm very happy because my family and myself, our father, all together waiting for you. In the meantime, I hope you like the jazz saxophone playing. And, I hope you like our Afghan food, which my mother and my sisters prepare for you.

Jean: Oh, we've been looking forward to this occasion very much. See, I'm all dressed up.

Basheer: Very good. I have a lot of words, but unfortunately, I cannot speak English well.

Jean: You mustn't apologize! Your English is very good, Basheer.

Basheer: But you know my pronunciation is not good, my grammar not good. But I hope by practise it will be better.

Jean: Exactly. You do not laugh at me when I speak Farsi!

Basheer: You know much better. But you don't have time, and there is no opportunity for you to speak Farsi.

Jean: Well, you speak to me. I will help.

Basheer: Okay.

Jean: Now we're sitting in the lovely lounge of the house where it's very cool and pleasant. We stopped off and picked up Shukriyah, Najibah's friend and teacher.

Shukriyah: Yes, I'm teaching her typing.

Jean: Every day?

Shukriyah: Yes, every day.

Najibah: About three months before, I was in Peace Corps course. I practise typing. I take one course.

Jean: With the Peace Corps?

Najibah: Yes.

Jean: Did they make you pay for the course?

Najibah: No, it was free.

Jean: That's good. Shukriyah, you're a student actually, aren't you?

Shukriyah: Yes, at Delhi University.

Jean: You just live here in the summer with your parents, is that right?

Shukriyah: Yes, yes. Do you like this music?

Jean: Yes, very much. Do you?

Shukriyah: I love it!

Jean: How do you like it compared to Afghan music?

Shukriyah: Indian music is richer.

Jean: In what way?

Shukriyah: It's technically more complicated, and I understand it better than I understand Afghani music. Afghani music is quite pleasant to listen to, but I prefer Indian music. Why do you like Afghani music?

Jean: I think that it's a little bit more melodic.

Shukriyah: Yes. Because it's so simple, that's why.

Jean: Yes, there are not as many instruments. What is your favourite Indian instrument?

Shukriyah: I like the sitar very much. But I also like the pure Indian instrument, the *veena*.[42] I don't know if you have heard of it.

Jean: Yes, I have.

Shukriyah: That is a proper Indian instrument. Sitar is actually more a Muslim instrument, you know, and more modified.

Jean: I think that's why the instrument here, the *rubab*[43], sounds very much like it.

Najibah: Yes, it does. It has fewer strings than a sitar, the instrument here.

Jean: Do you know many famous Indian musicians?

Shukriyah: Well, I've been to a few recitals when I was in India. I've been to a live Ravi Shankar recital and to a live Khan recital.

Jean: What is his name?

Shukriyah: Velaiz Khan. He's a Muslim.

Jean: There's another Khan, isn't there?

Shukriyah: Yes, Rais Khan. He's very good. Have you heard him?

Jean: Yes. He's the first one I heard in Delhi.

Shukriyah: Really?

Jean: Yes.

---

[42] . Similar to a sitar, but with a short, thick neck, often carved into a dragon's head.
[43] . One of the national musical instruments of Afghanistan. Resembling a lute, it is carved in one piece from the trunk of a mulberry tree.

Shukriyah: Have you heard Ali Akhbar Khan?

Jean: Yes.

Shukriyah: He plays the *sarod.*[44] That's a different instrument to the sitar.

Jean: The sitar is now very popular in the West. I went on one occasion to hear Ravi Shankar play with Yehudi Menuhin.

Shukriyah: Oh, yes! I heard about that. You have been to England also?

Jean: I live in England.

Shukriyah: Oh, I thought you were from the States.

Jean: I am, but I live in in England, in the country.

Shukriyah: You don't speak Farsi at all?

Jean: I have six, seven words, eight words maybe.

Shukriyah: You find it difficult?

Jean: Actually no. I find it much easier to learn than any Indian dialect, yes?

Shukriyah: Yes, quite right. I think if you know a bit of Hindi, it's easier for you to pick up Farsi because they are both in this same group—Urdu.

Jean: So, Najibah, Henry, and I are guests, and the custom in your house is for us to be seated in this room.

Najibah: Yes, that's right. Sometimes we sit on benches, sometimes on the floor, and we sitting talking and talking for two hours, four hours, then we eat.

---

[44] . Classical Indian stringed instrument similar to a sitar but producing a deeper, more resonant sound.

Jean: A lot of people to feed! You know in Basheer's shop there is that very tall, handsome boy with green eyes? He told me he has twelve sisters and eight brothers—twenty-one in the whole family.

Shukriyah: That's huge!

Jean: Yes! How many are there in your family?

Shukriyah: There are six of us in the family.

Jean: It's a lot different from twenty-one!

Shukriyah: (*laughs*) Certainly.

Jean: Najibah, does your mother get up very early in the morning?

Najibah: She gets up at four hours o'clock in the morning to pray at the mosque. Then she read holy Qu'ran, thirty pages, twenty-five pages.

Jean: And then she goes back to bed and rests.

Najibah: No!

Jean: No?

Najibah: She prepare something for breakfast, then tell the cook for lunch.

Jean: She gives directions to the cook?

Najibah: For lunch, yes. Then she clean the house.

Jean: She doesn't. The servant cleans the house.

Najibah: No, sometimes she does. Then she sews or does something.

Jean: Oh, here comes Basheer with a friend of his, also arriving for lunch. And his wife too! Sheema, you are looking beautiful! This is lovely. It's a very pretty dress.

Sheema: Oh, thank you.

Jean: English! You're saying thank you in English! So, now you have *yes*, *no*, and *thank you*, is that right?

All laugh.

Jean: Oh, we have just had the most fabulous meal. It was like a banquet! The table was all laden with all different kinds of Afghan foods, some of which I'd never had before. *(to the family)* Tashakor, tashakor! Thank you, thank you. Khoda hafez. Goodbye, goodbye.

At the Afghan Carpet Bazaar

Bamiyan Buddhas

Henry in Kabul

Jean Tape Recording

Lake Band-e-Amir

The Melon Season

PART 2

The Communist Coup

"And So the Stage Was Set ..."

Fund-raising talk given by Jean in the early autumn of 1978, at meetings of the Women's Institute and many other charity groups in the UK.

Mr Chairman, ladies, and gentlemen, good evening. Tonight I would like to talk about Afghanistan and the recent events that have taken place there, together with some of the slides which I took in the spring of this year. They may well be the last ones I am allowed to take owing to the new regime, following the most recent and bloody coup d'état in April. New rules, regulations, and a heavy censorship curtail a foreigner's movements, and even contact with old friends is suspect, so if I return in the coming spring, I am uncertain of my position. I would like to begin by acquainting you with some background information.

It seems hard to believe that, in this day and age, in 1978, any country in the world can remain as remote and isolated as Afghanistan. In spite of increased trade, developing tourism, and instant telecommunications, this landlocked country remains securely hidden behind the towering Hindu Kush Mountains high in the Himalayan Range in Central Asia. It is a Muslim country with 98 per cent of the ten million inhabitants being devoutly religious, and it is a non-literate country with 85 per cent being unable to read or write. But though it is impoverished and among one of the poorest nations in the world, it is of vital geographic importance.

Its northern neighbour is the USSR, who, long before the days of the czars, dreamed of having a warm-water port in the Indian Ocean. The only way to realize this dream was, and is, through Afghanistan. For as long as the British Raj ruled India, it kept Russia from its goal, but with the granting of independence and with the subsequent withdrawal of all US aid, a vacuum was created into which Russia jumped with both feet.

Afghanistan's three other neighbours also present problems. Firstly, Iran on the west is violently anti-Communist and has had difficulties with the southern province of Baluchistan, which wants independence; Soviet Russia continues to stir up trouble in this area near the Persian Gulf, hoping to dislodge Iran's grip. Secondly, a similar situation exists on Afghanistan's southern and southeastern border where anti-Communist Pakistan is another trouble spot. The Pashtuns[45] in the border province have always wanted an independent Pashtunistan, and it is to Russia's advantage to keep the pot boiling there too. Lastly, up in the northeastern part of the country is the Wakkhan Corridor, which touches Sinkiang Province in western China, one of Russia's bitterest enemies. It is easily seen, therefore, that Afghanistan, wedged in by these troubled and troublesome countries, occupies a key strategic position.

In July 1973, the constitutional monarchy of King Mohammed Zahir Shah was overthrown by a group of military insurgents led by his cousin and brother-in-law, Sardar Mohammed Daoud. The coup was easily accomplished, and the royal family fled to safety to Italy where, it was rumoured, money and servants were regularly supplied to them. Even without this added payoff, their bulging Swiss bank accounts, plus the hordes of illegally smuggled lapis lazuli, have supported the Naderi Shah family in sumptuous luxury.

President Daoud promptly renamed the country the Republic of Afghanistan, and at last the two-hundred-year old despised aristocracy was finished. Daoud established himself as president, prime minister and, in short order, added all the top ministerial positions to his collection: foreign affairs, interior, defence, treasury, and communications. Those he did not claim were given to members of his large family, which ironically was still part of the old royal Naderi Shah family. This array of official positions did not make a very convincing argument to his claim of a new democratic regime. Nor did his failure to keep many of his promises; in particular, a constitution for the people and free elections to parliament. So, the poor people of Afghanistan really gained very little under their new ruler.

---

[45] . Afghanistan's largest ethnic group.

However, some reforms were introduced in an effort to drag this isolated and still feudal country into the twentieth century, and women were being encouraged to discard their traditional burqa, or chadri as it is known in Afghanistan. Extreme liberalizing movements such as this, however, angered the devout and fanatical Muslim mullahs[46] who, early on, organized themselves into a league of brotherhood to oppose the already authoritarian Daoud.

One man who refused to help in the revolution to topple the king and destroy the monarchy was Mr Nur Mohammed Taraki. Some fifteen years earlier, together with Babrak Karmal, another Communist activist, he had been one of the founders of the Moscow-oriented People's Democratic Party of Afghanistan (PDPA). While he was just as anxious to put an end to the corrupt and nepotistic dynasty, it seemed pointless to replace one member of the despised Naderi Shah family with a relative. So, Mr Taraki withdrew into the shadows of the underground. During this time, the PDPA split into two Marxist-Leninist factions: the more moderate Parcham [*"Banner"* party"] led by Karmal and the more leftist, hard-line revolutionary Khalq [*"People's"* party] of which Taraki became the leader.

For five years, President Daoud skilfully played the world power game, upholding Afghanistan's traditional neutrality as he balanced and juggled the Eastern and Western powers to obtain economic aid projects, military equipment, technical aid, and huge loans, which sometimes became outright gifts of money. There were many attempted coups to depose him as he became increasingly more powerful. All were ruthlessly crushed.

Towards the end of his dictatorial rule, a disastrous drought and famine caused the economy as well as the people to suffer. In spite of massive injections of foreign aid and the so-called "monetary gifts", the situation grew daily more critical as the big powers—especially the US and the USSR—competed to prop up the poverty-stricken but critically strategic nation. Undoubtedly, much of the aid money was siphoned off into private bank accounts and, over the years, the dust grew thick on the growing and groaning piles of discarded plans for such vitally important projects as family planning, hospitals and nursing programmes, irrigation development, agricultural reforms, road building, and mining technology.

---

[46] . Islamic religious leader and teacher.

Under Daoud's regime, Russia became Afghanistan's biggest customer. The natural gas on the border was pumped across at far below world prices or bartered in exchange for military aid. But the most important Russian project was the building of the Salang Tunnel through the Hindu Kush Mountains at a cost of three hundred and fifty million pounds. This was certainly not for lorry loads of goods such as karakul sheepskins, raisins, and seeds that lumbered up and down the hazardous mountain passes. It was always intended for Russian military convoys since the road begins at the Uzbekistan border in Russia's southern region, continues through Afghanistan south-eastward to the Khyber Pass and on to Pakistan. From there, it is only a hop, skip, and a jump to that warm-water port in the Indian Ocean.

There were also extensive scholarships enticing students to study in Moscow, and military personnel were also Moscow trained. Upon their return, fully indoctrinated, they lent considerable support to the existing underground movement, swelling its numbers and spreading a Marxist doctrine. Beginning at the university, ugly riots and scenes of violence erupted as attempts were made to expose the now-hated Daoud and his obviously corrupt regime.

So, Afghanistan floundered on during these five years, as it had in the past: a buffer state being tossed like a political football between the Soviet Union, whose aims were always clearly visible as they armed, trained, and drained the already impoverished country, and the United States, who competed with perhaps a little more subtlety as they built a dam/irrigation project, a university, an unnecessary airport, and one internal road.

In the spring of this year, the first of two events took place that set the stage for the bloody coup d' état which was soon to follow, the so-called "Saur Revolution". *Saur* is the Dari name of the second month of the Persian calendar, equivalent to April, when the coup took place. On 17 April, a left-wing trade unionist and leading member of the Parcham wing of the PDPA, Mir Akbar Khyber, was murdered, allegedly by government forces. In the funeral cortège that followed, thousands of mourners marched, and there was a violent anti-American demonstration in front of the US embassy. There followed the immediate arrest of the seven top Communist leaders of both factions of the PDPA, including Mr Nur Mohammed Taraki. All seven were promptly thrown into prison.

102

President Daoud now made a fateful blunder: he announced that on the following Thursday at 1 p.m. he would declare whether the seven prisoners would be shot or imprisoned for life. This proclamation forced the already restless PDPA into action, and no doubt Russia was in the picture too. It was clear that they had to attack the oppressive Daoud regime before his deadline expired or lose their seven ranking leaders and more than twenty years of underground work.

Incidentally, the so-called "Afghan watchers" among the Western powers had been anticipating a coup for well over a year, and in particular, the monitor in Kabul for the BBC World Service had stated about two weeks prior that a coup was imminent.

The second event was actually a coincidence but it aided the coup plotters. President Daoud was preparing to play host to a major meeting of cabinet ministers from twenty-four non-aligned countries in preparation for a summit in Havana, where Cuba was rigged to take over the leadership from Sri Lanka. In recent months, Afghanistan had been seen surreptitiously lobbying against this shift—which no doubt displeased Russia mightily, for naturally she wanted her satellite in the leader's chair.

These twin events are seen as a likely cause for the actual timing of the coup, which began promptly at twelve o'clock on Thursday, 27 April 1978, exactly one hour before President Daoud's fateful proclamation and one week before the arrival of the delegations from the non-aligned countries. A cable from the American embassy to Washington apparently announced that what the British first and later the Americans tried to prevent for a hundred years has happened: the Russian Bear has moved south of the Hindu Kush. And so the stage was set.

I Am an Eyewitness

Wednesday, 26 April 1978: Arrival

As I step off the Aerflot plane in Kabul, the sunshine is brilliant, the sky a dazzling blue, and the smell of spring is in the air. The easiest flight ever, uneventful except for the wondrous beauty of the Hindu Kush Mountains as we soared over the snow-clad peaks at sunrise. Azad and his entire family are all on hand to greet me, with Azad himself beaming from the head of the queue. As we drive through the city to their house, where I am to stay, it seems strangely quiet and empty, but the noise of our chatter in the car as we all talk at once catching up on news sidetracks my thoughts. Invitation to dinner for later.

After settling in, I go make a few business calls in the heart of the city where, again, I am conscious of this normally bustling, noisy city of more than half a million people being oddly quiet. The shopkeepers are just sitting in their doorways, not even bothering to hawk their wares, and suddenly I realize that there are no foreigners about and not a tourist in sight. I puzzle over this as I return to the house.

Huge family dinner at Azad's! More members of his large family gather to welcome me, but in the midst of the festivities, promptly at 9 p.m., they all gather around the radio to listen intently to the BBC World Service News broadcast. They hang on every word, and after it is over, they tell me that, because of recent events, this is now their only reliable source of information.

It seems that a few weeks ago, a bigwig of the Afghan Communist Party, Mir Akbar Khyber, was shot and killed. Azad patiently explains that he was the leader of the more moderate Parcham faction of the

People's Democratic Party of Afghanistan (PDPA). He also says that it is being rumoured that the murder was at the government's behest. Some thirty-five thousand people demonstrated, carrying his body through the streets. The government retaliated by rounding up and jailing all seven of the PDPA party leaders. Azad blames the so-called scholarship students who were sent to Russia to be educated. When they returned, they set to work at the university and thus planted the seeds for demonstrations, dissatisfaction, and disintegration.

The family goes on to discuss the shootings, the riots, the arrests and imprisonments, concluding with their deep concern over President Daoud's proclamation to execute or give life sentences to the PDPA leaders. They explain that the city has been cleared of foreigners for security reasons for the forthcoming Conference of Non-Aligned Countries. The borders are to be closed from 30 April to 12 May. No hotel bookings are being made, no visas are being issued, and all tourists must leave before the first of May or they will be deported.

Only after all their deep concern is expressed do I realize what troubled times they are having.

Thursday, 27 April 1978: Under Fire

Invited to lunch at the home of Abiba, a young daughter-in-law of Azad's, who is widowed with five children and lives in the family compound. The women gather, exchanging gossip and opening the presents I have brought while we wait for the children to come home from school and the men from work. Our chatter and laughter are abruptly interrupted by the sudden, ominous whine of jet planes, and we hear explosions. We all dash to the windows, which look out onto the broad main avenue leading from the Ministry of Justice at the far end of the city to the airport at the opposite end. In utter, shocked amazement, we see waves of fighter planes overhead and, on the street, tanks rolling by with soldiers, heads barely visible, holding rifles with fixed bayonets.

Confusion and hysteria set in amongst the Afghan women. Our immediate concern is, of course, for the children. Three are not at home, and niece Soraya is also missing. We all gather in Abiba's room from about 2 p.m. onwards. We pace and worry, wondering at the events taking place beyond our vision. Our anxiety deepens as we hear the noise of the exploding bombs, rockets, and shells and the firing of guns, much too close for comfort. For nearly three hours we watch and wait, during which time the fighting intensifies. More and more tanks, spitting orange-and-red fire, lumber down the tree-lined street while overhead the planes dip and dive, dropping their lethal loads.

After what seems an eternity, the children burst into the house, the three little ones sobbing and shaking with fear. They had been kept after school, as we guessed they would be, until for some strange reason, the teachers turned them out, screaming at them to run home quickly. As they ran, they had seen the frightening spectacle of an army and an air force on the move, for the school is situated between their home and the staging post near the Ministry of Justice. Soraya is hysterical as she's had to run home through lines of soldiers shooting. Fatima, another niece, was barricaded in her government office at the ministry and had to take a circuitous route home when she was "released".

Our relief over the safety of the children is enormous, and shortly afterwards the men come, breathlessly giving sketchy news of an attempted coup d'état. Azad is the last to come home and reports that the airport is inoperable and adds that this coup is well organized and actually was planned for the conference when over 500 ministers were scheduled to be here.

Through the evening, there is intermittent heavy gunfire under the windows, and the glass rattles ominously as explosions go off just beyond the garden. Everyone is terribly concerned for his or her own safety and the country's future for there has been no mention of a Communist-backed army takeover.

At 8 p.m., the radio, which has been playing the national anthem non-stop between intervals of dead silence, suddenly comes to life. The first announcement is brief and to the point, in both Farsi and Pashto: "Tanks, infantry, and the air force," it says, "loyal to a military revolutionary council, have surrounded the presidential palace, killing President Daoud and his brother after they have madly resisted the People's Revolution." There are reassurances that Islam will remain as a religion, and nothing will be changed except to make the people and the country secure at last.

And so, briefly, we are informed that this landlocked country where, for centuries, political scores are traditionally settled through the barrel of a gun, is erupting once again. I am not afraid, just concerned that my family will worry, and I can't get a message out yet. And these poor people who don't want Communism and have no choice!

Now, at 11 p.m., we can still hear shots coming from the rooftops of the school across Darlaman Street. All during the night, we cling to each other as there are bursts of ack-ack firing followed by explosions, all very close. What will tomorrow bring?

Friday, 28 April 1978: The Coup

At about 5 a.m., when it's getting light, there is a very big explosion which shatters the glass in our compound and the neighbour's next door. We rush over as their windows look out onto Darlaman Street where we see more tanks on the move. Later we learn that there is considerable damage to nearby homes and, further up the street, the palace is on fire. Beyond it, there is a huge military base, so we are right in line of the bombing and strafing by the planes.

It is the longest day imaginable. We are pinned down here in the house, almost sleepless, forbidden to go out, rationing our dwindling food supplies and huddled together around the radio, which issues frequent bulletins. The rockets, shells, and gunfire shatter the air, and the noise of tinkling glass punctuates the short intervals between attacks.

At night we hear the BBC World Service. What a relief! Apparently, the soldiers first secured the radio station and then surrounded the Ministry of the Interior and began firing on both. Daoud has been reported killed, and his family in the French embassy next door. The new government, led by the hard-line Communist, Mr Taraki, claims it is Islamic and democratic, but the soldiers are the same ones who put Daoud in power. Things are quieter now.

Saturday, 29 April 1978: A New Government

The new military government says all is to be normal today and that business should be resumed as usual. But, of course, normalcy is far from the truth. No group gatherings are allowed, and a strict 10 p.m. curfew is to be enforced. The borders remain sealed; the airport is closed; the telephone cables and telex are not working, their headquarters damaged. I can't reach Henry at home in the UK.

The propaganda machine has swung into quick action, and the long preparation for this walkover is obvious. To whip up enthusiasm, all the tired old Communist jargon is cranked out, such as "The People's Revolution of the Glorious Saur Seven has finally wiped out the injustice, tyranny, exploitation, corruption, and the oppression of the boot-licking, mongrel, imperialistic, Naderi Shah family." The Saur Seven are those imprisoned Communist leaders who instigated the coup, now glorified with the name of the second month of the Persian calendar when they led the revolt. The Farsi broadcasts use the phrase "Afghanistan Democratique" like dripping water whilst Radio Afghanistan, in English, denounces the lies being told by foreign reporters when they refer to Afghanistan becoming a "satellite" Soviet state. The broadcasters here *never ever* use the words *Russian* or *USSR*. It must have a numbing, hypnotic effect, which I feel sure is deliberate.

I hear that many educated people are optimistic for their future and that of young people who, it is said, favour the new regime's policies and want to give "it" a chance. They seem convinced that the new government is *not* a Communist regime because it is already being drummed into them by the radio, and today, the press. The phrase the "prime minister and president of the Revolutionary Council of Democratic Afghanistan" is repeated so often it's hard to believe. But how can acknowledged Communists of twenty-seven years' standing have a successful "revolution" (they don't like the phrase *coup d'etat*) and then suddenly claim to be a democratic government?

There is a lot of anti-American feeling: "What did they give us? A little education, agriculture, but not the real support we needed and what they knew we needed! Weapons and ammunition." There is great bitterness expressed here at what the Afghans see as huge sums of money spent on

American staff and personnel to support them in a style they could never know in the US, plus the graft and black marketeering, trip expenses, and whims all granted. They comment on the term "hardship post" as they see booze, cars, bathrooms, every luxury in the commissary, servants, and much more. Afghans know they're being ripped off. The Russians too have looted the country *and* made them pay for it: Jalalabad oranges, raisins, and gas taken as repayment of loans but at lower than world prices.

Sunday, 30 April 1978: The Presidential Palace

We went to the palace today, now open to the public and renamed the People's Palace. Thousands and thousands of people, shoulder to shoulder in a human stream, swelled the streets, spilling over the dusty sidewalks and mingling with the vendors, who were out in full force for what appeared to be a gala celebration. Families were picnicking, mothers nursing babies, and crowds of people, ringed around every soldier, were clamouring for reports. Ice cold drinks, slices of melon, figs, raisins, nuts, kebabs, steaming samovars of boiling tea, streamers, flowers, and balloons were all available and added to the confusion as the roads approaching the palace were choked with people.

All the way from the Khyber Restaurant, which seemed to be an HQ of sorts, there was colossal evidence of the coup. Littered everywhere were the skeletons of burned-out tanks, twisted wrecks of steel amidst the rubble. Tanks and soldiers guarded the ministries all the way to the American Embassy. Huge holes could be seen in the ministerial buildings, and a cloud of smoke hung over this part of the city.

Gaping crowds of turbaned, bronzed men and veiled, ghost-like women milled about, pointing at the ruins. Over the noise of the multitude and over all the city could be heard the strategically placed loudspeakers blaring forth their propaganda messages of hatred against the Naderi Shah and Daoud families and their regimes. The constant drone of planes buzzing low overhead was a further reminder of the control of the Military Revolutionary Council.

Within the palace grounds, the press of people was almost unbearable, and the buildings thickly surrounded by such huge crowds that one could scarcely move. A loudspeaker was blaring and, from a platform, I could see children being thrust into the air one at a time, obviously separated from their parents. Soldiers were being garlanded with flowers and were only too proud to tell the awed questioners of their part in the glorious overthrow of the villainous Daoud.

My friend Nooria told me that Mme Daoud, one of her clients, was at her beauty salon at the start of the coup. She was called to the telephone and told to come home quickly, the pretext being that they had a luncheon engagement. Evidently, Daoud was a terribly proud, stubborn man who wouldn't believe what he was warned of. He sent two planes to quell any disturbance, but the revolutionaries called them back in Daoud's name, and they returned, only to be captured. Then the real air force strike began. The palace was stormed with Daoud beating his head and repeating, "How could I let it happen?" Of course, the coup had been well planned, but not for this early a date.

By all accounts, the battle in the palace was a bloodbath, and the fierce clash between several thousand loyal police in Daoud's private security guard and the insurrectionists utterly devastating. Only two hundred are said to have survived and ten thousand in all are reported killed. Daoud, his family, and all his relatives were brutally murdered. How quickly the bodies had been cleared and the wreckage tidied up for "the people" to see *their* revolution! And how quickly poor, uneducated people have been interviewed on the radio about the riches stolen by Daoud's family and the former king, so that it can be said that this is *their* palace now.

I finally saw the severity of the attack. The walls of the palace were riddled with bullet holes; shells and rockets had torn through the outer rooms, and the clock tower hung crazily atilt with a gaping hole. But what impressed me most was the incongruity of dozens of gorgeous Afghan carpets, washed but still blood-stained, lying drenched on the lawns to dry in the warm spring sunshine.

Sunday, 7 May 1978: The Immediate Aftermath

Within 24 hours, the loudspeakers were in top gear, blasting their message of "Revolution" and hatred. Propaganda in Kabul begins at 5 a.m.

and continues *non-stop* till the 10 p.m. curfew! The continuous barrage seems to have two prongs: to convince the "toiling peasants and labourers" that they actually did take part in the revolution (when in fact it was the small group of Communists and army chiefs who organized and executed it) and to discredit and whip up hatred against "the rich" and all the so-called "imperialist" enemies of the Democratic Afghan government, in particular the Western countries, with the UK taking the brunt.

About five days ago, the airport reopened and the first news reporters flew in from Delhi. I ran amongst them, anxiously trying to give and receive news. Their reports, although heavily censored, have still angered the new government, which condemns them as the work of the "vile imperialists". Especially in disfavour is the BBC, which the new government, knowing full well in what high regard it is held, attempts to discredit with the most virulent and vicious smears in order to destroy the faith people have in this lifeline of truth. So many people have pleaded with me to go to the BBC and beg for it to continue as before. It could be a total cut-off if the BBC is further reduced or dropped. Everyone is being so very careful of what they say, and there is one man to censor every message going out.

The facts point to Russia having had a heavy hand in the plans. The actual execution of the coup and its timing were uncharacteristic of Afghans, and there was the so-called hardware of Russian T-54 tanks, MiG-21 jet fighters, and Kalashnikov automatic rifles with fixed bayonets. It's being said that some of the fighter planes were surely piloted by Russians, for their manoeuvres were far too complicated for Afghan pilots. Then, too, Russia has been the first country to recognize the new People's Democratic Republic of Afghanistan within hours of its being born! Following Russia, all the Eastern Bloc countries will fall into line. Question: Why haven't we heard of a single country censoring Russia?

Monday, 8 May 1978: The Russian Bear in Sheep's Clothing

The first act of the insurrectionists has been to free the seven imprisoned Communists and immediately form a revolutionary council. Mr Noor Mohammed Taraki of the Khalq faction has been declared president and prime minister of the People's Democratic Republic of Afghanistan. The remaining released prisoners have been appointed to the top ministerial posts with Mr Babrak Karmal, leader of the Parcham faction, taking the number two position as vice-president and deputy prime minister. So, the new government is formed of the two wings of the PDPA. All the cabinet members seem knowledgeable, well-educated, and suited for their positions.

Two important announcements were made yesterday: one, that the government recognizes equal rights for women (!) and two, that the hoarding of wheat, bread, rice, and essentials will be dealt with according to the new military law whereby food staples must be distributed to the poor. Currency has been freed, and apparently there are no restrictions. The price of bread was cut a little, and meat even more. People are being asked to make contributions, however small, to the poor and to share books and pencils with poor students. In answer to the government's plea for money, nearly a million afs will undoubtedly be collected— already forty-five hundred afs today! Some people give land for schools or various projects. Everyone has been told to report immediately any acts of corruption, hoarding, or bribery.

One person said to me in broken English, "I will even broom the street. They can take all my land, my car, but not to put me in jail! They talk of rich people with the poor having to share, but many companies and single persons are giving much money to the government out of fear."

Afghanistan is to remain neutral, non-aligned, *and* Muslim. But the most worrying fact is that no representation has been given to any religious leaders. No mullah has a ministerial post. This does not auger well for the Glorious Revolution of Saur Seven which professes adherence to Islam and *denial of Communism*. It is being said that the government called the mullahs together today, one from each mosque, to show they intend helping the Muslim faith. If one thing were to indicate that the government is Communist, they've had it. Friends say that Afghans would perish to maintain their religion. There is a *very* strong group of mullahs whom I'm told would lead a revolt if their religious life were denied, and this I believe. These mullahs are fanatic, allied against this regime. No doubt they see it as a threat to their power. After all, if people are educated, they ask questions, and a declaration of equal rights for women is definitely "red flag" waving. We shall see, and everyone is afraid.

Tuesday, 9 May 1978: Lies and More Lies

It's already being rumoured that "the Russians are coming soon", and I say, "Watch out!" This country is very rich in minerals, in particular iron and copper, gas and oil, and none of it has been developed. (Where was America with its paucity of aid?) Azad believes that the Hindu Kush will be the natural barrier, dividing the country north and south, but it seems quite clear that the USSR will have no opposition in its march to the Indian Ocean.

Rumours are coming from Iran where the American forces protecting the shah are said to be alerted to protect the western Afghan border. There's talk of US aid coming through Pakistan and Iran, both uneasy with this very obvious threat on their doorstep. The fact that it's even thought of at this early stage is ominous. And what will China do up near the Wakkhan Corridor on the northeastern border?

In a matter of days, the nations of the world have officially begun to recognize the new government, knowing that it is a Communist one in spite of the blatant lies that it is not. Why haven't the so-called "big powers" got together and shown strength and honesty for a change? What a chance has slipped through their fingers. The foreign press reports gave the lead, and when they were blasted from here, that was the time to ask questions, not give in.

Many Afghan people, Azad and his family and I too, feel terribly depressed. My friends pray to Allah that the Western governments will not grant this stamp of official recognition. They see this, as I do, as an opportunity to stand up and be counted against such outrageous interference. But with memories that the USSR is actually composed of fifteen formerly independent countries, plus the events in Hungary and Czechoslovakia, not to forget Angola and Ethiopia and, way out there, Cuba … well, Afghanistan stands no chance at all.

Impressions I have: anger that no one stands up to the USSR—not one country, not one government with the courage to oppose Russia. What a fantastic chance to say, "*No!* We will not recognize the Afghan government. It is *not* democratic, in spite of what you say. If members of the new government were Communists, then they still are! We will not accept your lies. You say we lie, but *we* say *you* lie!" How foolish to miss the chance to say, "We'll wait and see what you do." It's sheer cowardice, weakness, and capitulation to the USSR. China today said, "We were *asked* by the Democratic Afghan Government to recognize it!" At least that's a little closer to standing up to the USSR than the responses of the other powers.

And I feel such sadness for what may happen to this poor, strangely beautiful, and ancient land. Will the proud and independent Afghans allow yet another master to control and dictate their country's destiny, exchanging the Naderi Shah regime for the Russians? The black, red, and green flag of the Republic is already being replaced by an all-red flag with a golden sheaf of wheat symbolizing the "toiling workers". Will we finally have to colour Afghanistan red?[47]

---

[47] . The symbolic colour of communism and a reference to maps of the British Empire where the colonial countries were indicated in red.

Life in the New Soviet
Puppet State of Afghanistan

Thursday, 11 May 1978

Henry arrived safely. We went to the American commercial attaché and later to the British attaché, who was very helpful regarding business. It seems "reasonably safe" to proceed now. Government control is predicted for the future, but for now, it is business as usual.

The next day at 8 a.m., we saw the secretary to the minister of commerce, who referred us to the deputy minister, then to the president of external trade, who advised us. A new company has been formed to export liquorice root, which, as of last night, is a government monopoly. All other articles we asked about are to be freely exported. We were directed to the Pastany Bank where we saw our vice president friend, then the vice president of the new company, and by 9:15 a.m., we were in the office of its president. Incredibly fast and efficient and open.

Dr Youmas is the professor heading the faculty of pharmacology at Kabul University and has for some years been researching liquorice root. Even under the old regime, he made proposals for conservation of this product and for government control. He's very knowledgeable. He says sizes will be standardized next year to world dimensions. The company has not yet had time to set a price, but will do so within three to four days. If agreeable, a contract can be negotiated. The price will vary depending on the percentage of glycerine content. Liquorice root must be clean and free of soil, packed in jute bags.

I am now what Afghans call a *nanawat* or "intermediary" on behalf of two friends, Azad and his son, Basheer. Azad is very depressed because he sees great chaos within the government. They are *not* of one mind. Some, being very extremist, presage controls in the offing. The business proposal for free import-export business has been tabled for consideration, and that's a setback. Some key industries have been nationalized, and the current anxiety is that the fur industry will soon follow. Since this supplies the most foreign currency and jobs to thousands of people, the anxiety is understandable.

Today I learned that a close associate and president of one of the Afghan banks was told he could *not* go to London for the fur auctions. To deny such an influential man in this way, after the minister of commerce had approved, is drastic! Later, another prominent businessman told us,

"I don't want Afghanistan to be the workshop of the world. Now I see competition in business being denied. This results in lower prices, fixed by the government, and we can't survive. I am being forced to trade with the USSR, thus eliminating my opportunity for free trade and cutting me off from competitive world prices! I don't like the system, but what can I do?"

Sunday, 14 May 1978

No tourists are here. It's deadly quiet, and the curfew is horrible evidence of the military presence, still after nearly six weeks now. Many devout Afghans believe that, because of their devotion to Allah and Islam, the USSR could never take over here, and they are convinced that it will not try, knowing they would fail. Do they say this wanting to convince themselves ... or me? I am told themselves, as they have great fear.

Following the coup, many changes have taken place under Mr Taraki's rule, although he has moved very slowly on the more radical Communist programmes. In a sincere effort to get at the roots of the traditional problems in this rigidly controlled religious society, the government has abolished the bride price, reducing it to a token 300 afghanis, about £3, so that no money or property or other form of wealth is allowed in payment to the parents of the bride to be. The new government has also sought to break the vicious circle of rural indebtedness with a measure designed to eliminate the hold of big landlords over small farmers.

Wednesday, 17 May 1978

Yesterday, I went by local bus to the town of Charikar in the northern Kohdaman Valley. I sat next to a soldier on leave for two days and going to Gulbahar. I think his opinions may reflect those of many. He actually doesn't know what Communism is, just the names of Socialism, Imperialism, and Communism. He feels the new government is the answer to the people's prayers for deliverance from Daoud and his false promises. "Land we work will be ours, not belonging to a landlord. Factories will be owned by all. A man with a larger family to feed and educate is entitled to more money; otherwise, how can he pay for food to get energy to work?"

He seemed almost hurt to think so many countries don't understand that this is a Muslim, not Communist, country, and his worship of Noor Mohammed Taraki was reverential. I think people identify with Taraki because he was so poor, worked so hard with no financial benefit, and became a brilliant student, US educated. People can look up to him for his achievements and leadership. And people feel that positive things are happening so quickly. Each day new pronouncements are made, which is important. I think it is only the educated people (and not all of them) who question the hard, so-called "Islamic" line. They are waiting for the axe to fall although hoping it won't. But there's something they can't quite swallow, a big question: Where did *those planes* come from?

Saturday, 20 May 1978

The outright confrontation between Marxism and Islam has yet to come, but it is no doubt close at hand. Comrade Noor Mohammed Taraki opens each speech with the words "In the name of Allah, the merciful and compassionate" in an attempt to pacify and convince the traditionally independent Afghans that the new government is not being run by godless Communists but by scientific Socialists who fully support the tenets of Islam. But this has done little to reduce the fear and panic among the educated bourgeoisie, the "vile, imperialistic dogs," who have been stripped of their property, had their bank accounts, possessions, and stocks of merchandise confiscated, and who have been put on public display to be made examples of to the "toiling peasants and labourers".

The old ministers who have not been killed are in a prison of sorts and "well cared for". They've been told that *all* of their "crimes" are well known and documented. Then, they're told to write down *everything* they've done, and that if they omit something or make a mistake, they'll be shot. Threats are also being made to the educated. Basheer told me that they say, "Do this or we will use *this* on you," pointing to a gun! The Russians are establishing a school for Marxist indoctrination and another for training in guerrilla warfare, both in Mazar-i-Sharif, the holiest of Afghan cities. And the East German police is now in charge of a "secret" KGB-type operation. Anyone belonging to the Parcham or Khalq party can challenge you with a gun, take your money and your documents, and "arrest" you.

I'm told that the various new ministers have visited all the departments and sections under their jurisdictions to allow staff to meet and see them in person and to clarify their availability to discuss and deal with any decisions. As all are being interviewed by their appropriate minister, they all are being exhorted to work together. The ministers say they are just like them and no different from any other workers. They even have the power to act independently of the president and prime minister. Opinions, advice, and ideas are being asked for, and it could be said that it is an impressive beginning.

The call to Azad from the minister of commerce must be typical: an appointment and a meeting after which, Azad said, it might not be so bad. "They are going to work with us and are for us." Despite his doubts, he is trying to believe that things will be all right. But while the "ordinary", uneducated, poor people are happy to see equalization, educated people ask themselves questions and can see beyond their noses. The new ministers, avowed Communists, are lying to the people, saying they are not so, to persuade the very religious that they embrace Islam.

Yet another lie, which is rather a contradiction, is that they *hate* capitalism, but they sure want every afghani they can get or blackmail for it! In the first month following the coup, no less than forty key trade agreements have been signed with the USSR, two or three reported every day in the renamed *Kabul New Times*. None with any Western countries and only two with Eastern Bloc countries, Czechoslovakia, and, the stupidest one, with East Germany. This one is for a cooperative air service, when neither country is currently issuing tourist visas!

One of the most fearful and devastating contracts for Afghans will be the one between the official USSR news agency, Tass, and the Afghan Bakhtar News Agency. It's the slow strangulation of any outside, unbiased news. The press and all publications, plus radio and TV, are all under strict censorship, repeating ad nauseam the lies not only about the last regime (awful and corrupt as it was) but also about present conditions.

Wednesday, 24 May 1978

Recently, there was a lunch for a group of workers, each carrying a picture of Taraki and wearing a red flag honouring him. They sang slogans and recited poetry. I ask myself why the pictures in the papers show people, forced to come from the provinces to Kabul, happily talking with Taraki and other ministers, and the answer is they are afraid not to. Although they smile and applaud, it means nothing.

True or not, I don't know. It's very touchy for an Afghan to be seen with a foreigner—again fear. The BBC becomes more of a lifeline than ever. I must get in touch with journalists Jonathan Power on the *Herald Tribune* and Miss Murad on the foreign desk at *The Guardian*.

Monday, 29 May 1978

A clean sweep has been made in the civil service, schools, banks, hospitals, and so on. Western-educated and trained Afghan personnel are now confined to their homes, no jobs or future, and they as well as the country suffer. Many young people and students are being sent to the USSR for training; about thirty-five hundred are already there. Unfortunately and very stupidly, key positions have been abruptly vacated and filled with incompetent but "hard-working, non-elite persons", young and inexperienced PDPA members and Russians!

Every day, three or more planes land at Bagram Airport as Russians flood into the country and assume key positions in the army and air force, swelling the ranks of the Russian technicians, soldiers, teachers, and advisers already here. They stand out in the empty streets, especially when they shop, for no one is greedier or drives a harder bargain or is as unfriendly than these non-capitalists! This is already proving disastrous as efforts to conduct affairs flounder. Business is at a standstill, prices are fixed, and there are now some government monopolies.

In all schools, teachers are being replaced and new Marxist programmes introduced. Examinations for entrance into high school and college have been eliminated, and those students who fail their critical exams will be given a second chance. Parents can already see the beginning of brainwashing. The children are formed into cadres, made to wear red ties, and are indoctrinated into the Marxist dogma. Their refusal to join a group means certain failure at examination time. One pupil per class is made responsible for obedience to the new system by getting the boys to sign a secret oath of loyalty to the left-wing Parcham Party. "Do you like Parcham?" This question is being asked of every pupil. They are told it will help them with school work and passing exams. Even if they don't understand or ask for help, they must *first sign* the paper and, if a boy refuses, the teacher comes to ask why!

Even worse, we are told that the children are given guns and instructed that they must report *anyone* speaking against the government, including members of their immediate family. There is a report of a boy, about nine years old, who, like many other children, was persuaded by the soldiers to spy, even on his parents, and to report everything. This child tape-recorded all that was said in his house, even the prayers of his parents. The mother pleaded with Allah to banish the Russians and perhaps said other unflattering things. The tape was given to an officer, and one night, soldiers came, took the woman away, and after some time, she was returned having had her tongue cut off. In a rage, the father killed his traitorous son and was in turn killed for the murder.

The university students are keeping very quiet, watching and waiting.

Wednesday, 14 June 1978

I had a forty-five-minute interview with Dr Anahita Ratebzad, minister of social affairs and culture. I believe that she is the first Afghan woman to play an active role in government. Dr Ratzebad outlined her ideas on the future programme for children and the development of women. She believes that divorce laws and their enforcement need revision and that health, nutrition, and more family counselling are priorities. There is talk of unionising, even among the women. Nursery care, including a crèche, will be *away* from the influence of the mother. Fantastic, but this would mean the lessening of the traditional, all-enveloping role of the mother as the core of the family. And in marches "Big Brother" with children literally taken over at nursery school age.

Dr Ratzebad believes it will take two generations to change the social behavioural pattern, the ideas of men towards women, and of boys to girls, and all other attitudes, and more. No outside influences are wanted with regard to the training of teachers or to teaching assistance in other fields. She said training in every field is necessary and will be slow. I conclude that, as Dr Ratzebad says, it must be done by Afghans but, it will take *too* long, the inference being that Soviet help for training is acceptable but from others is not.

Most people here do not understand why *only* the USSR offers aid, help and assistance, loans and contracts. And so many cannot understand US policy or "the deaf ear of America". Why did the US not recognize the direction in which things were going and counteract accordingly? Why desert Afghanistan? It is key to the whole USSR plan: through Pakistan to the Indian Ocean, all of Saudi Arabia, sweeping westward where strategic positions are already held. America should never have withdrawn aid under President Johnson.[48] Aid should have been increased but, now, it is almost too late!

Thursday, 6 July 1978

We are beginning to understand that there are two pro-Soviet factions in this government, the more moderate left-wing Parcham Party and the more radical Khalq Party. These formerly opposing views, which recently joined to undertake the coup under the name of the People's Democratic

---

[48] . Lyndon B. Johnson, US president from 1963 to 1969.

Party of Afghanistan, are now living uneasily together. In other words, the patched-up coalition is showing signs of an internal struggle for power. Purge has followed purge as ministers and lesser functionaries have been imprisoned, killed or exiled. Five of the released Communist prisoners who had been granted ministerial posts have been victims of the first purge when they were suddenly dispatched abroad as ambassadors. Almost before they had a chance to present their credentials, they were sacked and left stranded. One of the first to be purged has been the Parcham leader, Babrak Karmal, whose views on Islam, some say, were already suspect.

The vast majority of people are not for the government, and more and more opposition is being whispered about. Oh yes, the government officials speak of their "respect" for Islam but *not* of their belief in it, and religious people know the difference. Rumours are rife from the eastern Paktia Province on the border with Pakistan where tribal groups have not accepted the regime and are fighting, allegedly, with American or British tanks and planes.

There is only one possible outcome, as full acceptance of the coup has never come to pass. Discontent within the army, the air force, and the remote war-like tribes has grown as the Afghan people see their cherished religious customs and traditions begin changing, their freedoms vanishing, and far, far too many Russians moving in. Some people whisper about another coup because of the two factions within the new government and because of the devout Muslims' refusal to accept the government's claims that it is not Communist. Most of the intelligent, educated people are very distrustful of the heavy Islamic proclamations. Others express the hope that a combination of mullahs, Paktians, and dissatisfied soldiers from within will, with outside help from Pakistan and Iran, revolt soon.

If Western countries do not provide the initiative to assist the people here who are so ready to fight for their independence, all of Central Asia and the Middle East (including, of course, the oil fields) will fall and be crushed. With empty hands, what can these anti-Communists do? They *must* have outside help or perish under this system. As Azad and other friends predicted, less than six months after the first, fully fledged Communist state in this part of Asia was born, a major counter coup is in the offing. What will Russia's policy be when it takes place? How will the Western nations react? Will they continue to stand by, helpless and ineffective as before?

Jean Photographs the First Army Vehicle at 1.22 pm- Darlaman Street

Jean the Eye-Witness

After the Coup -The First Edition

The Day After the Coup

Driving in Triumph

The Bulletin Board - A New Government

A Hard-Won Battle

Viewing the Aftermath at the Renamed 'People's Palace'

Inspecting a Tank at Close Quarters

A Welcome...For Now

Clearing Up

A Russian T-54?

Life Goes On

Young, Modern, and Afghan

Jean was concerned about the impact of the new regime, especially on women of the next generation. She set out to deepen her understanding through tape-recording several informal, wide-ranging conversations with one of her younger friends, Sahar.

Kabul, July 1978

Jean: Well, Sahar, I believe the tape recorder is going now. We met earlier this year through our mutual friend, Najibah.

Sahar: Yes, we met at my office in the ministry.

Jean: Thank you for talking with me. I wanted to ask you, in Afghanistan do women have a vote?

Sahar: Yes, they do.

Jean: Have they had it for a long time?

Sahar: No, since about ten years ago, I think. Women can vote for election.

Jean: Have you had elections recently?

Sahar: Yes, for senate, and women voted for the candidates.

Jean: Are they interested in voting? Do they come out in numbers?

Sahar: Not very much. Just the young generation.

Jean: I see. What about women my age, of your mother's generation?

Sahar: Oh, no. They're not interested at all. They don't vote.

Jean: Do young people concern themselves with politics?

Sahar: Yes, mostly.

Jean: But mostly the ones who go to university?

Sahar: Yes.

Jean: Tell me, can women own property?

Sahar: Oh, yes!

Jean: That's Islamic, isn't it, that women can own property?

Sahar: Yes, it's legal. There's no problem at all to own property by women. Fields, houses, shops.

Jean: How do they manage to buy property?

Sahar: Somebody will look after it for you. For instance, if my mother owns some property, then my father or my brother will look after it.

Jean: Does a woman have the right, if she dies, to will this property to whomever she wants?

Sahar: Yes.

Jean: It doesn't automatically go to a husband or the children?

Sahar: It goes legally as much to the children as to the husband.

Jean: Can women sue people?

Sahar: Oh, yes! Plenty of cases. Also in criminal cases. If somebody kills her husband, or, if somebody steals her things, she can sue in court and ask for treatment.

Jean: I didn't realize that they had so many legal rights, you see. Now, could they own a business?

Sahar: Yes.

Jean: But could they run the business?

Sahar: Yes.

Jean: Would they appear in the shop or whatever sort of business it would be?

Sahar: They can, legal. Is no problem. They can run a business, or you can sometimes see women as shopkeeper, but mostly they don't like to do it. And because most are poor, they don't own the shop and work just for salary there. But if they have got the money and the opportunity and the capital, they will do it.

Jean: Then probably they have the right to have a bank account?

Sahar: Sure, sure!

Jean: Now, that's on the ownership side. On the employment side, what sort of rights have women got?

Sahar: The same as men, in any field of working.

Jean: *(surprised)* They do?

Sahar: Yes, but, in fact, you can see in the ministries; for example, there are less than one hundred women in each ministry. But if they apply the law, they must accept them.

Jean: Well then, why don't they?

Sahar: Well, maybe it's because most of them, they don't want to work because they are looking after the house, husband, and children.

Jean: What sort of jobs do women do?

Sahar: Any kind of work. They're doctors, teachers, judges, nurses, factory workers, at the ministries.

Jean: So, it's not just educated women who work?

Sahar: No, uneducated women, as cleaners, are also working.

Jean: But you wouldn't see a woman in a shop, would you? Like in a supermarket?

Sahar: (*surprise.*) Have you not seen it?

Jean: (*equally surprised*) No.

Sahar: Not in Azad bazaar? Or in department stores? You can see a lot of women working there behind the counter. At the supermarket, even at Marks and Spencer's, everywhere, the girls.

Jean: That's only recently I think.

Sahar: Yes, about four or five years ago.

Jean: Now that's in Kabul. What about in other cities like Zara, Herat?

Sahar: (*quickly*) No, no. Just in Kabul. Just a beginning.

Jean: Do they have training in advance for the jobs?

Sahar: No.

Jean: Now, if a woman works, does she get the same salary as a man?

Sahar: Yes.

Jean: She's luckier than in some countries. *(They both laugh.)* Well, I want to ask you something about family life and, of course, the big question that most people are interested in is arranged marriages.

Sahar: *(sighs)* Yes, we still have it here.

Jean: Even here in Kabul?

Sahar: Yes, we have plenty of arranged marriages.

Jean: Is that a religious law or is it just custom?

Sahar: Custom. Mostly custom.

Jean: The bride is bought, isn't she?

Sahar: *(laughing)* It looks like it, yes.

Jean: *(also laughing)* Is that what it really is? The groom's family gives the bride's family a price? Is that how it works?

Sahar: Yes.

Jean: What's the going rate? Once on a trip here with my daughter, Anne, I was offered one hundred sheep for her! *(They both laugh.)* I mean, use Azad's and Halimah's daughter, Najibah, as an example because she was married the most recently of all the girls we know. She was lucky because she met her husband, Hakim, in her job, so it wasn't really an arranged marriage.

Sahar: No, it wasn't.

Jean: It was only an arranged marriage in the sense that, if the family had not approved of Hakim, they wouldn't have let the marriage take place.

Sahar: Yes, that's right. But some young girls, they just say, "We don't like arranged boy." They are against their family. They say, "I go with that other boy." And their family tell that, if they don't want arranged one, they are not good girls.

Jean: Did Hakim's family contribute financially?

Sahar: I don't think so. I think just they paid for the wedding. But he didn't give any money to Najibah's father.

Jean: But usually that is the case, isn't it?

Sahar: Yes, usually. And usually most of them spend that money to buy some things for the bride.

Jean: What happens first?

Sahar: If a boy wants to get engaged with a certain girl, he sends his family to the girl's family to ask for that matter. If the family are pleased, they say, "We want this and that for our daughter." For instance, jewellery, a house, a car, or a big wedding for her. If they are engaged for two or three months and, in these three months, there are some of our religious feasts, the boy has to take good clothes and also sweets to the family.

Jean: What happens in rural areas?

Sahar: In the villages and tribal areas, the parents ask thousands of afghanis from the boy for the dowry, but mostly they don't spend that money for the daughter. The father just takes that money for himself. He might buy some land for himself or some animals—cows or sheep. Just a little bit spend on the daughter.

Jean: It doesn't go to the girl at all?

Sahar: No, not in the provinces. But in Kabul, asking the bride price is getting less. Just they give her some dowry and then spend a lot of money for the wedding.

Jean: Would they go into debt for the wedding? Or sell things?

Sahar: Yes. *(sighs)* Of course, they borrow from others, from their friends, or sell something to purchase these things for the bride.

Jean: What can a big wedding cost? Say for two hundred, three hundred people? Is that a big wedding?

Sahar: Yes. You know, for my younger brother's wedding, we invited six hundred people!

Jean: *(gasps)* Where was it held?

Sahar: At a very big club newly opened at that time. We invited six hundred, yes. Because everybody in our family likes my brother. He is a nice man. So, we invited a lot of friends and family relations for his wedding night. My father paid the club eighty thousand afs just for the banquet. And we bought jewellery and clothes.

Jean: Eighty thousand afghanis is ten thousand pounds?

Sahar: Yes, ten thousand pounds.

Jean: Just for the banquet at the club?

Sahar: Yes. And we bought twenty complete outfits for the girl. *(Peals of laughter.)* A lot of money!

Jean: *(also laughing)* You must be poor by now! It would take forever to find the money to pay it back!

Sahar: Fortunately, my father had that money. He didn't borrow. Many families don't have to borrow. But that's why most young boys and girls don't get married, because of the money.

Jean: And why they marry later?

Sahar: Yes.

Jean: How did your older brother meet his wife?

Sahar: He didn't meet her at all. My family found her for him.

Jean: How?

Sahar: My sisters met her and her mother. They were just talking together, asking about each other's family, and my sister told the girl's mother that we got a brother who we want to find a good wife for. And the mother said, "This is my girl. She's very pretty. If you like, you can come to our house, and I will give her to your son to be married." So, our family went there, and they discussed the matter, and they were engaged.

Jean: How long after they met?

Sahar: Within one week.

Jean: They didn't waste any time!

Sahar: *(giggles)* No, no.

Jean: Who went to her place?

Sahar: Just my mother and my sister, not my father. And they discussed the matter, and it was okay. They agreed to engagement with my brother.

Jean: Now, they didn't ask the girl if she wanted to be engaged, and they didn't ask your brother if he wanted to be engaged.

Sahar: We asked our brother because he saw her once. He liked her because she was a young and pretty girl. And that was all. They were engaged for two months and after that they got married. They have three children.

Jean: How long have they been married?

Sahar: Hmm ... ten years.

Jean: And it's been a happy marriage?

Sahar: Yes.

Jean: And he has only one wife?

Sahar: Yes. (*laughs*) She will get spoiled.

Jean: Now, just supposing he wanted to have another wife of his own choice. What would her attitude be do you think?

Sahar: Oh, she would kill him!

Both burst out laughing.

Jean: That's quick enough! She wouldn't permit it?

Sahar: No, no!

Both laugh.

Jean: But, seriously, can men still have more than one wife?

Sahar: They're restricted in the new law, but you can see a lot of men who have a second wife.

Jean: How do women live with more than one wife in the family? How do they cope with that?

Sahar: It's very difficult to find two wives in the same house living peacefully. They've no choice. One wife goes to court and claims she can't cope with the first—or second or third wife—and that the husband must get another house for her. The court tells the man, "If you hadn't the financial means, you shouldn't have married again."

When the husband goes to court and says, "I can't cope with the wives. They must be separated from each other," the court tells the husbands to separate them and sometimes they do, or they separate them in the same house, just give them separate rooms. But it's really difficult.

Jean: But why would a man want more than one wife really?

Sahar: I really don't know. If I were a man, I wouldn't! (*Both laugh.*) Maybe for a change, maybe they get bored with one wife.

Jean: (*surprised*) Does that have something to do with it, really? Because it certainly costs more money to have two families or three families.

Sahar: They don't think about the cost at all. Only they think about their wives!

Jean: But they can find a woman. They don't need the wife in the family.

Sahar: (*lowering her voice*) It's very difficult here.

Jean: In Kabul?

Sahar: Yes. And for a good man, he doesn't go to these places.

Jean: So, then what is the real reason? Do you think it's because he wants another woman?

Sahar: Yes, I think so.

Jean: Just for that?

Sahar: Yes, just for that.

Jean: Not necessarily because he wants to prove that he is a man and have a lot of children?

Sahar: Oh, no. In past time it used to be, but not now.

Jean: Well, if they have more than one wife living in one house and they haven't been to the court and haven't been persuaded to have separate houses, who runs it then, number one wife or the favourite wife?

Sahar: *(laughing)* The favourite wife, of course!

Jean: And what about divorce. Have women the right to ask for a divorce?

Sahar: Yes, legally, they can ask now, but it's very difficult for them to get it. One cousin, he is in family court, he tells woman there are some conditions, limited in law. For instance, a woman can go to court and ask for a divorce if the husband is disappeared for more than some years, or hasn't got the ability of being a man, or can't prepare the alimony and support his family. Also, I think if the husband has spent some years in prison or has got a very bad sickness which is not curable, then a woman can ask for a divorce.

Jean: So, it's really quite easy for a woman.

Sahar: It looks easy, but I think in the court it's difficult because it takes time to prepare the documents.

Jean: But for the man, it's not that difficult?

Sahar: No, nothing like that. Just he goes to court and says "I divorce my wife," and they'll prepare a document for him.

Jean: Just like that?

Sahar: Just like that.

Jean: What about when there is more than one wife?

Sahar: The court should ask the wife who goes there if she's unhappy or has any sickness or hasn't any children, but mostly they don't ask the wife. Just prepare the document for the man.

Jean: Well, now the big question. (*More laughter.*) Naturally, we know that a male child is the most important thing and that you have to keep on trying to have a male child.

Sahar: Najibah was lucky in that case!

Jean: Yes, thank goodness, because she was so afraid of having a baby, she may not have any more. Does it ever occur that a family doesn't want to have any more children?

Sahar: Yes, it happens if they have many children. But if a woman hasn't got any and her husband wants to have a child, she can't prevent it because, otherwise, her husband would not get merit.

Jean: But, again, only in the city, not in the rural areas?

Sahar: Yes, only some rural areas. In Kabul, most try to have small families because it's very expensive to have four or five children these days.

Jean: I want to ask you about family planning—birth control. When you get married, would there be a means available for birth control, and how do you feel about it?

Sahar: I think family planning is good. Now women have started to control birth, and they know why they should control it.

Jean: They know about contraception?

Sahar: Yes, they do.

Jean: How do they find out?

Sahar: There's an institution, the Family Planning Centre, that helps with preventing pregnancy and gives tablets and other contraceptives free to every woman.

Jean: But, I met a man who already has eight children and his wife's going to have a ninth child! I asked him, "Why don't you stop having children?" and he said, "I don't know how." I said, "Why don't you go to the Family Planning Centre?" (*She lowers her voice to a whisper.*) "Oh no," he said, "I couldn't do that." Well, he must represent a certain percentage of people here. Are there many like him?

Sahar: Yes, sure. In poor families, just the men decide, but, exactly, they don't control it. They say, "It's all God's fate. We can't change it. Why should we control when God knows we will have the number of children that God wants us to have?" And they just let children come. In educated families, men and women discuss the matter.

Jean: So, really, only the educated people know about it.

Sahar: Yes. Because most uneducated people think that if they take these tablets, they will get nervous and bad things happen and some of them put on so much weight. But it's not true, because if they take another tablet, like vitamins, it will be all right for them. There were courses to teach them how to use these tablets, how to prevent other children.

Jean: So, the teaching programme hasn't been all that successful.

Sahar: No.

Jean: But does it ever occur that a woman wants to get rid of the baby before the baby is born?

Sahar: Yes.

Jean: Can she have an abortion?

Sahar: Yes, but not legally.

Jean: Would she have her husband's consent? Or would she do it without his consent?

Sahar: The doctors, they won't do it because they say it's a murder. It's a murder after three months.

Jean: But what if it's before three months?

Sahar: They will do.

Jean: A doctor would?

Sahar: Yes.

Jean: But, if a woman was, let's say, six weeks pregnant and decided she had as many children as she could manage, would she tell her husband? Would she talk to him about it?

Sahar: Yes, some of them they do.

Jean: There is that kind of relationship with a man? That kind of open relationship?

Sahar: Yes.

Jean: But would that be true out in the country?

Sahar: Ah, no, no.

Jean: In other words, then, we come back to the same thing, that it's education that brings people to this way of thinking.

Sahar: Of course. Education is everything.

Jean: So, if education teaches you this and makes allowances for these sorts of things, does education also teach about sexual relations?

Sahar: No, it's secret! Everybody has to find out for themselves. (*laughs*) They don't teach that in schools at all!

Jean: Well, it's only recently begun to be taught in schools in Europe. It's something quite new. Now, how does a young girl become introduced to the physical change that is taking place in her body?

Sahar: Well, it's a very tough question because mothers never describe these things to their daughters. Sometimes, some educated woman will do that, or some girls may learn from their friends, but mostly, girls have to find out themselves when they're grown up. We haven't even got any books or any magazines. It's prevented to bring here magazines like *Playboy* or *Playgirl*. If we bring them in, they would put us in jail!

Laughter.

Jean: Stopped at the border! But that's on the extreme side. On the informative, educational side, when you and your sisters and brothers were growing up, nobody told you anything? Prepared you?

Sahar: Nothing.

Jean: But what happened to you, for instance, when you started?

Sahar: I was really shocked. I knew it meant I'm grown up, but I was so ashamed, I was nearly to cry. No one told about this. It's a very big shock to young girls.

Jean: How did you learn to take care of yourself?

Sahar: My mother and my sister showed me.

Jean: If you have to go into a shop to buy sanitary products, how do you do that?

Sahar: I go to the shop and buy just like that.

Jean: You're not embarrassed to ask for it?

Sahar: No. I go to the shops, and I know that they know about these things. So, I'm not embarrassed.

Jean: Now, is there such a thing as female circumcision?

Sahar: No, not here. It's really very, very important for an Afghan girl to be a virgin. If she's not a virgin, that means she's not a good girl and her husband won't accept her.

Jean: So, before marriage, even nowadays, young girls wouldn't associate in that way.

Sahar: No, no.

Jean: Then I suppose it's safe to presume that there isn't any preparation for marriage.

Sahar: None.

Jean: And what about premarital and extramarital love? Because I know of a situation where I feel quite sure there were premarital relations, and I was very surprised. I thought it would have been much more correct.

Sahar: Yes, we have some here, but just in the cities.

Jean: Does rape exist in Afghanistan?

Sahar: We have some kidnap cases, but not rape.

Jean: Would that be for the money?

Sahar: No, not for the money, just for the girl, that's all.

Jean: Maybe you give the name of the situation a different name. Maybe you call it kidnapping here, and in the West it's called rape.

Sahar: Maybe, maybe.

Jean: Tell me about the education system.

Sahar: Well, some people are so poor, they need their children to go to work for them. But, in the city, most young children go to school, even in the provinces. Then comes secondary school, but many stop before university.

Jean: You started school when you were six. How long is primary school?

Sahar: Six years.

Jean: And then?

Sahar: Secondary school for three years more and then high school. Altogether twelve years.

Jean: Besides Kabul, is there another city with a university?

Sahar: Just Jalalabad. There is a medical university there.

Jean: What is the size of Kabul University? Do you know?

Sahar: I think ten thousand students.

Jean: Do many students go abroad?

Sahar: Yes. If students have the opportunity, they go; they like to go abroad.

Jean: What happens when they return?

Sahar: If they have got a new idea from the country where they have been, they will use it. Otherwise, they will keep it in mind, looking for an opportunity to practise their new idea.

Jean: You went abroad, didn't you? Could you settle down fairly well, readjust, after you came back?

Sahar: Yes. I lived here for more than twenty years, and I was away for just six months. How could I forget my country and my customs? I wouldn't.

Jean: What about young people who stay abroad for longer periods of time?

Sahar: Yes, for them it's difficult to readjust here.

Jean: Are there opportunities at your work for you to be able to move up?

Sahar: Maybe when I get a bit older and get more information and experience.

Jean: So, there's hope of a promotion. But, is it limited where you can go and use your knowledge?

Sahar: Yes, it's limited for me here. But my cousin says, in the Ministry of Justice, there is one woman. She is a judge and will be a judge in a family court in the province. It's very strange—unbelievable—for a girl being a judge in a province. It's very new.

Jean: Is she the first one? How old is she?

Sahar: Yes, she is. I think she's twenty-five.

Jean: She's very young! What sort of preparation did she have to have to become a judge?

Sahar: First, I think the faculty of law for four years. Then one year of training.

Jean: Did you pass the exam for your job at your ministry the first time?

Sahar: *(laughing)* Yes!

Jean: *(also laughing)* Smart girl, smart girl! Then you got a scholarship to study in the UK for six months. Do many more students go to Europe than to Russia? Or, the other way around, do you think more students go to Russia?

Sahar: I think Russia because they give more scholarships and fellowships to Afghans. Every year, I think more than two hundred or three hundred go.

Jean: In Russia, do you think a lot of these scholarships are offered for political reasons, to indoctrinate the students?

Sahar: I think so. Must be.

Jean: What differences did you observe when you were abroad?

Sahar: If I compare an Afghan family with an English family, I can see some differences. For instance, children in an Afghan family are surrounded by their parents and relatives, and mostly they obey them. Even my brother, married with children, sometimes he has to do what my father says. But in UK, when a child is grown up and has his own ideas, he follows his own; he hasn't got to follow his parents.

Here also, mostly children are not open with their parents. They don't talk as free as they talk with their friends. If they've got some problems, they will just keep them inside. They won't say straight to their parents. I had a friend there, an English girl, and she had a boyfriend, and their relation was cut off. She was so embarrassed, but she just called her mother and said, "My boyfriend has left me. I am so sad and I can't study." It was so strange for me. I can't talk of a boyfriend to my mother or my father.

Jean: You couldn't talk to them?

Sahar: No. Something which is a very, very good thing in London means a bad thing in Afghanistan, like having a boyfriend. If a girl hasn't a boyfriend there, she might think why boys don't like her, that maybe she has some bad thing. But here, if I have plenty of boyfriends, everyone will think I'm not a good girl, that I'm a prostitute.

Jean: It's the opposite, isn't it?

Sahar: Yes.

Jean: But, if something were disturbing you at work, maybe a colleague is making you unhappy and you're not be getting along, would you talk about it to your parents?

Sahar: Yes, for that, I will. Also with my sisters and my brothers. Usually we sit together and we talk about how are things at our work, good things and bad.

Jean: Ah, you do. But most people don't.

Sahar: No. But these days, some families are beginning because they've learned that it's a good thing to discuss matters with your family and ask their advice.

Jean: Is that coming with education now? And contact with other people?

Sahar: Yes.

Jean: Do you think people talk more freely to their friends than to their parents?

Sahar: Yes, to their friends.

Jean: More observations, please.

Sahar: Of course, our customs, our religion, everything in UK was different. Even these days when the gaps are getting smaller because of contact, newspapers, TV, and radio, still, there are some big differences. For instance, our funeral custom.

Jean: How different?

Sahar: You see, for funeral custom, we have to spend a lot of money. For instance, we have to cook a lot of meals for our family who come with their sympathies. We have to cook lunch and supper for three days for more than one hundred or two hundred people. After that, every Thursday, we have to cook a big meal for forty days. Then, on the fortieth day, we have to prepare a big meal for almost two hundred people. And it means a lot, a lot of money to spend. Some families have to sell their rugs and furniture to prepare these things!

Jean: I can't believe it!

Sahar: It's really awful! Now the government tried hard to let people know that this spending is not good. It's not good for the community. It's not a religious law, just custom! They shouldn't follow that. I don't know how people still do. You know the woman who died just three hours ago? I assure you, because I saw that the family have already hired big pots from the shops to cook rice and all the food in. Now, their family and relatives will come from everywhere and stay for supper. A good meal must be prepared for them, even with two or three kinds of meat, rice, and puddings.

Jean: The woman's hardly cold.

Sahar: Yes! It's really odd. They don't think about the dead person; only where can they find the money. It's terrible!

Jean: What could an affair like this cost over the period of forty days?

Sahar: As much as eighty thousand afghanis.

Jean: That would be ten thousand pounds! Horrendous!

Sahar: Yes!

Jean: What about poor people? Will they go into debt to pay for these things?

Sahar: Yes, poor families do.

Jean: That's worse than spending all that money on a marriage, because at least in a marriage there's a future for the bride and groom.

Sahar: You know, my brother-in-law who died a few months ago, I think we spent sixty or seventy thousand afghanis.

Jean: As you say, it is a strong custom. That was so tragic, his death at only forty-one, and he's left his wife, your sister Azita, with eight children. Who is going to take care of this young family?

Sahar: Now my sister must also be a father for them. But it's a family problem too. My brothers, my parents, even me, all are caring for the children. I ask them, "How are your grades? What are your hobbies after school? Do you like football?" Sometimes I take them to places like the cinema. My parents are very worried about my sister also. They want to take care of their daughter.

Jean: So, you all contribute, not only financially, but with their education and the development of their character.

Sahar: Yes, sure.

Jean: That's wonderful for the children to know that they will not be on their own. But Azita is what, only thirty-four years old? Will she have to remain a widow?

Sahar: Yes, it seems so. Because if she gets married now, who's going to look after her children? It's a bit cruel if she leaves her children.

Jean: But another man who, for instance, may have lost his wife, wouldn't he have the responsibility of the children? Does that ever happen?

Sahar: Yes, sometimes it happens.

Jean: Why do you say that if Azita were to remarry, she would have to leave her children? Wouldn't they be taken into a second marriage?

Sahar: No, because the man wouldn't accept them. That's the problem.

Jean: I see. Is that the custom?

Sahar: No, they just don't like it. Maybe she finds someone who will accept them or who wants children, but most men, they don't like. Because they think the children will be trouble for them, they won't get along and they'll be enemies.

Jean: Would the family consider making an arrangement for her or, having been married, would she want to make this decision herself?

Sahar: No, I think if she gets married again for a second time, it's also a family problem. Now, she can't leave her children because, really, she loves her children. I think she prefers children to marriage. If the family thinks of arrangement for her to get married again, she won't accept it.

Jean: But presumably her children are going to grow up, and they themselves will get married one day and be gone. Being so young, would Azita still wait and continue bringing the children up now?

Sahar: Yes, she would wait. But at that time, she might be married.

Jean: But how is it possible for her even to meet someone her own age or a little older? And then, she's also so many years older.

Sahar: Yes, it's a real problem for Afghan women.

Jean: Now, I want to ask you some questions about religion. How religious are you? (*Both laugh.*)

Sahar: I'm religious. I pray five times a day if I get the time: in the morning, in the afternoon at the office, sunset, and the last one.

Jean: (*surprised*) Do you really? But you're a working woman. When do you get the time?

Sahar: On Fridays usually. Not every day of the week.

Jean: And, of course, you're allowed this time off when you're at work.

Sahar: Yes.

Jean: You're a good girl! *(Both laugh.)* Is that more or less prayer than your mother?

Sahar: Mine is less, of course. She prays more than me.

Jean: Do you pray because you feel it inside you, or is it a duty?

Sahar: No, inside me, a real feeling.

Jean: Do you think many young people feel that way, like you?

Sahar: No, not much.

Jean: What about your younger sister? She's thirteen now. Does she pray five times a day?

Sahar: She doesn't pray at all!

Jean: Does it make your mother sad?

Sahar: Sometimes, yes.

Jean: But she can't force her.

Sahar: No, she can't.

Jean: And what about the boys?

Sahar: They pray five times a day and study the Qu'ran every day. They're very religious.

Jean: What about teenagers? Are they more like your brothers or like your sister?

Sahar: Like my sister. They're moving away from it.

Jean: But perhaps not in the provinces?

Sahar: I think they're very strict in the provinces.

Jean: Is there a difference in religious beliefs between someone like yourself and, say, someone from a nomadic tribe, like the Kuchis?

Sahar: Yes, because nomadic people accept things just which they have heard. I believe in things which I read and can justify for myself. I can't accept things which I don't think are real. Maybe their religious leader tells them something and they believe it because they can't see which is right and which is wrong. They just believe it because a religious man has told them so. I think there's a big difference.

Jean: Yes, of course, because you're approaching it from your knowledge.

Sahar: Yes. They believe just because somebody has told them.

Jean: Are you separated from men in your religious worship?

Sahar: Yes, in mosques.

Jean: Have you or your mother ever been to a mosque?

Sahar: No, never.

Jean: So, no women go to mosques?

Sahar: No.

Jean: I thought in Mazar[49] they had a place upstairs for women. Can a woman go to her place in a mosque?

Sahar: It's not really a mosque; it's a holy place for women to go there just to pray. I don't know in Mazar, but women always pray separately from the men.

Jean: Do you ever pray in a group of women? When you're at home, or at your office, do you pray with other women then?

Sahar: No.

Jean: Never with your mother or your sisters?

Sahar: Never.

Jean: It's always a private thing?

Sahar: Private, yes.

Jean: And at work, it's private?

Sahar: Yes. Men can pray in a group but, women don't do that.

Jean: Take the situation where you work. Supposing there are ten women working in your office. They all pray separately. Doesn't that disrupt your work?

Sahar: Most of them, they don't pray. Just they leave it. Because for prayers, we have to wear a long scarf and trouser and we have to wash, and all these too many things to prepare make it very difficult at the office. For men, it's easy because they just have to wear a hat.

Jean: So you make up for it at home?

Sahar: Yes.

---

[49] . Afghanistan's holiest city.

Jean: If you were married and had children, would you bring them up to be religious?

Sahar: I will tell them the facts which I have learned or have heard from others, but I won't force them. I will lead them to find out themselves.

Jean: Would you instruct them or allow them to be instructed in other religions?

Sahar: *(laughs)* No, I can't do that.

Jean: *(also laughs)* That's a tough one, isn't it?

Sahar: Because we Muslims, we believe so much in God. If somebody believes in other religions, it's a bit strange for us. It will be accepted as a fact because we know there were other prophets and we believe in all of them. But we believe Islam is the last religion in the world, so everyone should believe in Islam. If it's the last religion, it's the best one, so why should we change our religion?

Jean: You have never worn a veil, have you?

Sahar: No.

Jean: But your mother did and does.

Sahar: Yes, she still does.

Jean: Did you ever think it was strange that she did? Or did you just accept it as that was the way.

Sahar: No, because when I was young, I saw all the adult women wearing it. *(laughs)* The strange thing was seeing a woman without a veil!

Jean: Oh, so the other way around! Of course. What do you think it's like to live behind a veil?

Sahar: I think it's a terrible thing!

Jean: Why?

Sahar: Because it restricts your view. You have to look just in front of yourself and nowhere else and why should we hide ourself?

Jean: But that's a Muslim law, isn't it?

Sahar: Yes it is. But circumstances change. Then, you must adjust yourself. Now, can I go to work wearing a veil? It's impossible. So we should adjust ourself to our generation, to our circumstances and conditions.

Jean: Do you ever talk to your mother about that?

Sahar: Yes, but she doesn't accept it. She says you shouldn't show your face to others, or even your hair. It's really a big sin to show your hair. But I can't follow that. I am not scared from the religious point of view. I can't understand wearing a long scarf.

Jean: It's a custom which is quite baffling to Western people. I notice that many young girls here aren't wearing a veil but continue to wear a scarf on their head. Now, why do they do that?

Sahar: Because their parents are strict and they won't allow them to go out without a long scarf. They've grown up in a religious family and are used to that.

Jean: But your mother doesn't think ill of you because you've decided not to wear the veil.

Sahar: No, no, she accepts the situation.

Jean: She accepts a change, but that she can't change. Your mother sounds very liberal.

Sahar: Yes, she is!

Jean: I wanted to ask you some general questions about women and doctors. How do women feel about going to male doctors, because there are not many women doctors?

Sahar: Because it's about their health, they won't mind. They will go.

Jean: Would a woman in a village or a tribal situation, like a Kuchi woman, would she mind going to a male doctor?

Sahar: Some of them, yes.

Jean: What do they do when they have babies? Just have them?

Sahar: Yes, of course. They don't look for a nurse or a doctor. The woman sits and waits for the child to be born.

Jean: I want to ask you what women do all day. If they haven't been educated and they take care of their house and their family, is that all they do?

Sahar: That's all. When they are finished their work, they might go to see friends or relatives, or go shopping. Nothing else.

Jean: Who has the say in the house about bringing up children?

Sahar: The father, because he thinks he's master of the family.

Jean: And the woman will obey him? She's quite obedient?

Sahar: Sure.

Jean: Sahar, this is a personal question. Do you consider yourself inferior to men?

Sahar: No.

Jean: What about women who aren't educated?

Sahar: I think they do.

Jean: And they obey, instead of feeling equal?

Sahar: Of course.

Jean: Do you think that men in Afghanistan, in general, regard women as inferior?

Sahar: Uneducated men, yes.

Jean: But an educated man?

Sahar: Some of them still do, but most educated men don't.

Jean: That's interesting. I didn't think that would be the answer really. Afghanistan, as I understand, has a very strict Muslim religion, and it is the mullahs who are in charge. How do they regard women?

Sahar: They consider women as a thing, to stay at home and cook for them, wash their clothes and do housework, bring children for them, and not go out and not have equal rights.

Jean: How would a mullah feel about women going to school and becoming educated, having jobs and working?

Sahar: I think they wouldn't like it. No. They believe that if a Muslim woman goes out, it's a dishonour because other men will see her figure, will hear her voice, and the mullahs are against these things; they don't like it.

Jean: So, the mullahs will obviously be against this new regime who want to educate.

Sahar: I think so.

Jean: Sahar and I are at her home and we are talking now about the people who have just dropped in, guests who have arrived—uninvited I might add—because ... well, you go on.

Sahar: Usually Afghans cook a big meal, you know. If it's dinnertime or lunchtime and the guests just drop in, we always have extra food so we can entertain them and not feel embarrassed. If it's just teatime, we bring out some cookies or cakes and sweets. If it's mealtime, we have to treat guests with whatever we've got. Sometimes, people prepare special things for guests because we say it's not just for our family, we should cook something else for our guests. For us, it's not polite to serve them just an ordinary meal.

Jean: Even if they come uninvited?

Sahar: Yes!

Jean: Is this not very expensive?

Sahar: Yes. If there are no guests, we just have curry with bread. If a guest comes, we have to cook rice because it wouldn't be polite to put just a pot of curry in front of him. We have to cook something else and prepare some salad and such.

Jean: So, you're always really at the mercy of these people who may or may not drop in. And you have to be prepared in advance.

Sahar: Yes, that is the way.

Jean: This is the last time we talk. Certainly, a lot of things have happened, haven't they?

Sahar: Yes. Good things I think, for the best.

Jean: I think one of the exciting things today is the publication of the newspaper.

Sound of paper rustling.

Sahar: Yes. And you know, one of the important things is that they haven't changed the name of the paper. It's the same as before.

Jean: Which is?

Sahar: *Anis.*

Jean: What does it mean?

Sahar: *Anis* means "one who talks with another". When I'm always with you and I'm good to you, I'm your anis.

Jean: Why do you think it's good that it's kept the same name?

Sahar: Because I think the man who established that newspaper wasn't a bad man, so they didn't want to change the name of the newspaper.

Jean: The news is very encouraging, isn't it?

Sahar: Yes, so encouraging.

Jean: In spite of all the rumours that are going around.

They both laugh.

Sahar: Yes, a lot of rumours.

Jean: That's to be expected.

Sahar: It's normal when a government changes that you hear a lot of rumours against the new people of the government.

Jean: Have you spoken to colleagues in your office about it?

Sahar: Yes. They're in favour of the new government. They hope a lot of good things will happen to Afghanistan now. They're waiting and we will see.

Jean: What about your family? How do they feel?

Sahar: Oh, my family's happy because, you know, my parents are so religious. My brother and I told them that their religion won't change. The government hasn't got anything to do with religions, so now they are happy. Everybody wants Afghanistan to be an improved, wealthy, and good country, so if the government says they will do something good for Afghanistan, why should we be against them? That's what we want from them. They say they will do for us, so we like them. My family will respect them, will accept their ideas. They will follow them if they think it's for the benefit of Afghanistan.

Jean: So you have to give them a chance.

Sahar: Yes.

Jean: What do you think the Russians will want from Afghanistan for helping to develop the country and improve the life of the people?

Sahar: I have no idea.

Jean: Have you thought about it at all?

Sahar: No, I haven't. Maybe the Russians will be happy because their regime extends to other countries where they think it will be good, and then some other countries will start to follow their regime and they will be happy with these things.

Jean: You can't tell. Inshallah. God willing. Thank you, Sahar, for these wonderful conversations.

Sahar: You're very welcome.

PART 3

The Soviet Invasion

"There I was: steeped in Afghanistan until the Russian invasion. Afghan friends quickly became Refugees and it was natural for me to want to help." —J. H. W.

Am I Too Old?

In her notes for one of her talks, Jean wrote, "I dream of going to Pakistan, to that part where the refugee camps crowd against the borders of Afghanistan offering shelter to those unfortunate people who have had to flee from their native land in fear of their lives." How many women Jean's age would have such a dream, much less live it? Despite her doubts and the dangers of war raging just beyond those borders, Jean embarked on another new journey.

Thatched Cottage,
Buckland Newton

To the First Secretary of the Embassy of Pakistan, London

21 August 1986

Dear Madam:

I very much enjoyed meeting you on Thursday, 14 August, when we discussed my proposal to visit your country. As perhaps you will remember from our conversation, the object of my visit would be to travel in Pakistan to find out as much as possible about the fate of the Afghan women refugees. When we hear news of the war, it is usually a report about military happenings or political implications, but rarely, if ever, do we learn of the unique problems confronting the women who have been thrust into a strangely alien way of life. What has happened to them since the coup d'état took place in 1978? I'm particularly anxious to discover how they are coping with life in the refugee camps which your government has been so intensely humanitarian in providing for them.

One of the most important issues must deal with the various aspects of aid already being given. The question of whether it is enough and of the right kind is undoubtedly a consideration. Health, social welfare, opportunities for education, preservation of the handicraft skills and the cultural heritage, employment as a means for supporting an independent life, these and many other aspects requiring assistance from outside sources must be assessed. Since our talk, I have been in touch with Global Village and they have agreed to sell items embroidered by Afghan refugee women.

Under all these circumstances, is not there a need and an opportunity for assistance from women's groups such as the National Federation of Women's Institutes and/or the Associated Country Women of the World? I would welcome the opportunity to spearhead such an investigative mission for I sincerely believe it would have important and far-reaching results that could lead to a more satisfying and acceptable life for these unfortunate women.

I hope it will be possible for me to go to Pakistan before the end of this year, perhaps in November. You were kind enough to say that you would write a letter on my behalf to arrange for me to visit some of the refugee camps. Thank you very much for your help.

Yours faithfully,
Mrs. J. Heringman[50]

Friday, 6 February 1987

Departure from Heathrow. The EgyptAir plane was grotty and creaking with age and no supervision of safety: no seat belts fastened for children, huge parcels and suitcases slithering about, and many adults standing to open the luggage compartments during landing.

---

[50] . Jean's letter was answered to the effect that her request was being forwarded to the appropriate ministry in Islamabad.

The route was long with many stops: Cairo, Dubai, and then Karachi, where there was a lengthy check-in with endless forms at immigration control. *Control* is the optimum word. Once over the European borders, one feels that freedom has been left behind and privacy is unknown.

Although Cairo was a transit stop, we had to leave the plane so it could be cleaned (thank goodness). But we then had to wait about three hours before continuing on to Dubai. Whilst our luggage stayed on board, we were instructed to carry our hand luggage off the plane and to form a queue on the tarmac. Over three hundred of us had to wait a turn to enter the tiny room where our hand luggage had to be searched and our passports taken away for bureaucratic officialdom and forms to be filled in. There was *one* man to deal with the luggage and *two* to stamp the passports and reassign boarding passes. It was exhausting and helped no one.

In Karachi, two earlier planes scheduled to depart before my own 4 p.m. flight had been delayed and combined, so I grabbed at the chance to leave, fearing my flight might also be delayed. Therefore, I arrived an hour or so before I was due, and no one was there to meet me. There must have been hundreds of people meeting the other passengers. The brilliant setting sun shone directly into my eyes as I emerged from the arrival section. I was momentarily blinded, seeing only a mass of silhouetted shapes. How would I recognize my driver or be recognized, I wondered? I made a badge and stuck it on my chest and stood right at the exit door.

Sure enough, at the scheduled time, two young men came up to me and identified themselves. One was Shapoor, a relative of my good Afghan friend, Laila, who, back in London, had kindly arranged for my transport, accommodation, and meetings. His friend, Hewad, is a physiotherapist who lives in Paris. Shapoor said, "We are going to drive straight to Peshawar instead of staying over in Islamabad as you thought. Many comings and goings of the people you are to meet are there, okay?"

So, off we went in a beautiful, big new Jeep, driving on a bumpy road for another two and a half hours to the house of another relative. Afghan people are not only hospitable but believe it's their duty to look after everyone who is brought to their attention. It's a very deeply embedded part of their culture.

Shapoor, like many other Afghans, has given up his career as a promising engineer, with an extensive education abroad, to fight for jihad, the holy war against the enemies of Islam. He is with the National Islamic Front for Afghanistan (NIFA).[51] He deals with arriving refugees and resettlement, registering them with the Pakistani government, finding and setting up tents, and procuring them blankets, food, clothes, and medicines. Some NIFA men are military mujahideen, guerrilla resistance fighters; others locate and buy arms and ammunition—it's said, CIA-funded—and then arrange for transporting it; others represent political aspects. Of course, they must speak English as they deal with various foreign governments. It's a staggering and monumental problem.

Some refugees have come with a little money and are helped to start work in a bazaar shop, or to gather wood to build huts, wool to make carpets, cotton to make quilts, flour to make bread. I've already learned that there are more amputees than ever recorded before, so this means getting wheel chairs and crutches as well. Stories are endless about smuggling, gun running, bribery, corruption and, above all, despair and hopelessness.

On our 9 p.m. arrival at the house, I was faced with a huge Afghan meal which protocol required I eat. Then conversation straight away: what is it that I want to do here? Who would back me? Then I was shown to my room and fell into bed.

Saturday, 7 February 1987

Next morning, we were joined by two Norwegian ladies connected with a church group and an American girl from London writing for *Newsweek*. Off we drove in two Jeeps to a border camp where refugees were crossing over. Crude tents house 396 families, and they averaged two children to each family. Shapoor has worked with these people, and they are at rock bottom. Bare, rocky scrub land, no good for even the most primitive farming. A few chickens, one water well, a few latrines, and unending desolation. It's so bleak and depressing, so grim.

In the night, there is a drenching rain, and I can't sleep for thinking of those people and others out there trying to cope. It makes one really

---

[51] . The most moderate of the Afghan political parties founded in Peshawar in 1979. Led by a prominent Sufi family, it favoured a constitutional monarchy and nationalism rather than communism or Islamism.

wonder if Gorbachev, Reagan, and all the other leaders and their families had to change places, what would the world be like? Can they have any real conception of what their programmes do to humanity? I am sure they do not.

Sunday, 8 February 1987

I was assigned a car and driver and went to investigate a secondary school set up for women, then to Hayatabad Camp. Same grim conditions, but there are two schools, one for boys and one for girls. Of course, no supplies. I wonder if I were to bring them crayons, paper, and pencils, might they want to make some drawings of their experiences?

Dinner was at a brother of Laila's, a handsome, smooth, sophisticated chap, UK and US educated. They are really all well educated and well off. And all are working with the resistance cause.

It was decided that, since everything would be closed in Peshawar the following day by government order, I should return to Islamabad. There was concern because of a visit from Benazir Bhutto[52] against whom a demonstration was planned. All roads were to be closed, no buses running, and the airport also closed. So, at 6 a.m., a driver in a Jeep drove me in the pouring rain to Islamabad. We had to hurry to leave Peshawar before the roadblocks were put up.

In Islamabad, another driver took me to the British Embassy. I was bursting to use the loo and embarrassed to be meeting one of the consulate staff for the first time. He seemed a dour Scotsman but diverted me first to the ladies'. Then we arranged an appointment, and he told me of a hotel. Driven here to the Ambassador Hotel; made some calls and plans.

Monday, 9 February 1987

D-Day, or rather accident day. I took a bad fall at the mosque, and my sunglasses cut my face. Lots of bleeding as I walked across the parkway

---

[52] . Pakistani politician who later as Prime Minister became responsible for the Afghan refugee policy of voluntary repatriation.

towards the hotel when, among the bazaar shops, I spotted a homoeopathic doctor's sign. The medic cleaned the cut with disinfectant, and then sent me, with a man to show the way, to a nearby doctor who cleaned it some more and said it needed stitches. He sent me to a hospital emergency clinic where a neurosurgeon, no less, examined it.

There were hundreds of people, all needing looking after as it was a huge clinic, but I was treated as an emergency and, being a foreigner, was pushed forward to the number-one position. I could call the American Embassy if I preferred to go there because the doctor said the cut would need five to six stitches. He kept reassuring me in the kindest way.

I put in a call to the embassy and learned their health unit deals only with staff, but I was assured the clinic had good doctors. Sooo, I now have six stitches—after being shown the sterile equipment every step of the way! I was told to rest and not worry about the inevitable vertigo, headache, black-and-blue eye, swelling, as if I wouldn't! I was given a tetanus shot and prescriptions for antibiotics, pain killers, and vitamins B and C. I was charged nothing and only paid for the medicines at a chemist's shop near the hotel and for another pair of sunglasses.

I rested all afternoon and watched the horrible sight developing. I think it will take two weeks to disappear, but the stitches will come out in five days when I'm back in Peshawar. I hope there will not be a scar. Curiously, I'm not as upset over this setback as I'm over the move I think I must make from Thatched Cottage.[53]

Tuesday, 10 February 1987

The eye is hardly visible, as the swelling obscures it. The discolouration is purple, black, blue, and yellow—a horrible sight. How lucky that the eye itself had no glass in it. I rested this morning, felt okay by noon, and took advantage of the weather, which was gorgeous, to hire a car and driver for sightseeing in the city and then on to Rawalpindi, or Pindi as it is known by the local people. It's a crowded town of bazaars and tiny shops, very colourful, noisy, and busy. The driver looked after me, and I returned to

---

[53] . Jean's beloved, rural Dorset home in Buckland Newton. Although loathe to leave, as she got older, she knew it made sense to move to a nearby town.

the hotel to rest before dinner with an English couple who've invited me through a mutual friend back home. Jill and Steve are a super couple, especially Jill, a warm-hearted, friendly, and helpful girl.

One of Laila's nieces, Aisha, has called to introduce herself, and is also a help. Her grandmother has had a heart attack and her own daughter is just recovering from a month's illness, yet, apologies for not being more attentive!

Wednesday, 11 February 1987

Jill picked me up and we went to a place where she works as a volunteer helping an English doctor administer to a group of about four hundred squatters who are mainly sweepers. The doctor's husband heads the Church of Pakistan Christian Mission and has been here for five years. Living conditions are appalling, and all major necessities—medicines in particular—are hard to come by, but they are trying. Jill has three children, and her husband is with the British Embassy. We spent the rest of the day together, including buying me a *shalwar kameez*, the traditional tunic-like shirt and loose trousers worn by women here and in India and Pakistan, so that I can be respectable!

Got exit visa for Peshawar. Went to the French Cultural Centre to see the great artist Ghiasuddin's fabulous paintings, and he was there—older, frail because of a heart condition and waiting for nearly two years to go to one of his sons who lives in the States. His escape with his paintings is heartbreaking: twenty were stolen, and the Iranian Embassy, for which he worked, has confiscated some of his biggest pieces. I shall try to contact someone regarding his time to leave, as he's confused.

Aisha said she can give me a lift on Friday to Peshawar where there are excellent American and French doctors. I will see one Saturday to remove the stitches. I'm fearful of a scar. I hope I can find a reasonably priced place to stay.

Thursday, 12 February 1987

It's hard to keep my courage up, mostly because of the accident. I feel it's an indication that I should not go further. I'm very worried about removing the stitches and seeing the actual damage. How lucky, lucky, no glass went in the eye. The swelling is almost gone, and the discolouration is disappearing. This was a real blow, which has made me nervous, but I can't help but compare it to what is happening "out there" to those refugees or the mujahideen who have no doctors or medicines for much more terrible injuries.

Islamabad is a beautiful city in its layout of broad avenues, a good grid system making it easy to locate places. Lots of trees and parks and a lot of building taking place, trying to make it another Brasilia. Except for the foreign buildings, the architecture is unimaginative, and the materials used are not going to last. The signs on the building fronts, to my eye, are gaudy and very tasteless.

After some paperwork this morning, I went to the Super Bazaar area and found a tailor to alter the garment I'd bought with Jill yesterday. Then to the hairdresser (passable but patient), and then to chat about Afghanistan with my friend Abdullah at his carpet stall. After some discussion and some hesitation on my part, we walked about twenty minutes to the house of Professor Aminullah, one of the members of Hezbe i Islami Party.[54] The politics are too complex to discuss here, but he said I could do more good in London, acting as a link to push the information coming from inside Afghanistan to the media. I feel sure he's right, for language is a problem, and what is needed are doctors and teachers. I feel my age terribly.

I then went with Alistair and Carole Crooks for tea, an intro by Jill. More learning about the situation, but this time, from an articulate Englishman with a clear insight and knowledge of his field—the refugee problem. He suggested that I might collect and stockpile the photo slides which are lying about here and need cataloguing and editing before they are presented to Western news sources. He feels the perspective should not be that of the smuggled-in news reporters and journalists based in Islamabad, but that of the Afghans, as documentary material of what has happened. We shall see.

---

[54] . Islamic fundamentalist organization, founded in Kabul in 1975, to fight the communist-backed government and the Soviet Union.

Friday, 13 February 1987

Face definitely improving. Went to Jumma Market, a huge bazaar with primarily a glut of oranges, and people in colourful clothes selling, selling. Hewad, who had met me at the airport with Shapoor, called for me. We had tea and left at 4 p.m. The driver dropped him first at the home of a friend as he's returning to Paris tonight.

Then I set off for Peshawar with the driver and lots of packages. Two hours of very interesting but daredevil driving, and we arrived at the house of Shapoor's father where I'm to stay until I find quarters. Father is in the US for medical reasons. I have my own sitting room, bedroom, and bath which are Pakistani style, but the price is right.

I was brought tea and sweets as, one by one, the other residents arrived. They are all young mujahideen. Samandar, living in the room next door, speaks good English and is a real gem—polite and helpful. He explained that they go in and out of Afghanistan frequently—in to fight some battles, and out to find work to support their families who are now refugees in Pakistan. Jobs are scarce and poorly paid. All supplies are hard if not impossible to come by. Corruption and black marketeering flourish as both Pakistanis and Afghans get their hands on goods intended for refugees. These they then re-sell on the black market in order to survive. The very sick, poor, and crippled people perish.

Samandar is a good photographer and has worked with US film crews in Afghanistan. He also worked at the Palm Beach Clinic for Afghans, a small medical facility here in Peshawar endowed by the citizens of Florida. Now it has been destroyed by bombs and needs to be rebuilt. Funds are not forthcoming until the clinic is registered by the Pakistani authorities. They refuse to do so on the grounds that such clinics already exist—another catch-22.

Samandar's mother, a teacher, is visiting him from Kabul for one month during the school holidays, taking advantage of the new government amnesty policy. She has come by bus and will be here another week. Nice for me to have a woman around. Bad news is that Shapoor's father is returning, and although no definite date is known, it's best I vacate. Long talks and dinner with Samandar and mother: rice, cauliflower, tea, and naan bread. Hot shower Afghan style, and I feel okay.

Saturday, 14 February 1987

US Consulate was closed, so I called UK Aid to recommend a doctor, as the stitches must come out. Nothing is easily accomplished in countries like this. The phone didn't work, so I tried to hire a rickshaw. Even attired in my Pakistani ladies' clothing, no luck. So, the *chokidar*, or gatekeeper, walked me to one of the new Peshawar schools where I know the principal. He introduced me to his accountant, Mr Usmani, an old gentleman who speaks beautiful English. He was detailed to accompany me to find the French lady doctor, Dr Ariel, recommended to remove the stitches.

It was very difficult to locate her surgery, which she runs for Afghan refugees. It was far out and almost hidden in clouds of dust. I scribbled a brief note to her, and it was taken by a messenger through a throng of huge Afghan men. In about five minutes, a black-bearded young Afghan appeared and escorted me to a consulting room. He spoke to me—thank God, in English—and told me to get onto the cleanly covered table. He was a nurse and cleaned the wound, removed the stitches with nary a twinge, and then Dr Ariel had a look.

She's a delightful, twinkly, friendly young woman from southern France. She has worked in Afghanistan for two and a half years. An anaesthesiologist actually, but she established this surgery! I think the scar will be minimal. A bandage to keep it clean is all. I'm being *so* careful.

Called on a few people in the afternoon with Mr Usmani to help. They will not allow me to wander, a good thing too because this is really quite a wild place, tribal in make-up, no law enforcement, and gun-toting Pathans everywhere. Mr Usmani informs me that this is a British term used to refer to the Pashtun people who are the largest ethnic group in Afghanistan and second largest in Pakistan.

Dinner with Samandar and mother. Plans made for me to teach him basic photography.

Sunday, 15 February 1987

Goodbye to Shapoor, who is off to a conference in Sweden and then on to the US for talks following the Geneva Convention[55] on 25 February. So much depends on the questions which are asked and how they are worded. Slanting is so easy.

A phone call to Mr Usmani to organize a car with his son, Asif, to drive me, and within half an hour, they appeared. Mr Usmani's background of many years with the RAF and with the Americans has given him perfect English, and he is known to be of high moral integrity. Asif works for a pharmaceutical company and drove me on lots of errands today. I would be lost without their supervision. I'm not sure whether it's due to my age or the changed conditions in Pakistan, but I'm not nearly as free as before.

We took my belongings to the Afghanaid guest house where I've rented a room. It's freshly painted, and while I waited in the garden, two workers stitched some curtains together and nailed some hooks to the wall. There is a bed, huge wardrobe, extra bed-settee, night table, and a carpet. Toilet is across the garden, and all is very clean, being British I suppose. One hundred rupees a day with breakfast, including sweeping and laundry. Altogether about £47 a week. I hope I can stay for a month or so and then join the Bales[56] tour of the Himalayas at the end of March.

Today, Asif drove us out of the city, and I could tell immediately where the so-called Afghan village began. It has been there about three or four years: a self-sufficient surviving group allowed by the government to develop this land, no doubt in return for favours from various governments.

Monday, 16 February 1987

Eye is mending well—scar won't be too bad, mostly in the eyebrow area.

---

[55] . One of many rounds of negotiations between intermediaries of the governments of Pakistan and Afghanistan to secure the withdrawal of Soviet troops and the voluntary return of Afghan refugees.

[56] . Jean's preferred travel agency.

Collected this morning by Mr Usmani's older son, who drove me to interviews with various aid agencies and also showed me the old city of Peshawar. It teems with people and is so crowded with tiny bazaars, goods of all sorts, lorries, cars, bicycles, rickshaws, and tongas,[57] that one can scarcely move. It's dirty and crumbling, a sea of confusing sights, sounds, and smells. I would surely have got lost on my own and, with no women about, it was more than scary. So many tribal people, and the Pathans are wild.

We visited the house of Asif's new wife who didn't appear. They married a year ago, but have only spoken on the telephone since. In March, they will have a huge party with a thousand guests, and then the bride will move into Asif's house.

We had delicious elevenses.[58] At 2 p.m., we collected Mr Usmani and his daughter from school and went to his house for lunch. It's in the old Muslim quarter of the city, and all his huge family live there in apparent harmony. As it was chilly, we all curled up on a huge bed, covered our legs with a sensible quilt, watched cricket on TV, and waited for the meal. It was served on the floor of this big bedroom, Pakistani style, and was delicious and very informal.

Back at the Afghanaid Centre, Samandar came and we had a long talk and made plans. He's going to the Panjsher area in Afghanistan for a jihad stint of about four to five days. Most of the mujahideen cannot sustain a continuous battle because they must provide for their families. So, many of them come to Pakistan for short spells to earn enough money and then return to battle. Sometimes they bring Russian arms with them, which they sell at a profit. Or, they may receive aid goods and sell them on the black market. Peshawar is a glut of goods, much illegitimacy in business, and a buzz of intrigue. The refugee crisis has become *big business* for Pakistani merchants and for some Afghans crafty enough to capitalize on the misfortunes of their countrymen.

Dinner with my old Kabul friend, Nasir, who's been here four years and works with Bruce, my contact at Afghanaid, to earn for his family. They are still living in three tents in a mud compound with no toilet facilities. Yet, the women produced a fabulous meal, which we ate sitting on beautiful Afghan carpets with comfy bolsters behind us. After lots of

---

[57] . Light, horse-drawn vehicle with two wheels.
[58] . Traditional English morning coffee/tea break.

fruit, they brought thick wool blankets and steaming tea. Later, I went to visit the ladies and, oh, how I regret being such a dummy about the language! I'm fairly hopeless, and it really matters.

Tuesday, 17 February 1987

Asif and his brother came again helping me out. It's embarrassing, but finding places here is very hard and time consuming. I worked it out so that they dropped me off at Samandar's in time to say goodbye to his mother, who is returning to Kabul by bus tomorrow. Then, he, a friend, and I squeezed into a rickshaw to go for a photography lesson.

Dinner, via intro from Jill, with Barbara, a fabulous American girl speaking perfect Pashto and here on a Fulbright.[59] More talk about plans for children's drawings and an exhibition. Bruce walked me there, and they both escorted me back to my quarters.

Wednesday, 18 February 1987

Trying to check on this idea of children's drawings, but it will have to wait till next week when I've made appointments. More photo lessons for the young men.

An SOS from one of the hospitals for a boy needing brain surgery for the third time. He's being flown to Paris, but they need funds. I gave 1,000 rupees. I saw the hospital and the splendid work being done training Afghans. This is a combined French, Belgian, Swiss, and Swedish venture. People of different nationalities seem to work together very well here.

Thursday, 19 February 1987

Still making calls and checking things out—how to be of use. I must try to keep in mind what Nancy said in her letter, "The problems are so immense that one *can* feel that one is squandering time as you say. But I believe firmly that every person who openly shares a commitment with the

---

[59] . Prestigious American scholarship program for international study and research.

Afghan people, in any way whatsoever, makes a genuine contribution and strengthens individual and group resolve. Yes, it takes time to penetrate the 'muddle' but every minute (both positive and negative) is a learning experience."

Went to Save the Children and the Danish Commission. Photo lessons each day with my five students. Just basics are needed.

Life here is so basic. No toilet in this cosy room, so I've rigged up a two-gallon tin for a night-time loo and have a huge bucket which I fill each night for my *bath*. One bottle of boiled water lasts till toothbrush time in the morning. Jonathan, who is in charge while Bruce is away on a five-day holiday, is quite thoughtful.

Everyone out here is so young that often I must disappear to let them get on with parties and such like. It's a bit awkward.

Friday, 20 February 1987

Jumma, Friday prayers. I helped organize sandwich making for a cricket match: tuna, crab meat, and a lovely local smoked veal like Parma ham. Watched the game on the Ismalia University grounds. Went to Saddar Bazaar to check on Greens Hotel in case I have to leave here, and bought a blue shalwar kameez.

Went to see a video at the American Centre and stayed for dinner so as to see some others. All astonishing as the TV crews get in so close with the mujahideen. They are very brave and risk their lives. It's hard being here on the fringe and not knowing fully what is going on. Film director Jonathan Ali Khan is waiting to go in. His film on the State of Eritrea in Africa was great. Met Peter Juvenot, a brilliant TV photographer, and Floris, a Dutch chap here soon to set up an information service inside with Julian Gearing, the British war correspondent. I am the wrong generation for all that is taking place here and inside Afghanistan too.

Saturday, 21 February 1987

Letter from the travel agency confirming I can go with the Bales tour. I think it will be good for me. It gives me five weeks here and allows me a couple of days to do some sightseeing in Quetta besides. If I can get permission for the children's drawings, I will still have time to join the tour in Lahore on 30 March for fourteen days and return on my own ticket.

Met a young nurse today for lunch, Finola, an Irish beauty and sweet, working so hard in a medical unit. She explained how funds with so many aid organizations break down over time, leaving even more problems: how to pay the Afghans employed, plus the staff, plus the running costs, all with no money, while the board at home meets to discuss redoing budgets. At this end, the Pakistani government, so heavily burdened with the more than four hundred thousand refugees, increases the rates on the aid agencies for electricity, gas, and rent in order to deal with *their* financial refugee costs. Catch-22.

More trouble today with roads blocked. Demonstrations prior to the Geneva Conference are putting pressure on the Pakistani government to return the Afghan refugees by putting pressure on the Soviets. Whilst helping out on the reception desk at Afghanaid, I took a phone call from a Swedish agency. Seems all voluntary agencies or VOLAGs have a subsecurity network for passing on just such info. The tailors who are given work here had to be taken home in Jeeps in order to avoid trouble for them. Yesterday's demo was the worst so far with twelve killed and seventy hurt.

Afghans long to go back home, but not under Russian rule, and who can blame them? If the USSR refuses to leave Afghanistan, then Pakistan will be next. It's a real pushover; the land is flat, and the people not tough or willing to fight.

Sunday, 22 February 1987

Met a super young woman, Margaret Segal, head of education for the International Rescue Committee. Now I feel I'm getting closer to a good project. Had a talk about the drawings from the children and an exhibition. She could get me to more remote camps that have guest lodges and interpreters and schools, of course. Directed me to Gabi Steiner at the Austrian Relief Commission (ARC).

Julian Gearing arrived, and five of us went to the American Centre where I was the only American. Dinner was delicious, and a video afterwards, an old but good spy film.

Must talk to Julian regarding a story on the VOLAGs of Peshawar. All their workers seem to be dedicated, sincere, and hard working, giving years of their lives for little pay. No recognition and hardship conditions. They seem to overlap and work with each other in mixed ethnic, national groups. They are the unsung heroes and heroines, facing alien problems in an alien world.

The real issue they all grapple with is the need for total education, as 98 per cent of the Afghan population is non-literate. It's not just dealing with the immediate refugee catastrophe as Afghans flee the destruction of their country. It extends from basic reading and writing to sanitation, health, pre- and postnatal care, family planning, occupations, and training to enable the refugees to earn a little here and prepare for their eventual return to Afghanistan. Because of the near extermination of the small, educated elite of the country, perhaps the biggest programme of all is to educate the children. The tragic void must be replenished. I can't recall in all of history another such monumental undertaking and, as far as I can tell, the people of the VOLAGs are bearing it on their shoulders.

Monday, 23 February 1987

Appointment with Gabi Steiner of the ARC, another super young woman. Spent two hours there and got lots of valuable information. Towards the end, she discussed her idea of a book written by an Afghan refugee woman named Habiba. The three of us share a deep concern for the plight of women, especially widows. The idea is for Habiba to interview different people and families in the camps, tape the conversations, and write them in Pashto. I've Pashto-speaking friends who could translate them into English. And the stories could be illustrated with the drawings I hope to get from the children! Gabi is very enthusiastic about it and has arranged for me to meet the lady on Thursday. It's such an exciting prospect!

Steady downpour of rain. Went to the Pearl International Hotel where it was warm with a nice atmosphere. Caught up on some correspondence.

Tuesday, 24 February 1987

Everything is very quiet and tense because of the bombings and killings two or three days ago. Workers have not come to the Afghanaid Centre as they are vulnerable when going to and from their homes. The same situation prevails at other VOLAGs. It's the Geneva talks tomorrow, and lots of questions being asked, as the Pakistani government is under intense pressure.

Still pouring and damp. Lack of drainage on the roads hampers walking. Spent morning at Danish Centre, which deals with an embroidery project for women. I shall try to take some items back for Oxfam and Global Village. A little extra income helps restore dignity and lifts spirits. Some of the women I met were smiling and even telling jokes.

Wednesday, 25 February 1987

I'm told I must move, as many new Afghanaid people are coming. Will contact Finola about renting a room, as her co-worker is leaving. I'm quite spoiled in this cosy setup; even with no bath or toilet, I've managed, and very comfortably too.

Tonight I am uneasy. Each day I've been seeing and talking to the various aid agencies, trying to find my way. Tomorrow is a meeting Gabi has set up. If only I could stay with Finola just one week, then go to the camps for two or three weeks, during which time I could do the children's art project, photographs, and Habiba's book.

Re-read Nancy's letter where she says, "I agree that vignettes of Afghan life can say volumes more than flogging the bombs and bullets bits. After all, what exactly is this culture the mujahideen and their supporters want to preserve? How many people know about that? The whole world should. Go to it!" I hope it works.

Thursday, 26 February 1987

I met Habiba, who walked from her camp to talk with me. What a unique young woman! She had horrible experiences escaping. She was bombed, shot at, and badly injured during a night-time mountain trek. She lost all her belongings and became ill, cold, and hungry. Nothing but misery. Married with one baby daughter who is, tragically, brain damaged. She works as a nurse with one of the aid agencies. Yet, she wants to write a book! This must be special—the refugee story from an Afghan woman who will brave the disapproval of her people and especially the men.

She said, "Afghan people have been sleeping too long; now it's time they wake up and assume their responsibilities." She's so angry and wants to shout. She needs an audience.

Question was, how to get the Afghan men to agree to a *woman* doing this? Gabi asked me to speak to the two ARC subdirectors, Afghan men, to seek their approval for Habiba to tape stories of Afghan families just in the refugee camps under their auspices. I did a super job—playing it just right. Gabi and even Habiba were very pleased.

Gabi has proposed that I stay in the ARC guest house near the Mardan refugee camp. There is transport to Peshawar twice weekly, but by staying in the camp, I can work on the children's drawing project and get close to some of the families. At the same time, what an opportunity to help Habiba shape her book towards the realization of her dream. Now we must wait until I get the necessary permits to go into the camps.

Friday, 27 February 1987

The chap about tent supplies arrived from London here at Afghanaid, and I acted as hostess. Packed and wrote letters. Finola came at 6 p.m. We took Bruce to the English couple who breed Alsatians to see about a friend's sick puppy. Then we took Floris to a German doctor friend of Finola's for a shot, as he was suffering all day from the most appalling allergic attack.

The doctor asked us to dinner with another nice German man, so after I settled into my new quarters at Finola's, we collected them and dined at the Pearl International. Lovely evening, and Finola is amazing. The things she's done and is presently doing. Quite a gal.

Saturday, 28 February 1987

New quarters quite okay; not so cosy as at Afghanaid, but comfortable and the same price with all food included. Off early today to change money: rum deal—down from 18.40 afs to 17.20 afs to the pound. Did jobs. Went to see Samandar and met an Afghan doctor, one of the mujahideen, just back from California with more chilling stories. Went with Finola to an Indian evening concert at the French Cultural Centre, then back to her quarters. Still waiting for the permits.

Mujahideen 'Going in'

The Harsh Landscape of Battle

The Target

Ready for the Attack

In the Line of Fire

Grim Justice

In the Midst of Battle

Will Anything Be Left?

No Sign of Life

Back to Camp

Martyrs

How Many More...

Map of Refugee Camps in Pakistan

"There is no hopeful heaven to asylum, just a bunch of bureaucrats throwing paper to each other. To be a refugee, more than losing your country, more than the losing your history and your culture, you lose the right to choose your way of life." —Ghulam

Into the Camps

Sunday, 1 March 1987

Went at 9 a.m. to the ARC, and lucky me—I can go into the camps! Gabi arranged it all: written permission to visit the camps, accommodation nearby, and transportation. She even provided a sleeping bag. Leaving on 2 March at 4 p.m.

The plan is for me to work with Habiba, interviewing and taping the conversations with different refugee families and individuals, especially the widows. I see it as a collection of vignettes. My next job will be to take Habiba's first efforts—an introduction and one story—to London, find a publisher and a contract with an advance for Habiba. We have one month. If necessary, Muriel Pike, my Dorset English friend and author, could help polish the writing and guide me to the right publisher. A thrilling and daunting task for me, and that's just for starters!

Spent the day with Finola—bazaar shopping, photographing in a nearby village, supper at Finola's, and preparing for the time away at the camp.

Monday, 2 March 1987

Left by Jeep at 5 p.m. for a one-and-a-half-hour drive accompanied by an Afghan doctor, his wife and their two young children. With introductions made, I learn that Dr Ghulam and Shazia, are stopping overnight on the way to their camp's clinic. I can't believe how primitive my "quarters" are at this team house. Because a so-called "delegation" of

Afghan men is here, I must sleep in a room with two Afghan lady workers. What passes for a toilet stinks and is near my bed.

Habiba arrives from her camp, and together we write a working draft for her book entitled *Time to Wake Up* with the following interview questions.

Habiba's And Jean's First Draft

Introduction: Why do you think an Afghan woman should write this book?

Life in Afghanistan Before the 1978 Coup

1. A brief personal background for each of the women (for example: place of birth, childhood, education, career or job, marriage, present family).
2. The plight of women in prison.

Exodus: Why, who, when, how and to where?

Refugee life

1. What aspects of culture shock have you experienced and how have they changed your social and economic status?
2. How do you cope with your feelings; for example, of frustration, anger, despair, the inevitable compromises which must be made?
3. What do you tell your children?
4. Have you or anyone in your family had to beg?
5. What is your attitude towards aid projects and foreign aid workers, male and female?
6. How did you feel having to register with a political party as a condition before receiving your registration and rations?
7. How do you cope with the lack of freedom without passport or travel documents?
8. Is this the first time you are wearing a chadri? If so, why? How does it make you feel?

9. Traditionally, when a man dies, the widow must be looked after by the eldest male, who could even be a young boy. What happens in the camps?

Your future

1. What do you think about repatriation back to Afghanistan?
2. Does education and westernization influence your decision to return? Does the feeling of obligation diminish or remain constant?
3. How does your exposure to different tribal customs affect you?
4. How do you feel about Afghans who take refuge in the West?

How do you see the future of Afghanistan?

1. Your country can be rebuilt, but can your culture survive?
2. What do you think of education for girls?
3. Are you afraid of being pushed back into a fundamentalist society and losing what little ground women have gained?

Habiba explains the title, "After seven years of sleeping, it's time to wake up. We must ask, to what? To the realization of what has happened to the people and the country. Of where to turn now. And where and how to begin."

Both Habiba and I are very pleased with what we've written together, especially as there is a power failure later. This meant dinner with Dr Ghulam took place by candlelight—sounds romantic, but wasn't! A fitful night.

Tuesday, 3 March 1987

Up with the mullah's call at 5 a.m. Over to Habiba's camp for breakfast at 6:30 in her "room". An old crone tending the baby also sleeps there with her husband. Habiba's baby is tragic, lying on the bed, head covered, twitching and making odd, whimpering sounds. Her name is Farishta, sixteen months old, brain damaged and hopeless. Medicines cost a fortune; earnings don't cover such "luxuries".

At 8 a.m. we leave for the clinic at the first camp, collecting people on the way. The huge camp is a cluster of many mud-daubed buildings. There are six schools for boys, four for girls. The clinic consists of a lab, research room, vaccination room, and treatment rooms.

Twice a week, Habiba teaches prenatal and delivery care to about thirty women who sit on benches or crouch on the ground. They arrive fairly promptly, some drifting in slowly. Ages from young teenagers to older women, all holding babies, and most are pregnant as well. Tribal clothing and good luck charms decorate their peaked and beaded bonnets, their bangles jangling and ankle rings winking in the sun. One five-year-old sitting next to me has a thin leather thong laced through her pierced nose.

Here they distribute enriched cereal, boiled water, and milk. All is carefully rationed. You must be registered and have a card, which is not easy, as the Pakistani government does not want to reveal accurate statistics. Medicines for the clinic are bought in the local bazaar, manufactured in Pakistan. Corruption reigns supreme. Pakistanis are "slightly" worse than Afghans, as they are on home ground, and immigrations officials along with police and security officers are flagrant in their abuse.

A cooking demonstration of vegetable stew: how to peel, cut, and clean carrots, turnips, onions, potatoes, tomatoes. Rice contains mice and rat turds, which are hand removed, but all the rice must be infected and filthy with germs. Vegetables are washed in who knows what kind of water? Aha! Potassium permanganate is used to rinse everything. Almost every child coughs, sneezes, or has a runny nose. Small wonder: they all are barefoot, rags barely cover them, flies abound, but at least these women here learn to wash and clean.

Later, at another camp, Dr Ghulam lets me sit in his office at the clinic while he deals with patients, an endless stream of men and women, all with several children. What pitiful sights. The aid agency has established a wonderful system with everything recorded, charted, graphed, and analysed. He is the only doctor for more than 28,000 people. His wife also works here. There are a few female helpers and nurses. There is no hospital.

We took some pix at the ladies' and children's request. Photographed Dr Ghulam with his wife. Had tea, left at 2 p.m. for the team house and lunch. About 5 p.m. I went for a lovely walk up a country road but on the way back, an ARC car came hunting for me. Just security precautions;

they really look after foreigners. Tea with Pakistani neighbours, and more tea with Dr Ghulam and Shazia who, laughing, wish me to drop the "Dr" and use just their first names.

Wednesday, 4 March 1987

Up early again—important to be first in the stinky loo. Breakfast at Habiba's. Farishta is a sweet bundle but has tuberculosis meningitis. No sign of mobility; she can't even hold her head up. Medicine costs 1,800 rupees or $100 per month. Habiba's and her husband's combined salary is 3,100 rupees. They need 800 for food, so how can they manage? They can't. I will help as I have helped others.

Pickup at 8 a.m.—off with the education team to Jalala camp. It is situated on a lovely road leading to the Swat Valley. The land belongs to one of the big Pakistani families. Beautiful approach to this rolling hillside village next to a river, reached by walking over a rickety log bridge. Long walk to the first school with four classes, all outside on the hard, mud-baked area. I asked to see the children's drawings. Good start.

All the people have blackboards, and today's lesson is on the building of pit latrines. They have been learning the necessity of and the reasons why this is important. Now comes the practical part. We are all laden with crates, tin cans, poles, nails, hammers, saws, and knives. Each group is to construct a pit latrine following diagrams drawn on the blackboard. I sit in the "chair of honour" with tea being brought.

The teachers gather on cushioned charpoys and then dig and build. Jolly good efforts. But I'm told that, whilst many illiterate Afghans have learned how to dig pit latrines, it has been discovered that they don't use them, continuing their age-old practice of shitting in fields or in streams. So pollution has become a terrible problem, and the government has had to realize that an education programme must be implemented.

Afterwards, I am taken to two other schools. All the children are boys with only two girls so far. The Qur'an says that women should be educated equally but the mullahs, most of whom are uneducated, say not so. They say, "Who will look after the children and keep the house if the girls are educated?" So, because the girls and adults can't even read the Qur'an, they can't query the mullahs. But this is slowly changing. One positive factor in this whole terrible catastrophe is that, for the first time in their history, there is mass education.

I think this school, which is supervised by Gabi, will produce drawings. Wouldn't it be great if the UNHCR[60] supported the idea regarding a grant? What doors I've opened since those first depressing days!

After classes and observation by the team, we drive to another school where the teachers all sit on the floor. Twenty of them are receiving more information from the instructors, mostly Pakistanis, for the teachers to pass on to their students. This is Habiba's lament, that the Afghans never tried to educate their population, that only 2 per cent went to school. Now, not only do aid agencies have to deal with the basics of food, shelter, medical aid, clothing sanitation, health, and nutrition programmes, but also with schools for everyone of all ages. In other words, the total education and social reform of an entire nation. What a task.

We drive back in billowing clouds of dust with long traffic delays. Lunch at team house. Four ladies in one room, six men in another, and one toilet. I haven't been yet, but I bet it stinks too. I shall have an early night because there will be another early morning. Samine, one of the few female teachers, invites me to a wedding tonight, but I decline—better sleep. She will help with the drawing project.

Thursday, 5 March 1987

What a night! Dreams and an Afghan widow praying loudly three times during the night, twice with the light on. Terrible rain in the morning, and I've left my raincoat behind in Peshawar. Drive with the aid team to Jalala camp and tried to walk up to the makeshift houses for home visit assessments, but it was too muddy and slippery. We had to get the vehicle out quickly owing to the disappearing road, which was slowly sliding into the river. Sat in a chaikhana, or tea house, while the team wrote their reports.

Then, drove to Peshawar, arriving about 12:30 p.m. Walked to Afghanaid to get mail in drenching rain. How wonderful to hear news of loved ones. Bruce invited me to lunch, then Olivier Roy and his wife came

---

[60] . United Nations High Commissioner for Refugees.

by; they're a French couple who travel a lot in Afghanistan. He is a brilliant sociologist, writer, and an authority on Islam. I must get his newest book.

Back at the ARC. I have a lovely room, bath, closet. Everything clean. I am going to spend half an hour in the shower.

Friday, 6 March 1987

Rained all day yesterday and still going strong today. A lousy Jumma (Friday prayer)—no cricket, no walking. Habiba came, and we took a rickshaw to one of the hospitals to make enquiries about her little girl. Doctor hasn't shown, so she must return next week. When Farishta was one year old, she took sick with convulsions. Up till then, she was quite normal, so these six months have been a real blow.

We took another rickshaw to a huge refugee centre where Habiba's family live. They occupy a dreadful mud hut with tiny so-called rooms—cold, damp mud floors with a few mattresses, and a paraffin cooker. Millions of flies swarmed everywhere; the baby was kept covered. Habiba's mother, looking eighty, is only forty-four. All their large extended family were eating on the floor –rice, chicken salad, spinach, all well cooked. Thank God I had given Habiba the money, though intended for herself, not for a family meal. Oranges and bananas, a real luxury, then tea. Afterwards, we made a tape recording with Habiba telling her own story.

I left at 4 p.m., and Habiba's husband, Aziz, took me on a bus. I was the only woman, and it was a hair-raising ride. As he was going to his brother's, I walked alone to Gabi's. Finola came later and stayed through supper and on till about 10:30. Her education programme for nurses is threatened with closure because of a demand for bribe money. There is *so* much corruption, blackmail, and threats. "Pay up or else get out!" This VOLAG business here should be written about. It is obscene and from all quarters! Stories on so many levels make one's head reel.

Saturday, 7 March 1987

Have got a lousy cold, *again!* No doubt from sitting in Habiba's house and being in the rain. Lots of errands and a hair wash, which didn't do the cold any good.

Went with Finola to meet a friend she hadn't seen for some time, a young Afghan woman named Mahzala. What a reunion! She lives in a very strict Muslim house and can scarcely move. I will see if I can help her, as she wants to go to the States.

Dinner here, and later Dr Rahman Zamani and Gabi returned from Quetta. He is a soft-spoken doctor from Kunar Province and director of the medical programme.

Sunday, 8 March 1987

This morning we collected an Afghan girl currently studying nursing in the UK. Perfect English, well travelled, and probably the one to do Habiba's translation. Habiba is going to be given one to two weeks off to do preliminary work, and this is very important as her crone-nurse has left to look after a grandson. What to do with Farishta? So far, no one to care for her. Habiba brought her to the clinic this morning, and I was there too. We also went to a new camp for tuberculosis patients. The agony is endless, and the percentage of Afghans able and/or willing to help implement programmes is small.

Dr Zamani will help with the children's drawings, and the ARC will supply the materials. We will go to schools in the ARC camps near here.

Am invited with Gabi, Habiba, and other female aid workers to a big ladies' meeting in Peshawar. We leave on Wednesday.

Monday, 9 March 1987

Staying overnight at Habiba's. From her room, I can see two little girls outside playing. They are blowing up "balloons" from condoms bought in the bazaar. I tell Habiba this is a shameful rejection of family planning to make toys of something so important to the health and strength of the nation.

Slept in Habiba's room. Aziz went to sleep with the three doctors across the compound. The baby was quiet, and I slept okay. My cold is gone as is my sense of smell, which I'm sure is a blessing. If everything smells as bad as it looks, I'm in luck.

Up and ready to leave at 8 a.m. to the camp. Habiba brought the baby along and made calls on families. These two poor people, Habiba and Aziz—what can be done for them? Maybe I can find a way for Farishta to be brought to the UK for examination and treatment.

At his camp, Ghulam was very kind and took me to six schools. This is really the story I want. What is happening to the children of this war as refugees? What is their daily life? What do they do? How do they pass the time? What do they think about? What do they remember? What about their school, their teachers, their homes, etc.?

I consulted the teachers in charge and explained that I would supply the necessary paper and crayons. I would then collect the drawings to take them to England where I would show them to raise money for their books and school supplies. Every headmaster likes my idea, and all have agreed to what will be an enormous task.

I must make an audio-visual component with a tape recording of children's voices—singing, laughing, and chattering in Pashto. One storyline will narrate a child's activities in the camp from waking up until bedtime; another will be a child recounting his or her memories of escape. My photographs will provide the visual part portraying the arrival of refugees, medical attention, ration time, men and women's work, daily activities, and the lives of widows and orphans.

I must work hard to show the exhibition of drawings and photographs to women's groups in the UK and elsewhere, as I am convinced that changes in our society will only eventually come from women. And I must work hard to make it a success—very hard—but I really believe in it, and so many have helped. I must also do it for them.

Lunch, a rest, and a walk. To bed early as we rise early.

Tuesday, 10 March 1987

Arrival of the French aid group. All these teams of people having to be shown round and given VIP treatment takes time away from dealing with patients.

Habiba had an awful day, as her helper did not show. A bad day too for Shazia, Ghulam's wife, as she had a three-month-old baby die from tetanus as she was examining her. No vaccination of course. Again, the story of corruption and vital medicines.

Some conclusions after this time of observation: Many people, especially women, from all over the world, are working desperately hard in an alien land under substandard conditions of health and comfort for very small salaries. They form part of a dedicated and humanitarian group loosely called VOLAGS or voluntary agencies. The percentage of Afghans working in a similar way is very small due mostly to the traditional lack of education, particularly among women. How can some sit by *idly* and let others do things for them *and* do nothing to help themselves?

It seems it's their culture and their religious mullahs who interpret the Qu'run to keep women as slaves/prisoners, making babies, looking after them, and providing for the men. "Don't learn to think" or a woman might become as or more powerful than a man. Then, he would lose control. It just does not occur to these women to volunteer to help, to ask to be taught, to look after each other's babies, to organize a play activity for children. Nothing. Nothing except for the very few who have had education but not nearly enough, and even some of them marry men who have the age-old hang-ups. The clinics ought each to have an Afghan who could do simple tasks like queue forming, keeping order, weighing babies.

Dr Zamani has gone to so much trouble for me to have a better room than my sleeping in Habiba's that I must go there tonight. She is angry and sad for me to go, but I know it is right, as he has been so kind. It is a wrench for me too, but it has been a shockingly tragic experience for me—to have to live as she and her family live, day in, day out, with the heartbreak of that baby, and all the time her working to help other mothers and their babies. What irony to have that job.

Dr Zamani brought books of paper, crayons, and coloured pencils. I gave the first ones to Rozamon, the head teacher at Camp 1 Primary 2.

Took photos of the team house area, and then we were driven to the house of his Swiss friend, who has a huge double guest house shared with two German-based programmes. These are businesses, I think employed by Pakistan, and not refugee work. It will be a hundred rupees a night.

No one is staying in the house at the moment, so I have the choice of four immaculate rooms, each with tiled bath, fresh towel, new bar of soap, and toilet paper. There is a real toilet here with a clean *seat*, and it looks like new. I can't wait for a luxurious shower—I must stink, but I can't smell as yet.

The chokidar made the bed—not a charpoy (the low bed strung with ropes)—and with clean, pretty sheets and a blanket. Large wardrobe, all new vinyl, nice décor, electric lights, a desk, outlook onto a covered terrace and garden. Boiled water. I think of poor Habiba, Aziz, and their poor baby, Farishta!

No food tonight, as we had late lunch. I shall blow up eating so much rice and naan, but oranges are plentiful and delicious.

Wednesday, 11 March 1987

Had a super sleep. Breakfast and off at 8 a.m. and then to the camp. Habiba, Aziz, and baby took sick in the night, so it was a good thing that I wasn't there.

Went to schools to distribute supplies, and at the first one, when I approached and the children recognized me, they produced the first drawings. They waved them at me from the windows. It was great! Visited two widows with awful stories. Gave both some money. Left in special Jeep sent for Habiba, her mother, and me, and we just made it to the UNHCR meeting.

It was most interesting, as many nationalities were represented, including Afghan and Pakistani women. Discussion about women and female problems, very open. For first time, Afghan women were strong and offered to present next month's programme. There is hope.

Dinner with Gabi and children. Babysat. Dr Zamani and two French aid people in Quetta came over for the evening.

Thursday, 12 March 1987

Went to Saddar Bazaar to shop. Bought baby clothes for Habiba, postcards, and odds and ends. Gabi and her husband, Gustave, won't take any money. I buy bits and pieces, but I will give the couple money. It's always a question of how much.

Friday, 13 March 1987

Mahzala came early this morning, and we talked for four hours. What tragic stories refugees have. I cried again. How I hate what religion imposes on women. It's really *not* the religion but some mullahs, and therefore some men's interpretation. It's how some keep control, and when I see what it does, I am overcome with anger! Mahzala is a case in point. She needs lots of help. She brought me a lapis necklace, earrings, and a ring packaged in a Kabul version of Bond Street.

I walked to the Spin Jamat Bazaar and around to Afghanaid. Had a meal with Gabi and Gustave. Our plans changed for Saturday, as Habiba must go back home for the day.

Saturday, 14 March 1987

Habiba showed up at 9 a.m. She didn't go home because Farishta was sick. She was supposed to be put in hospital with oxygen, but it was impossible to leave her to go and get the medicines, which the hospital does not supply. Too late to alter plans again, and besides, Mahzala was due at 10 a.m. Big mix-up. Habiba returned to take care of Farishta. Mahzala and I did more talking, errands in Saddar Bazaar, and finally, lunch at a Chinese restaurant.

She had never been to the bazaar or any other places in Peshawar. The story of her life in a *very strict* Muslim family is yet another indictment of that religion. I *hate* what the extremists believe in and enforce on their ignorant people. Examples: the abuse of women, the threats and instillation of fears. All horrible and backward, no logic, just superstition and blaming Allah for everything bad, expecting everything good to be bestowed by him, not by hard work or aid.

Sunday, 15 March 1987

Have been stuck in a hopeless traffic jam for over an hour. Pakistani people in the village are demonstrating. I'm not sure of the reasons yet, but it's a helluva inconvenience *and* in the pouring rain with appointments to meet. No way to telephone. Pakistan, oh Pakistan—*always* something is not working. Two hours of detours with huge loaded lorries, buses, rickshaws, tongas, motorbikes, aid Jeeps, and masses of people walking, all slithering and sinking into the clay-like mud. It was a traffic jam to end them all.

UNCHR meeting was very satisfactory with the PR director and the overall director. They will support my plan financially, and have advised me how to get further help in London. I can't believe this luck—the chain of circumstances working yet again. When told of Habiba's baby, the director immediately offered the services of her paediatrician sister at Lady Reading Hospital *and* the supply of medicines.

Met Finola at Afghanaid, and then for tea at her house where an Australian chap spoke with great cynicism of the Afghan mujahideen and civilians. I cannot agree and think he is off base, also about the CIA causing disruptions and creating confusion. But why? For what purpose? I don't understand.

Money mix-up as the payment I made has arrived in Karachi, and now the Peshawar branch must locate it. Mr Usmani will help, but at least it's here. Rumour says that the banks hang onto money for as long as possible, as they earn foreign exchange from dollars or pounds. The degree of corruption is almost total, even Pakistanis say it is their way of life.

Monday, 16 March 1987

Life in Gustave and Gabi's house is interesting. An Afghan couple do all the housework, the cleaning, and cooking. The husband is the one who looks after the children, ages four and two. He always speaks quietly and, physically, is on their level, squatting or sitting cross-legged and speaking softly in Farsi, which the children also speak, plus German and English.

Collected at 9 a.m. by a driver, Sardar, and went via another route to the camp. We drove into the rural part of the country where his sister has a huge farm. It was to see about renting a house for Gabi's team. It could have been a gorgeous house, but it's a third-world attempt: smelly loos; dark and musty cavernous rooms; no real taste, quality, or knowledge of building or architecture. Several plump Pakistani lady neighbours sitting around, eating and drinking very sweet milky tea. They do this every day.

The countryside was lovely, and the rural scenes tempting to photograph, but no time. Went to the camps, then back to team house. At 6 p.m. went to the guest house and was invited for dinner by Erika, the Swiss wife of the agricultural programme director. Dinner was lovely with *salad!*

Tuesday, 17 March 1987

Off at 8 a.m. to Baghicha camp. Sardar took me to the six schools to distribute supplies. It was gratifying. I collected drawings from four schools—a beginning with much enthusiasm. I notice latrines, water supply lorries, lots of bored children, but many in schools. The girls' school will not allow pix. The girls scratch the alphabet on boards like cricket bats using old-fashioned nib pens and bottles of ink or tiny slates and stencils. They embroider beautifully at young ages.

Then to the guest house for mediocre dinner. Again, light fuse blew, cold shower, early to bed.

Wednesday, 18 March 1987

Collected at 8 a.m. as per plan. Driven to Jalala to distribute materials, but one school was closed and the others were having exams, so I just left the materials. I can return to collect the drawings after 13 April. Only one headmaster has given a negative response. He was greedy and wanted coloured pencil packages for all his 150 pupils. We talked him down. Now there are four schools in Jalala and six in Baghicha.

When finished there, it was time for lady home visits. I saw how the women live and how the lady health visitors are trying to change nutrition, health, and environmental ways. I couldn't take photographs of the ladies, as the men would not allow it. But they were so colourfully dressed and bejewelled that it cried for a photograph! The light was beautiful, and they were naturally graceful and assumed positions—almost poses—without guidance. When men or boys appeared, they were chased away as the talk was of female problems. Also, of the hold the mullah has over their men.

At home with Gabi and Gustave all is *not* well. They have received a letter from the Vienna ARC saying they must vacate by the end of May instead of August. It puts them in an awkward position regarding leaving, new jobs, and schools for the children.

Thursday, 19 March 1987

Rain in a steady, grey downpour since midnight. ARC car took me to Habiba's where I decided Farishta was too sick to risk the damp weather. Then to the bank.

Still they denied receipt of the remittance. I demanded they call Karachi. Things got hot as I was in possession of a telex which clearly showed the first error was Karachi's fault and the second was Peshawar's, who failed to check with their four measly branches.

When the remittance was discovered in the Old City branch and I had to go there, my problems really began. Forms and papers and more forms and signatures checked and rechecked. It took nearly two hours. Of course, I lost a lot on the transaction; my letter, many rides in rickshaws to the bank, and in the exchange rate from dollars to rupees at the lower bank rate. It's been a pain. Oh, well.

I hired a taxi and went to Habiba's to take her and Farishta to Lady Reading Hospital. After examinations and no hope, we went to the house of a friend of Mr Usmani's whose brother is a top consultant. They phoned the doctor, who came straight to the house. Again, no hope. Poor child will probably become a vegetable—and then die young. Too, too sad. The conditions in which Habiba lives are appalling. I wonder how many VIPs really experience what living the life of a refugee is like. Another power cut, twice tonight.

Friday, 20 March 1987

Mahzala came today, and she talked for hours. She is really so naïve I fear for her. Her Muslim upbringing and indoctrination will land her in trouble if she is unable to accept a Western culture on emigrating. She is due for big shocks.

The new director of ARC, a nice Scotsman, arrived.

Babysat for four children. They are very misbehaved. I think they are overindulged, not really allowed to cry, but are pacified or mollified so that, if as unfortunately often happens here, they die at an early age, they will not think ill of their parents when they are in heaven. There seems to be no real rebellion against "authority" leading to independent thinking, which is a contradiction in terms because this nation has a history of being unconquered and independent.

Saturday, 21 March 1987

So difficult to arrange things: either there is no telephone, or the lines are out of order. Went to Habiba's in the pouring rain. Farishta very sick, throwing up. I suspect too much medicine and congestion in her chest. It really looks so hopeless in spite of my financial contributions. Aziz is working, but it's a token job at the clinic, and if Habiba goes, so will his job.

I suppose I should be happy, but the other news is that Habiba is pregnant. How will she cope? I am more than a little cross, as she should have been able to prevent it. What if the new baby suffers the same dire fate as Farishta? Habiba will have to stop work if she can't find a woman to look after her, and she will have to stop in six months anyway for the new baby!

Here, then, is the *real* trouble. I sat in that tiny, cold, damp, dark room with one small glassless window and one small door amidst millions of flies swarming over everything, one kerosene cooker, a couple of pots, and food stashed under a charpoy. Under another on which the baby lies are perhaps twenty bottles of medicine, and she is immobile under a black *chador*[61], which at least protects her from the worst of the flies. In one corner, rolled up, are four cotton quilts used at night for bedding. In another corner, a sack of rice. Relatives living nearby are somewhat better off, but do nothing to help.

Sadly, as in all cultures, some people are selfish and greedy, envying the foreigners but not doing any—even menial—work. Instead, they beg. Others are well to do and arrogant, flaunting their education and money spent on bangles and expensive wedding celebrations. Almost none would forfeit the pomp and ceremony of a wedding if it meant helping refugees or anyone less well off.

I hear often that Afghan mujahideen are also disunited and not helping each other. Tribal differences flourish, and each commander is jealous of the others. The Russian spy network plays on this, and none can match their cleverness with propaganda. One faction controls the Pakistan-Afghan border and often keeps supplies from getting through because another leader may gain a successful mission. The Russians also take advantage of this and add subtly to the confusion. The situation is exacerbated by the mutual hatred between Pakistan and Afghanistan.

Sunday, 22 March 1987

Habiba came in the pouring rain. We went to Mr Usmani, who claims he can find a caretaker for Farishta. Then to the bank to open an account for Habiba. I deposited 4,000 rupees for twenty widows' stories at 200 rupees each, 1,000 rupees for April, and 2,000 rupees to cover the amount required in the account. 7,000 rupees = $390, and 100 rupees per month is about $55. If this will help produce the book, it's a good investment all round. And it isn't charity, so Habiba's dignity is spared. Then we shopped at Saddar Bazaar and had lunch at Greens Hotel, a financial shock for Habiba: the bill was $2.20.

---

[61] . The loose, full-length and all-enveloping outer garment worn by Muslim women in public. It is draped over the head and held closely in front under the chin with only the face showing.

Back to UNHCR where the director has got the grant and an appointment for me with the Commission of Afghan Refugees, a real coup. Also, I can get flip health charts free from the health director. Next days are packed!

Monday, 23 March 1987

Early start at 8:30 a.m. *Everything closed* for Pakistan Day. I phoned Mr Usmani about the babysitter, but he was out. Went to Habiba's. Aziz accompanied us to Nasir Bagh Camp by bus and Jeep and I damned the hated chador.

Last month, 1,500 families arrived. Unloaded onto a barren, flat, rock-studded plateau on the farthest edge of Nasir Bagh, they fill the seven camps. Registration is linked to a political party before rations are issued. Refugees are forced into a political decision in order to survive. To get rations they *must* join a party! And they must pay mullahs to register them.

Afghans are not allowed administrative positions, thus allowing unscrupulous Pakistanis ample scope for siphoning off supplies. A refugee, who wishes to remain anonymous, told me that the Pakistani government man comes and checks up twice a year and threatens, "If you don't pay me between 500 to 1,000 rupees, I will cancel your rations." With no administrative experience and worse still, no training programmes, Afghan administrators will be scarce upon their return when they will be sorely needed.

The International Rescue Commission is the only pure aid organization, others give with strings. Wells and latrines are slow to be dug owing to VOLAG's administrative bureaucracy. Must ask if tents, ground cover, and tools for building mud-type houses or more permanent *katchi*[62]-type squatter settlements are available here. My observations of what is needed: mosquito netting and fencing for chickens to prevent faeces mixing with the cooking area. Also, too much time is required to fill in forms and not enough spent on the families themselves.

---

[62] . Usually one-room dwellings made of a combination of mud, thatch, canvas, tin, or timber.

First, we visited a sister-in-law, quite an improvement on Habiba's hovel. The husband is paraplegic and had to remove his prosthesis when he came in to sit down. *Had* to have lunch, but with my tummy, I insisted on boiled eggs. Nice visit in yurt-like house, neat and clean.

Then to see three widows and write their stories. Tape recorder did not work. At the last house, there were so many children following us that we attracted the attention of a security officer. He demanded my permit, which I did not have and, after a brief argument, he warned Habiba and let us go.

One niece, age eleven or twelve, was to go with Habiba to look after Farishta till next Thursday week. After an initial agreement, the mother changed her mind saying what she had known all along: a brother had just returned from fighting with the mujahideen, and she wanted to visit him for a couple of days. Too late then to go to another widow.

Everything involves big and long discussions, repeated many times over when logic could make matters simple. Poor Afghans, for the most part, are not like Habiba and cannot and will not change their basic cultural habits, such as male domination and the inability to speak of the shared problems of women. It really is too much to overturn this nation. Whatever will happen on their return? There is no foundation on which to build.

Habiba is caught between understanding me and hating male domination, but feels helpless to rise up and shout in her own voice. Maybe some history books of other exceptional Afghan women will help. In so many cases, education stops with menstruation.

Tuesday, 24 March 1987

What a day! Again, things always seem to happen. I forgot to write about the dinner last night with Bruce, Finola, Jonathan, Gabi, Gustave, and me. Went to a new restaurant, Spogmai, in the old city, but it was a meatless day so we had scrawny but tasty chicken, just not enough, but it was fun.

Wednesday, 25 March 1987

Drove in the ARC car to the Commission for Afghan Refugees. Lucky, as it was pouring with rain. Got the permit to go to Nasir Bagh. A public information man, Mr Wahidi, accompanied me. He hired a taxi, and we went to Gabi's house to collect my chador. By that time, we had discovered that Mr Wahidi lives near the taxi driver, Nasim, and they knew each other. First coincidence. Immediately, the fare went down.

At the house, great confusion. There were three nannies, or *ayahs*, and lots of children. One woman had been brought for Farishta. Of course, she wanted too much, but I took her to Gabi's office for a chat. We decided to send a note to Habiba to see if she'd like to hire the woman on a trial basis. Answer: to come on Monday at 3 p.m.

We began, therefore, rather late for Nasir Bagh, had difficulty navigating the floods, and had to check in first with the security officer. One look at each other, and we both recognized our having met before when he had told me off for not having a permit, and here I was with the number-two man. Well, by the time the official greetings were over and we drove to the school, it was closed because of the rainy day.

So, we had to return, but our way was blocked by the river flooding. We took a detour, though longer, through back country roads and incredible mud villages. Many houses were being washed away or collapsing even as we drove by. We finally wound up on the top end of a road that I recognized as that of Samandar's house. As we approached, I asked Nasim to stop. He was astounded that I knew Samandar, who was a close friend of his and someone he often worked with taking VIPs about or making TV documentaries. Again, a very small world. We stopped, and Samandar was there, happy to see me. We waited while he and an Afghan engineer, recently returned from America, completed their prayers, and then he and I chatted for ten minutes or so.

Off again, taking Mr Wahidi to his house in the inner, inner part of the Old City. Nothing would do but I *had* to meet his daughter and all the available family. He considers his home a great one. He inherited the site and built the house, which has separate quarters for a brother and family, a daughter and family, and his own bunch. The so-called kitchen is in a cupboard on the upper terrace. Although the toilets are typical Indian ones, at least there are three and one for the servant.

Back to Gabi's to prepare for the henna party this afternoon being given for Mr Usmani's future daughter-in-law. Nasim came back sooner than expected and dropped me off at the Usmani's home early, so there I was watching the incredible preparations for his son's wedding. Brilliant, clashing colours of paper, tinsel, foil, sequins, and braid everywhere, and everything seems garish by our standards. In the pouring rain, the gaudy tent was raised, chairs brought in by the hundreds, and the cooking took place outdoors in huge pots with logs as big as trees for firewood. Smoke carrying the smell of wood and curry curled over the awning, and the air was filled with the raucous, shrill, almost angry sound of the music. It's this way at every wedding. No variation because it is a matter of pride to show up one's neighbours. It is a deep cultural custom.

When all the guests had arrived, we made our way through oozing mud to a rickety old bus. Everyone crowded in, and we were off to the bride's house for the henna party. Never did actually see the bride, who was under a hood, huddled in a heap. Then, back to the groom's house, more sitting around long into the night with the women shoved into three upstairs rooms. Under the tents, loud music with drums and singing were taking place, and dancing girls spun and twirled until the rupees showered down at their feet. Some people were already sleeping, but after much arguing, I insisted on going home to sleep, refusing to stay as other guests would do.

Thursday, 26 March 1987

This has been a hummer of a day, and that it should happen as I prepare to leave is significant to me. Nasim collected me at 8:30 a.m., and off to the office of the commissary to collect Mr Wahidi. He was apologetic, saying that he couldn't come as his boss was away and he was left in charge. Besides, it was a VIP day with Lord Cranborne[63] from the UK at the top of the list. I phoned Afghanaid and asked if there was a

---

[63] . Conservative anti-communist MP who worked to support Afghan refugees and to fund the Afghan resistance.

chance to meet him. Come for tea was the response, and I didn't even feel cheeky for having done it.

Then off to Nasir Bagh. Nasim said he had a pain in his shoulder, would I mind if his brother drove me? We made the switch and started again. My suggestion to go via Warsal Road to avoid possible floods was ignored, so I suspected this "he-speak-very-good-English" brother-driver did not. Past Afghan Refugee Bazaar, crowded to bursting because of the beautiful day at last. The third river was really running high, and although we had four-wheel drive and huge lorries managed to careen across, the driver refused and said he'd go the long way. Much to my surprise, he headed for the Khyber Pass. I had a real thrill, as the Khyber Range got closer, and I knew that just the other side was Afghanistan. It's very strange how I feel so attracted, like a magnet.

At the border, I showed my pass and, after an argument, we were given a security officer to accompany us. Then to Jamrud Fort and its huge gate at the entrance to the Khyber Pass[64], yet another thrill. Last time I saw it, I was coming from the opposite direction with Henry. Another check, only this time a flat refusal to go further. It's all a tribal area and *is* dangerous, and even though we were not going into the pass itself, I was told that special permission from another bureaucrat was necessary, and he was back in Peshawar. So, back the same way to the flooded area, and this time the driver went through. It was scary to see the water cover the bonnet and have it sloshing on the floor, and also to see the near-capsized position of other cars. But all kept moving on, and so, to the camp.

It was a farce. After another argument, I was taken to the school, and as I knocked on the gate, our security officer said, "Business closed. Examinations." Why he didn't say that before the long walk there? Who knows? Anyway, I managed to see a young teacher of 280 refugee girls. But I will have to return with Habiba.

Back to the house to freshen up for tea. The ride was most interesting, and with so much rainfall, everything is now very green and muddy, although soon to be covered again with dust and diesel fumes.

Good news is that Mr Usmani has found a woman for Habiba and arranged for a ration card back-dated to the time of her arrival. The

---

[64] . Historic fortress and massive stone gateway that spans the highway between Peshawar and Kabul.

Pakistani government has stopped all ration cards in existing camps, which forces the incoming refugees to settle in the Punjab, or else no rations.

At Afghanaid, I was taken into the sitting room and met Lord Cranborne. He is a nice-looking, forty-ish man, proper Englishman but very easy manner. Said to call him Robert, and I was Jean. He asked questions which show his interest, which I think is genuine, and he listened to the answers. I was so relaxed, and he really seemed to like what I was doing. He asked if I would be interested in starting an Afghanaid group in Dorset, and I said I'd consider it. He will be an invaluable help and has kindly given me all his phone numbers and times to reach him.

In the final few minutes, there was a phone call for me from Islamabad. Such a crazy coincidence that I just happened to be there when the Joint Voluntary Agency called regarding Mahzala's application to the US. I was able sort things out for her on the phone, obtaining the much-longed-for approval, then resumed tea with "Robert".

Afterwards, I walked as fast as I could to where Mahzala lives to give her the good news. She was overjoyed, and there was much crying. After about an hour, I noticed a tall boy outside the curtained doorway. He called to Mahzala, and when she returned, I could see she was upset, and I guessed why, although it took a lot of forcing to get her to say it. He was one of her brothers and wanted me to leave. Why was she sitting with an infidel? A foreigner and a woman on her own! The neighbours were shocked. This was a Muslim community, and I was not to be allowed there, etc. etc., with much emphasis on Western godlessness.

What can one say? None of them has asked what has driven her to such despair or helped her to pursue what she wanted. I must keep on helping.

The Khyber Pass

En Route

New Arrivals at Baghicha Refugee Camp

Rationing Ghee

Ayun Refugee Camp

At the Clinic

Waiting for the Doctor (Ayun Camp Chitral)

A Temporary Refugee Village near Peshawar

The Struggle for Literacy for Girls

The Water-Carrier

Jean at Habiba's House - Refugee Camp Pakistan

The Human Cost

Why Won't 'They' Listen?

PART 4

Torn Apart

"Their stories must be told to show the world that it is not merely enough to have escaped tyranny and oppression. Promises must be kept. Those who preach compassion must also show it in a practical way. Political expediency must never be allowed to override moral obligations." —J. H. W.

Habiba: "We Are Always Afraid!"

Jean and Habiba first met in one of the refugee camps. An immediate bond was forged, and, as Habiba opened her heart to Jean, their mother-daughter relationship grew to be especially strong. When Habiba needed help looking after her baby, Jean stayed in the family shelter, gaining grim, first-hand experience of camp life. Together, they worked on Habiba's idea for her book, tape-recording Habiba's own story for one of the chapters. She told Jean, "No money for me—I want to put it together on behalf of the women, to give them a voice."

HABIBA SPEAKS OUT

Pakistan, 6 March 1987

Habiba: Here is the microphone for the tape recorder. Now, if we want to speak, we should know if it is good or not good. I want to give you my story this way.

Jean: Yes, let's hope the new batteries work!

Habiba: First, my name is Habiba. I am twenty-five years of age. I come here from Afghanistan when I was nineteen. I come by walk because, in the first night through the mountains, the donkey I ride stumbles, and I fall off injured, so walking with lame five days. It was so difficult for us to come to Pakistan.

Jean: Why did you feel you had to leave?

Habiba: *(vehemently)* Because there was too much reason for leave! There was the Russian come to Afghanistan. They killed people! They put them in the jail! They bombard us! Then we saw the future as very bad for Afghan people in Afghanistan. I am sorry I have too much mistake in the English, but I hope you understand what I say.

Jean: I do. Your English is very good. Tell me, when you left, did you leave some family behind or did all of your family come with you to Pakistan?

Habiba: That time, close family come with me, but rest not coming at that time. Many families cannot leave in the one time together because, if the Russian people know that we want to go to Pakistan, maybe they took us and put us in the jail, and this was very difficult for us. So, then we came family by family, not in the same time, but stopping by stop. Also, because for money, we cannot have enough money to come to Pakistan. I have brothers, young and older, who fight against the Russian people. They are mujahideen with jihad. They do not come. When we came to Pakistan, we lived in the tent in the camp. A very bad place; it was not good. But every other refugee live like this.

Jean: Did you get blankets, food?

Habiba: Yes, we had some money from Afghanistan. When it is spent, about one year ago, we take rations with ration pass. Then it was little better. Now, my father is jobless. One brother in jihad, they give him seven hundred rupees to pay money for salary.

Jean: Who pays him?

*Habi*ba: His mujahid leader pay him.

Jean: Are you working now?

Habiba: When I come from Afghanistan, for one year I was jobless. After one year, I find a nursing job at hospital. Was good job. There was Islamic, very good people. But the salary was too little, the work was too much. I like it, but when I married my husband, Aziz, he didn't let me continue my job because there was too much night duty. He said, "Please stop your job here and start in another place." I start again job here as nurse in this camp. They give me room in staff house and salary.

Jean: Tell me about your work.

Habiba: We have Mother and Child Centre. The mother, pregnant woman, come there and we have them from seven months until delivery. We care for them, we dealing for them. I examine them and I make for them cards after examination.

Jean: Do you help them with how to look after themselves before the baby is born and what to do when the baby is born and after that? Do you explain these things to them?

Habiba: We care for pregnant lady before birth, how they should care for their selves before delivery, then how they should delivery, how they should clean, how they should everything. Then, for under-five-years children, we make also cards for malnutrition in the Nutrition Programme.

Jean: You keep records of everything?

Habiba: Yes. We give them clothes. We give them supplementary foods—dry skim milk, high-protein biscuits, everything.

Jean: And this comes from the aid agency?

Habiba: Yes. From agency. It is a good agency. They help much to Afghan refugee, and also I am happy from that. Since one year five months that I have work with them.

Jean: You feel you are really helping the women in this big camp?

Habiba: Yes. Twice weekly we go to their home for visit. We search pregnant lady. We search malnutrition children. We search TB patient, and also other diseases. And we send to the hospital. We shift them to the hospital, and they come, and we make card for them.

Jean: Who are the doctors in this hospital? What is their nationality?

Habiba: We have two doctors. Both are Afghan.

Jean: And you are Afghan as the nurse!

Habiba: *(laughs)* Yes.

Jean: Are there other nurses there too, or other workers?

Habiba: Yes.

Jean: And are they all Afghan?

Habiba: No, two is Pakistani. One is "vaccinator" and one is malaria supervisor. Another are registrar, pharmacist, laboratory technician, lady health visitor, assistant *da'yi*—she is delivery to the baby.

Jean: Do you mean a midwife?

Habiba: Yes. Now, what can I say? Since four years, I am married, here in Pakistan.

Jean: Who arranged the marriage for you?

Habiba: *(laughs)* My father and mother, not me. I was not agree with this, but my father and mother wanted to marry me. Then, I say okay, if you like, I will not say anything. Now I have one child, a daughter. She is ill; she is sick.

Jean: How old is she?

Habiba: Now she is twenty months. When she was nine months, she have measles. After measles, she have fever—high fever, many times, without reason. The doctors say they do not know about this child. After three months, she had high fever and convulsions and after, she go in the shock and she was unconscious. I was in the hospital with her. After twenty-two days, they discharged her. Now, since six months, she's some better. But she cannot see anything. She cannot walk. She cannot say. She cannot hold up head.

Jean: Can she move her body or do you have to move her?

Habiba: Her all right side is paralysed. I help her all the time. I am *very* sad about her, but ... (*Sighs.*)

Jean: What was the diagnosis?

Habiba: Tubercular meningitis, but I think—I am also nurse, and I think that this diagnosis was not good because I have no family history about TB. I have not TB, Aziz was not TB, how she get TB? I do for her, for her TB vaccination, BCG, which is good for TB.

Jean: The doctor told me that, because of the crowded conditions in the refugee camps, there are many more cases of tuberculosis, which people might not get if they were living in their homes. Perhaps she developed this disease because of that.

Habiba: Maybe. I don't know. But she's not good still.

Jean: The doctors you took her to see, did they charge you money or was this free medical help?

Habiba: No, no, not. I spend my money. I buy every medicine, and I buy everything in that hospital. This was not for refugee; this was Pakistani hospital.

Jean: So you had to pay for all these expenses?

Habiba: Yes, I paid for all things. Aziz worked with me in the camp. He took salary, but it was not enough to buy for eating, for clothes, for

231

everything, also for medicine. This was very difficult for me. Then, I took from money person, and then, every month, I gave again for this man, money. It's very difficult for refugee. But I am better than other people because I have job.

I am from poor family. When I work for Afghan refugees in the camp, I see from near their lives, their situation in the camp, especially widow lady. And they are in very bad situation in the camp.

Jean: Why is their situation worse than other women in the camp? Why is it so very bad?

Habiba: *(bitterly)* Why? Because their husband is died! They have nobody to give them food. This everybody know. Everybody! Then, I wanted to write one book about this people. We have too much newspaper, magazine, and radio cassette and television and everything, and everything about Afghan mujahideen, but we don't have anything about woman who live in the camp without husband, who live without anybody to care of them.

Nobody know about them. They have small children, they have many person in the home, but they don't have men to bring some food or some money for them from outside. This is very difficult for Afghan widow lady.

Jean: Do these women not get money from the government?

Habiba: No, not from government. Just rations—some, not all, rations. It is difficult to make for everybody rations. They give them wheat and tea, milk sometimes, sometimes sugar, oil, not rice. The food they prepare by themselves. When somebody don't have men in the home, it is very difficult for them. I know more widow people who don't have ration until now. It's so difficult for them, life.

For that, I have to write something. I know I have no time because I have ill child, I have sick child in the home. I should care for this child. I should not let her be like this. When I come from hospital, from the camp, I care for my child, and I have no time to write the book.

But I have to write because I want to tell every Afghan woman who live in the camp is in a very bad place. Then I hope I am successful in this writing. This is the first time I want to write book. I don't know it will be good or not good.

Jean: But you want to tell the story of the Afghan women, in particular the widows. Because in the West, nobody really knows what life is like in a refugee camp. Isn't that true?

Habiba: Yes, because those visitors who come here, those newspaper people and politician people and other visitors from the voluntary agencies, they come here and they spend so little time. They are shown those special camps, those camps not as bad, but where they taken by officials.

Jean: Yes, I don't know how many are here for humanitarian reasons as they claim. I do know that the statistics cross and double cross as proof must be given to donor countries to justify their programmes here. Experts sometimes have little real sensitivity or understanding of individuals' problems, and then, there are too many refugees to allow for personal contacts.

Habiba: So really, the people in Western don't know the hard lives the way we do because we are living now six years in the camp.

Jean: Thank you, Habiba, for agreeing to share your story on tape. I sincerely hope you can write your book.

HABIBA UNDER THREAT

"You brought me life again, so, how I'll forget you?"—Habiba

Jean greatly admired Habiba's courage, but she was also often deeply concerned for her safety. Although there were inevitable gaps, Jean kept in close touch with her, perhaps the most vulnerable of her extended Afghan family.

Back home, following a visit to the States, I've been trying to sort out Habiba's material. She's been finding it hard to make time to visit the widows and take down their stories. Not surprisingly as, just a month after daughter number two was born, to our great alarm, the baby started running a high temperature and having convulsions and stiffness—just like her sister. Habiba managed to get her quickly to hospital where, after a few days, the dreaded tubercular meningitis was eliminated as a cause. The diagnosis was a febrile seizure and, to everyone's relief, Zarmina, as she's been named, has made a full recovery. It's also a relief to know that Habiba was able to get the money for the medicines she needed through the arrangement I'd made with people at Afghanaid.

"Wish I was a bird to fly to see you."

August 1988

I haven't been able to reach Habiba for some time, and when I do, I understand, for she has sad news: tragically, but not surprisingly, Farishta, that sweet little bundle, has died. Inconsolable at first, Habiba now seems resigned to her fate. I think it is a blessing, for what future would that poor creature have had, blind and paralysed and living in a refugee camp. The irony is that Habiba is pregnant again. I worry for this family and won't forget them as she has entreated me.

"May God bless you, my dear."

January 1989

Habiba has asked me to help one of her patients, a fighter with the mujahideen, who has lost sight in one eye completely and partially in the other from a firearm injury. The eye specialist has prescribed a certain injection to improve this man's eyesight, but it is unavailable there. Habiba wants me to send the medication, as it is available only in England. I have approached one of the aid agencies based in London to see if anything can be arranged.

"My dear and very 'deariest' mother, Jean! Salaam alaikum!"

June 1989

I knew that Habiba was expecting, but have only now learned that she has been through a very dangerous pregnancy with several stays in hospital. She has been unable to work. Delivery was long and complicated, but thankfully, mother and baby are well. Only, this third child is another girl. This caused such a rift with Aziz that he didn't speak to her for two weeks after the birth! It makes me so angry. But, I have to laugh too, as she told him it was his fault for "putting in her abdomen".

"You always give me the joys of the whole world."

November 1989

Habiba has a new nursing job with another NGO[65], but she is not sure how long she will last. The director seems to be harsh and unpleasant and sounds to me like a "hatchet man", waiting to find something wrong with someone's work so he can give him or her the sack! Whilst Habiba is at work, Aziz stays at home looking after Zarmina and the new baby girl, whom they've named Kashmala.

"Tell your daughters, my sisters, we are very lucky our mother is alive!"

June 1990

I hope I can continue to help as before my accident.[66] Habiba has instructed me to recover like a twenty-year-old girl! Now the shoe is on the other foot, and it is Habiba encouraging *me* to overcome my physical and

---

[65] . Acronym for non-governmental organization: a non-profit, citizen-based group which operates independently of government to address social and political issues.
[66] . Jean was badly injured in a car accident in February 1990. After several months in hospital, she made a good recovery.

emotional difficulties! "Before accident, you mentioned you would send me gifts, but, you see, only I need is your recovery. That will be a massive cheerful time for me. Thanks Almighty God that saved you from such a terrible event. I do not want to lose you!"

Well, that's not going to happen! How could I let her and so many others like her down?

"I really miss your 'advisings', your ideas, and mostly you."

August 1990

Unfortunately, Habiba is finding life in the camp too dangerous, and, after several cases of looting, the family is moving to another camp, even though it will now take Habiba almost an hour to walk to and from work. It is still too risky for them to return to Afghanistan, despite the new repatriation policy negotiated between the UNHCR and President Benazir Bhutto to "encourage" Afghan refugees to go home. It is their "unlucky time" with war raging now between the different factions of the mujahideen.

"We are always afraid."

November 1990

Habiba fears that, because of the Gulf War, the plight of the Afghan refugees will be forgotten. She has seen angry crowds of people demonstrating on the streets in support of Saddam Hussein and against the US.

The level of violence is also increasing in the camps. Afghan women working with aid agencies, like Habiba, are being harassed, threatened, and intimidated; some even kidnapped. Many international organizations are stopping or restricting their work, making jobs even more scarce. Even medical teams are being attacked. It is shocking.

As a result, Habiba is starting to feel compelled to leave Pakistan. "My dear Jean, please, please, pave me a way to leave this country. I am here free, but feel I am in a jail." I must find a way forward for her and her family. They have lived in the camps for ten years! I am in touch now with a most helpful Canadian man, Jim, whom Habiba met through her work. We shall see.

"I have already learned that human beings must be very patient."

January 1991

Habiba has been without a job now for several months. Just as well as she is expecting her third child in the spring. I am trying to respond to her pleas, but so far have not yet found a sponsor for the family that would allow them to go to the States, Canada, or Australia.

They have had to return to their first camp because everything was too expensive elsewhere. At least Aziz has a part-time job, but he's earning only twenty rupees a day.

"Wish I had a home which I could receive guests."

May 1991

Habiba has proudly given birth to the longed-for son, Asadullah. Aziz is overjoyed, and streams of guests are pouring in with congratulations. I am very happy for them, but where were these people when the girls were born! It is Ramadan now, but Habiba is being sensible and not fasting. As always, I have sent a parcel with baby clothes and treats for the whole family.

"My goodness, how happy I am to receive your letter!"

September 1991

At last, Habiba has been able to find a new job—and a good one actually—at another hospital. No night duty! When she went for the interview, she thought the director resembled me and started crying. I had sent her a photo of myself as she had asked, and she confessed to me that she looks at it several times during the day, talking to the picture as if I were sitting in front of her, and laughing and crying.

She says when she goes outside and sees someone my age on the street, she suddenly remembers me. She even talks to me in her dreams. Her prayer for freedom in Afghanistan includes her being able to invite me to her home and write my name again on her doorway as when we first met. I am quite overcome by the depth of her affection.

"If I had thought it would be like this, I would rather have died."

I can hardly believe what I've just heard from Habiba, as it is so distressing—especially as I think it's partly my fault for encouraging her to write her book! Despite moving camps, she continued to receive warnings from the fundamentalists, commanding her to stop working. As before, she continued to ignore them and been quite outspoken, especially about the equality of women. Unfortunately, she did so in the presence of some international reporters.

Although they promised her anonymity, her name was in the news. The next thing she knew, a demonstration was staged outside her house, and then a death threat was actually thrust into her hands. Her poor older brother was attacked and badly beaten. Most shocking and terrifying of all, an Afghan colleague at one of the clinics was stabbed to death on her way to work. If only I can help Habiba's application for asylum to move forward. It is time to go, and none too soon!

"My all family send you best wishes and Salaam from Canada!"

March 1992

What wonderful news! At last. They've made it! Together with some church people, Jim and I were finally able to arrange for the family to be granted political asylum in Canada.

Habiba is so relieved to have escaped and so happy to be safe. But she has asked me still not to say anything about her or her family because of repercussions to her parents and other relatives who have had to stay behind.

At least, "our" Jim is also out of danger now. He had been receiving threats for having met with Habiba at his house, which is close to the headquarters of one of the factions of the mujahideen. If they were ever to meet again, he and even his chokidars were to be killed. It is truly chilling. What Habiba has seen has badly traumatized her—how women's lives are simply disregarded, how people are being killed like flies. She kept bursting into tears down the phone.

"We begin to start over our life."

May 1992

Making a new life for this family in a foreign country is a huge challenge, especially as only Habiba can speak English. Aziz will start English-language classes soon, but she is worried that he may not study hard enough to be able to get a job. They have had to borrow quite a lot of money from friends and relatives to be able to leave Pakistan. Habiba hopes to repay them as quickly as possible by working hard.

I am sending them another cheque with some gifts, but whilst she is always grateful and thanking me, she remonstrates that I must take care of myself and have money for the future. She tells me that she and her children are still young and will manage somehow, whereas I am "sick and old"! I have to smile, especially as she wants so badly to do something for me.

"My children and I send you warm hello and special hug."

July 1992

Habiba has given birth again! And, again to Aziz's great disappointment, it is another girl. They have named her Rokhana, which means "light" in Pashto. I have sent warmest congratulations and some gifts. Happily, two cousins who were fighting with the mujahideen have just been given refugee status and will be living nearby. Now she doesn't feel so alone.

"Show me a good way to succeed."

September 1992

Habiba and the family are more settled now. She is very proud of Zarmina, who has started nursery school. Kashmala goes to daycare, and she is looking after Asadullah and the baby. But she misses her parents and hopes the younger members of her family are looking after them.

She has decided to sit for the registered nurse exam. She will first have to take the English-language exam and then a refresher nursing course for nine months. On completion, she must work in a hospital until completely qualified to get a job. The whole process will take two years. Even with studying and looking after the children and the home, she is determined to succeed.

I haven't told her, but I think it will take longer because, with Aziz still not working, she has had to get a small, part-time job just to keep the family going. I wish I could do more.

"Confidentialness!"

November 1992

What a shock! There has been terrible news about Habiba's family in Pakistan: a close relative has been kidnapped! I had briefly met the members of this family when visiting their camp. Habiba has implored me to do something as soon as possible, and she herself is on her way to Peshawar. She must have borrowed the money for the ticket. She first tried all the different government and international agencies, even the church, but the answer was always, "We're sorry, but …"

Before leaving, she sent me all the pertinent documents, including a letter of warning to be translated, but not by an Afghan she admonished me, so as to safeguard the family. She does not know who or if any of the many factions might be responsible. I wonder if the kidnapping is in retaliation for her outspoken political views from when she was working in the camps.

"I waste of your nice time and make you headache."

January 1993

Now I know the whole story. Habiba's relative was held for many weeks. She and other members of her family frantically searched everywhere, again receiving little or no help from the authorities. Habiba thinks the motive behind the kidnapping was simply to extract money. And strangely, she's not surprised and explains that, after having lost everything back home, some refugees, with no money, no job, no prospects, are driven to extreme acts: "This is only way for them, only for money."

Eventually, the relative was released and the family reunited. Such a relief, especially as the victim was unharmed! It is a wake-up call to me to work harder to find a sponsor for these people so that they can join Habiba in Canada. She cannot sponsor them herself because of receiving welfare.

She is becoming more desperate and depressed and frets about not getting a job in her field. I try to persuade her not to be so hard on herself, but she feels so ashamed of sitting at home and "eating from government". The weather is cold and miserable, although she says that the children enjoy playing in the snow.

"Please, please, be quiet about our case."

July 1993

Nothing has happened to move forward the asylum petition for Habiba's family in Pakistan. I am still waiting to hear from the Canadian High Commission in response to the confidential letter I immediately wrote in support of their application. I certainly could vouch for their honesty, sincerity, and for their being upstanding citizens!

Thatched Cottage
Buckland Newton

To the Consular Officer of the Canadian High Commission
Islamabad, Pakistan

21 July 1993

This request for asylum is based on the fear that, due to a journalist's indiscretion, this family may be murdered if they remain in the refugee camp in Peshawar. The family home in Afghanistan has been burned down, and conditions there are such that they cannot return. They have already moved house several times trying to avoid persecution, but it is becoming increasingly difficult to avoid detection. The men are afraid to go out to work, as they are constantly followed, and the women, although veiled, are at great risk when in public. I am sure that one of the enclosed warning letters with its translation will be strong supporting evidence, but it must not, under any circumstances, fall into the wrong hands.

I beg you to treat this matter with the utmost confidence and urge you to give this request your most serious and immediate attention.

Sincerely yours,
Jean Heringman

"You give me courage for whole aspects of my life."

August 1993

Excellent news about Habiba's family! Again, Jim and the church group came to the rescue and are in a position to bring them out. It has greatly lifted Habiba's spirits, even though it will take a long time for the authorities to process the application.

For now, Habiba is studying as best she can, as the next English assessment is very difficult, and she must pass it in order to take the refresher course. It's so hard with no less than four small children underfoot!

"I am struggling with our life every day."

October 1993

Oh, I feel so sorry for Habiba! She didn't pass her exam and now must wait another year if she wants to try again. She is so upset and disappointed, especially as welfare has been drastically cut by 30 per cent! I've made several suggestions, such as looking for a job as a medical receptionist or in some other related field. I will try to help her buy a typewriter as to acquire that skill could be useful for her. Professional courses are expensive, but I will see if there is one that would suit.

Aziz is still not working. Habiba rarely complains; she only sometimes sighs and says, "I don't know how and why our world turned upside down." It's hard to tread the fine line between helping her and maintaining her dignity.

"I dreamed we were together again in Peshawar."

February 1994

Habiba has, at last, found a part-time job as an aide in an old people's home, and even Aziz is working, although it is a seasonal job. But, to my astonishment, she wants to go back to Pakistan and start work there!

She wonders if she and I could start a small organization that will benefit both her and the refugees. Having worked in Pakistan for such a long time as a social worker and nurse, she is, of course, used to working with refugee people and understands their problems better than most.

Perhaps she would be happier there. I will try to think about what kind of work or which organization would be helpful to her and her plan.

"You were a dream, and I'll not see this dream again."

August 1994

My heart has skipped a beat on hearing of Habiba's accident. Of all things, she was knocked over by a cyclist! Her leg has been badly damaged, so she cannot go to work, but she is managing the pain and coping at home. Aziz is again without a job. Everything—all their hopes and dreams—seem to have been destroyed, and they are very homesick now.

Yet, she always asks cheerfully after me and my own family, wishing me good health and happy times and thanking me, always thanking me. It is all I can do to keep her spirits up.

"Still I don't know who I am! Where I have come! What my future is!

October 1994

Habiba, for the first time, speaks openly of how their life is getting worse and worse. She cries out that she doesn't want to feel like a "disabled person"— to be a refugee victim any longer. She wants to be "something"! She asks me to show her the way to do something where she can use her knowledge and experience with her long-suffering people, especially the poor women and children in Afghanistan and Pakistan. She fears that her feelings are being "killed" and she will forget everything that she has seen or is hearing right now.

She really is at the end of her tether. Still without a job and very little money, she is so very disillusioned and frustrated because no one knows what she is capable of, and she has so much to offer. She feels that time is passing her by. If I can manage the journey, I will try and visit her in the spring.

"My heart, Jean! I am very, very thirsty of your visit."

January 1995

It's been a few days now, but I am still in a state of utter disbelief. It can't be true! It's just too, too awful, too ghastly. The visit will never take place now. Not ever. Habiba is dead! I can barely write the word. As yet, I do not know why or how. How in Canada, where she was safe? She is just … no longer.

As depressed as she was, I am absolutely certain she would not have taken her own life. As far as I know, neither was she ill. But surely, it couldn't be foul play. Was it to do with her beliefs? With returning to Pakistan and doing something in the refugee camps? But who would do such a thing? What in the world happened? This poor woman and her poor, poor children.

Disconsolate, heartbroken, I cannot begin to describe the infinite sadness I feel. The numbness. What could I have done differently? Such a promising young life, overcoming so many obstacles, so intelligent and compassionate a woman, to be cut down like this. The cruelty of it. The bitter irony.

How I shall miss her, this lovely and loving young woman who always signed herself, "Your daughter, Habiba."

Seeta: A Widow's Struggle

This is Habiba's first tape recording, translated into English, for the book she hoped to write with Jean, to be entitled Time to Wake Up. *They met Seeta, a young widow with six children, in one of the refugee camps in March 1987. By publicizing testimonies like Seeta's, Habiba and Jean believed they could raise awareness and possibly alleviate the particularly harsh conditions suffered by widows in the refugee camps. Jean wrote, "Without the protection and social acceptance provided by their husbands, these women could be compelled to marry a brother-in-law, often as a second wife, or they were left to endure an impoverished, isolated life of mere survival."*

Six years ago, I moved to Pakistan with my family from our home in Afghanistan. I have six children—two daughters and four sons.

In Afghanistan, I had a very simple but happy life. My husband was a farmer growing different crops. Unfortunately, we could not continue living in Afghanistan because, every minute, our lives were in danger. We had to hide from the bombings, and we were afraid of the cruelty of the Russians and the Afghan Communists too. So, we had to leave our dear and beautiful country and start life in a strange land.

It was an autumn night when we started our sad journey. How hard it was to leave our beloved country. We walked for five days and six nights, and during our tiring journey we had to confront so many problems. On the one-hand side, we were so scared of the Communists and the aeroplanes we saw circling overhead, and on the other-hand side, we feared that the children would become ill from a lack of food and not enough warm clothing. I worried so very much about the children. We were all hungry, cold, and feeling very weak.

Finally, after travelling for these five days with many more problems, we arrived in Peshawar. I couldn't believe how many other Afghan refugees were already there, so we decided to go into Kacha Gari Camp. We were so tired because we had so little sleep, and we were all shivering with cold from being in the night air of the mountains.

For the first two months, we were not allowed to register as refugees and so did not receive any ration cards for food and shelter. These were very hard days for our family, as we were forced to depend on other refugees to share what little they had. It was because of this that we decided to leave and go to another camp further away from Peshawar where we heard the situation regarding of ration cards was better. The name of this camp is Baghicha, which is near to Mardan but further from the Afghanistan border. After two months, we were officially registered as refugees and given ration cards.

During this long period of waiting, my husband became very ill. I could not afford to take him to a doctor for treatment. At last, I had to take him to a hospital where he was finally admitted. I had to pay for all his expenses, including medicines and the fare money for me to visit him. I had to borrow the money, which I still owe to the people. The doctors told me he needs an operation for which he must have blood. I very much wanted to give him my own blood, but I could not because the doctors said our blood groups did not match.

The doctors called his brothers to ask if they could provide the blood, but, without even testing the blood groups, these brothers said, if my husband might die, he might as well do so without their blood. They didn't want to weaken themselves, and besides, it was probably God's will. The doctors operated on him even knowing that there was a lack of blood, and he died a few hours afterwards.

I was at home that day, and I wanted to go to the hospital to see him, but I had no money to pay for the fare to get there. It was getting towards nine o'clock in the morning when a car stopped near the front of our door and I had a sudden worried feeling that something dreadful had happened. "Oh, God," I whispered to myself, "I hope everything is all right. What can have happened?" The next thing I saw was a coffin being carried inside, and I just can't remember what happened next. The children were crying a lot and asking me to wake their father. They asked, "Why he doesn't talk to us? Is he sleeping? Why he is so quiet?" And as the day wore on, they became hungry, and their father just lay there instead of providing them with food as he usually did. They became frightened, and their cries grew louder.

The day passed, and my brother-in-law borrowed the money for my husband's burial. That night was the first night of Eid,[67] but there was nothing in our house for the celebration, not even a small amount of flour to bake bread for the children. By evening, the children were terribly hungry, and the neighbours, hearing their sad cries, brought some dry bread for them to eat.

The night passed. Morning came and still I was facing the same problems: crying, hungry children, but the most terrible and saddest thing was that my husband was dead. I thought, "How will I manage?" Again, I went to a neighbour and asked if they could let me have a small amount of flour, which I would return from the next month's rations. But they said they had run out of flour themselves. Then I went to the baker's and asked him for flour. He said, "Go away. Your husband, who borrowed from most people, has died, and you must pay those people back before you ask for more." Then I went to the commander of the area to tell him that I have no wheat. I told him all that had happened and asked if he could give me some of my next ration's wheat, as my children were becoming ill, and I feared that they might die of hunger. After many persuasions, he gave me a sack of wheat, which really saved our lives for a few days.

Approximately two months after my husband's death, my son became very ill, and once again I found myself helpless. First, I took him to our camp's doctors, but I was not satisfied, as my son was becoming worse. Then, on Friday, I took him to the doctors at Shahaq Camp. One doctor examined him. I cried in there, in front of him, and begged him for God's sake, "Please do something for my child! What can I do? I have no money, no property to pay your fees and buy the medications." The doctor was a very kind gentleman. He gave me some bottles of syrup without having to pay for them.

---

[67] . The religious holiday celebrated by Muslims that marks the end of Ramadan, the Islamic holy month of fasting.

I come back home, and during the night my son was very uncomfortable. After midnight, I suddenly realized that he was dying. I woke up and, as I held him in my arms, he died. I felt like it was an earthquake and both walls were coming towards me to squeeze me. A black patch was spreading in front of my eyes, and I screamed. Most of the neighbours heard me and came to help me. They were all telling me, "Never mind. Be patient with God." In the morning, all people came and took my son to be buried. I've lived all sorts of problems like hunger, cruelty, cold and hot weather, but nothing like this. However, I am patient with God, send hope that He will help us in the next world.

Many of years dragged on. Then one night, very late, suddenly, there was a big flood in the whole camp. It had been a horrible evening with a lot of "lightenings" and cold winds from the storm. Everybody was sound asleep when, suddenly, with the noise of the hail and heavy rain, I woke up. When I got out of bed, all I could see was water, which was up to my knees. I was so scared!

As I went to wake my children up, I found that the walls of my other room were completely destroyed. Therefore, I needed to hurry up because I thought this room too might be soon washed away. I tried to be as calm as I could in order to reassure my children, and I called to my neighbours to help us, but they could not. My brother, who was living at the same area, came and took three of my children, and I took the other three children. We fought a lot of difficult, windy weather, icy cold rain and hail, but we managed to take the children up to the front of the camp.

When my brother finished helping me and my children, he then ran to help our mother and sister. He found that the room where they were sleeping had collapsed, and they both were dead underneath the mud and flood. He screamed for help to catch the bodies, which were floating in the water. Nobody came to help us because everybody was busy with their own problems. Therefore, my brother had to bring mother's body first and then sister's body.

When the darkness finished and the morning light came, everybody was looking for dead bodies. The flood and rains were over, but they left us filled with sorrows and grief and also left everything ruined and destroyed. Many people had been killed, and some people couldn't even find their relatives' bodies, and others would find bodies from underneath the mud left by the floods. People were searching every ditch and rubble to find the bodies.

It was an awful night, and I think God was angry with all us Muslim refugees. From one side, the cruelty of the Russians and Communists, and from the other side, hunger, thirst, hot and cold weather are our enemies. Some people have been killed, their houses bombarded, their children martyrs. Others, some died on the way coming out of Afghanistan, the rest died of no food, no water, and dehydration in the deserts of Pakistan. I don't know what sin we had made that God is not forgiving us for it. We pray and ask for forgiveness, but still he's not kind to us.

In the morning of that day, many Pakistanis and Afghans came to help us. They all came from the other parts of the country. They helped people with burying their relatives and also they accommodated everyone in some schools which belong to Pakistan. We all stayed in these ruined schools until we found somewhere to start living again. They also buried mother and sister.

My brother, who had injury in his leg, was taken to a hospital where he stayed for a few days. At the moment, I am living in the house which was ruined, and now I am building it again. I am spending my life on people's charity and their leftover foods, which they bring to me.

Ghulam: "We are Being Deported!"

Jean knew only too well that for Afghan refugees, worse even than living in limbo for years on end, was living in fear of being forcibly returned to their ravaged and war-torn country. What happened to Ghulam typifies this nightmare scenario. Jean's task was to protect this family in any way she could.

Thatched Cottage,
Buckland Newton

[Address of recipient undisclosed][68]

26 April 1993

Dear Sir,

As you are the attorney for Dr Ghulam and his family, I'm faxing this information to you as quickly as possible in the hope that it may help to reverse the Canadian court's decision to deport them back to Kabul. Briefly, my connection with Afghanistan is as a result of having lived and worked there from 1968 to 1978. In the aftermath of the war, I became committed to helping Afghan friends and their families in any way I could. I have sponsored numerous refugees to the US, Germany, and Canada, and I have worked in the refugee camps in Pakistan, particularly with widows and orphans, independently of any international organisations.

---

[68] . To protect identities and privacy.

I have known Dr Ghulam and his wife, Shazia, since 1987. I first met them in an Afghan refugee camp in Pakistan where they were working as doctors for one of the NGO aid programmes. They were providing medical care for over 100,000 refugees. Their total dedication and untiring efforts on behalf of the refugees were clear to see. However, should they be deported, their excellent reputation will be of no use to them with those now in power in Kabul. This is because Dr Ghulam belongs to one of Afghanistan's minority ethnic groups that all still suffer ruthless and relentless persecution.

Shazia herself is a target simply for being an educated, working, and professional woman. In the refugee camp, she was continually followed and harassed on her way to the clinic by members of the fundamentalist parties, especially the Hezb-e-Islami party of Gulbuddin Hekmatyar, the present prime minister, known as "'The Butcher of Kabul'". His views on the role of women are extreme even by the standards of the fundamentalists. Dr. Ghulam's and Shazia's association with me—a woman and a foreigner from the West—has only made things worse and increased the danger to them.

Furthermore, whilst they were working in the refugee camp, one of their relatives in Kabul was caught trying to escape to Pakistan. He was arrested, and at first, no one knew if he was in jail or even alive. It has since transpired that he is in the custody of the KHAD, the infamous secret police, and is awaiting trial. This has brought the family under even more suspicion.

It is for all these reasons that, if forced to return to their homeland, they will, undoubtedly, face certain death.

In Afghanistan itself, the civil war rages on between the Soviet-installed government and fourteen factions of the mujahideen who are now fighting each other despite numerous efforts of reconciliation. The situation in Kabul is chaotic, and the provinces are ruled by local warlords. The Islamabad Accord[69] is the latest peace effort, but is liable to collapse as the mujahideen are divided on ethnic and sectarian lines. The ethnic minorities, such as that of Dr Ghulam and his family, do not automatically

---

[69] . Truce and power-sharing agreement brokered by Pakistan between the Afghan government and the various parties of the mujahideen. Signed in March 1993, it lasted only a few days.

enjoy the protection of or alliance with any of the major factions and are caught dangerously in the middle.

The fighting has been particularly bloody in Kabul which has been constantly bombarded over the last three months. Huge areas of the city have been devastated and thousands of residents displaced, killed, or maimed. The part of Kabul where this family had their home has been bombed, and family members living there have not been heard from since.

I am not exaggerating when I tell you that this splendid family, having done so much for their own people at their own personal sacrifice, are in terror of their lives if they are returned to Kabul or anywhere else in Afghanistan. For these reasons, I therefore feel it would be disastrous and inhumane and even fatal to send this family back to Kabul where the situation is so unstable and terrifyingly dangerous.

Yours sincerely,
Mrs. Jean Heringman Willacy

June 1988

I immediately liked Ghulam and Shazia from the first time we met a year ago in Pakistan. We shared a Jeep on the way to one of the refugee camps where I was going to enquire about the children's drawing project. Ghulam was taking up his post at a medical clinic there. They too have quite a story: I think theirs is a love match.

Shazia's mother was widowed with nine children, the youngest six months old. She had to sew to earn money to feed her family. They all lived in one rented room and were always very poor. Yet, all her children have completed university and are doctors, engineers, or teachers.

Ghulam escaped to Pakistan to join the Afghan army after two years of being hounded by the KHAD, the Afghan secret police. He wrote surreptitiously from his refugee camp to propose to Shazia via a brother in Kabul. Shazia says she always loved him, so agreed to the marriage. She had to wait in Kabul until a guide was found, and then one night, clad in a chador and taking nothing with her, she left with some other people known to her family.

They travelled by bus to a town not far from the border, and then another wait until the bombarding lessened. Then on foot to where Ghulam was to meet her. But he had not been able to get time off, and no letter reached her at that place to tell her that he wouldn't be coming! After more waiting, she and the others began the walk to Peshawar, hiding by day and moving by night.

The couple had a *very* happy meeting and then a simple wedding, minus all the traditions, and no honeymoon. Ghulam continued to work, and Shazia began teaching health education classes and doing medical work. As I recall, they never grumbled or complained, but life must have been like a prison for them, living in one dark room and working so hard with the refugees all the time. Money saved was sent to the family in Kabul. Still, they considered themselves lucky to be together, so made the best of things.

Nonetheless, shortly after we met, I discovered that they were at a critical junction in their lives. The threats, intimidation and constant fear of attack were making their situation increasingly desperate, especially with two very young, vulnerable children, one just a baby. News from Afghanistan continued to worsen with everyone compelled to praise the Russian troops and their Afghan allies. During what became a momentous visit, they confided to me that they had decided to seek political asylum, and could I help.

I immediately contacted the US, Australian, and Canadian embassies. The answer was for them to make an application in Islamabad, but the irony was that to travel there was very difficult. Furthermore, Ghulam was worried that, with so many Afghans applying to leave, the backlog would be such that it would be a long time before their own application could be considered. I wrote to several health foundations where they might be able to find work, even, much to their amazement (and mine!), to His Highness the Aga Khan.

Ghulam was already aware of the very strict and complicated process for entry to the US, but also knew, as did so many other refugees, that Australia and Canada were, at the time, granting asylum from Pakistan far more easily. He had been told that sponsorship by an individual or a welfare organization was all that was needed. Perhaps I could find a church or a friend? He didn't have to ask for my help on a "humanitarian basis", as he deemed it because, of course, I was prepared to make all possible efforts to find them a sponsor when I returned to the UK. When the time came for me to leave, Shazia wistfully remarked, as we were saying our goodbyes, "I nearly forget how lovely are such visits and chatting with friends and relatives."

November 1988

Back home, I managed to stay in touch with Ghulam and Shazia whilst we waited anxiously to hear from the various friends, agencies, and consulates that others and I had contacted on their behalf. What next I learned of their fate was far more than we had dared hope for: they had emigrated to Canada! They were safe! Hearing Ghulam's voice on the telephone felt like a small miracle. Thank goodness I'd left them a reasonable sum of money, as the Pakistani government doesn't allow refugees to take more than $10 per person. I'm not clear as yet how it all happened, but it doesn't matter if they can start a new and better life, free from persecution and fear.

February 1989

Ghulam and Shazia can't stop telling me how well they have been treated and looked after during these past few months. They have been accommodated in a furnished rental house and given a monthly allowance for their expenses: $250 for food, $560 for the rent and telephone, and vouchers for purchasing clothing. The vouchers will be extremely helpful, as the children will need snowsuits! Even so, prices are very high, and Ghulam and Shazia are budgeting carefully, especially so as to provide the children with "high-calorie food".

They have been given one year in which to find jobs and are required to attend English-language classes. The government allowance will stop should they find employment sooner. Shazia is first to go to the language school, as with such high demand from so many different refugee groups, there aren't enough places for both of them. Ghulam's English is somewhat better, so he stays at home and looks after the children. He wryly joked with me, "Really, I didn't think looking after a baby is so difficult!" He studies his medical books and is also looking assiduously for work, hoping to practise his own profession at some time in the near future.

Even with the beginning of the longed-for withdrawal of the Soviet troops, he is still wary about what will now happen in their beloved, beleaguered homeland.

July 1989

Ghulam followed Shazia at the English-language school, and both have now finished the course successfully. They do not want to accept a "congratulations gift", but finally have agreed to my arranging for Shazia to take a computer course, which may help her job options. For now, she is working part time as a cashier.

Ghulam's efforts have finally got him a job as a porter in a small medical facility. Together, they are just about able to make ends meet. But, having to work in a menial capacity in a clinic is a terrible, demoralising blow for Ghulam. He is a very proud and traditional Afghan and has sworn me to secrecy lest anyone in his family should find out! Yet, he is determined to work hard at this job and equally determined to prepare for taking the many qualifying exams required of foreign doctors. I do so admire them both.

October 1989

Ghulam likes me to telephone since he can't talk to his own mother, who is still in Kabul, whilst it is easy between Canada and the UK. I am honoured that he feels he can confide in me and share his worries. I try to boost his morale, but he is deeply concerned about the future of their children. It upsets him when he sees refugee children forgetting their ancestry and heritage. He says that some of them can't even speak their mother tongue, and he fears they are losing their culture through assimilation.

Nonetheless, he still feels that it was incumbent upon him to leave Pakistan and save his family by finding an alternative place to live. He fears that Pakistan cannot not stay as it is and won't be able to absorb the ever-growing number of Afghan refugees who are already so different in language and culture. "Canada is not heaven-paradise, but it's good. We're free and have hope for better life for kids."

July 1990

Ghulam and Shazia have been so worried when they heard of my accident. Even shy Shazia was on the phone, telling me how they wish they could be my doctors and look after me! I hope I have reassured them enough, as I did with Habiba.

Ghulam tells me that he has been without news from Afghanistan for three months, except for the newspaper clippings and bulletins from Afghanaid and other related journals I send him. He is extremely worried about his mother, from whom he has lately heard nothing. Without a radio, he is unable to hear the BBC and feels that his homeland is being forgotten by the Canadian and American news media.

August 1990

From colleagues in Peshawar, Ghulam has heard that nearly all of the volunteer organizations are closing down or will be very soon, and I know this to be true. What will those poor people do? Ghulam bitterly deplores what he sees as the success of the Kabul regime and how it seems to be getting stronger and stronger. In Pakistan, the same intimidation that Shazia suffered in the camps is happening to a female cousin. She has been threatened by unidentified men to stay away from work. All women workers are apparently now being "policed" and forced to stay at home. Such a very dangerous time.

September 1990

I am in utter dismay after the brief telephone call from Ghulam telling me how, a few days ago, he and Shazia were woken early in the morning by an immigration officer and an officer of the Royal Canadian Mounted Police knocking at their door. Terrified and protesting their innocence, they could only try to keep the children calm as all their papers were seized.

They were ordered to report to the police station where Ghulam has been interviewed several times.

Apparently, acting on information that he and his family entered the country illegally, the immigration authorities are preparing to deport them, and they now have no papers, no legal status! Although late, I have made some phone calls and will see what more I can do tomorrow. What a shocking, frightening state of affairs! That poor family and their "dark, tragical fate".

October 1990

It is a few weeks now since Ghulam's "arrest", and thankfully, he has been allowed to remain at home and can continue to work. There is also time to mount an appeal with a government lawyer who has been assigned to the case. Now it is a question of waiting for the trial date to be determined. But the crushing nightmare of living in limbo has begun. "For us," he repeats, trying hard not to weep, "there is no place to go."

Ghulam isn't worried about himself. As much as I try to encourage him, he feels his own life is almost over. But he and Shazia do worry for the children. They know that there is no kind future for them in Afghanistan until there is peace. News from Kabul describes the situation as worse than before. Ghulam continues to deplore how the media and international community are attracted by other affairs around the world and Afghanistan forgotten. "They think Afghans as a bunch of uncivilized, uneducated people killing each other, so let them go ahead. Who will care about Afghanistan? Probably nobody. Who is suffering? Afghan civilian innocent people."

February 1991

The months have dragged on and on, still with no news from the immigration department. Shazia has become depressed and struggles with illness, exhaustion, and homesickness whilst poor Ghulam has almost had a nervous breakdown. Full of apologies, he confessed to me, "Because you are unique with your compassion as a mother who always gives hope and courage, I can share that I almost go crazy. It is the time of falling apart."

Even so, they are still both working, studying, and caring for the children, who are doing well at school!

At last, Ghulam told me what really had happened in Pakistan. He had been tricked by a husband and wife who were selling Canadian visa application forms. The wife, apparently, acted her part to help allay any suspicions. The husband instructed Ghulam to use the name of one of his wife's relatives who was already living in Canada to claim right of entry. He reassured him that this "your slight name change" on the form would go unnoticed. Like so many other refugees, Ghulam was desperate enough to pay for this.

There followed an interview at the Canadian Embassy in Islamabad and a medical examination. Just a few months later, Ghulam received the longed-for letter with their flight date and confirmation of their status as convention refugees. And all might have, indeed, gone unnoticed, except that, later, the man responsible for the falsifications was caught, and the whole ruse came to light.

The Canadian immigration authorities were alerted and acted swiftly, catching many other innocent refugees, all of whom had been duped. They, too, must now wait in a kind of no man's land between the letter and the spirit of the law, facing the horrendous prospect of being forcibly returned to a homeland where only death and destruction await them. It is a complete nightmare. And how bitterly ironic, after having secured a new life in a free country.

July 1991

I have been able to learn that there is actually not a problem with Ghulam's and Shazia's refugee status as such. The charge is misrepresentation because of the name change, making them "illegals". This is causing more delays because of the huge backlog of several years to be reviewed by the refugee board before the trial. The lawyer explained to me that there is also uncertainty about which jurisdiction is responsible for their case, the one where they reside or the one where the trial is to take place. Ghulam gave such a sigh from his heart when he lamented, "I think there is just a bunch of bureaucrats throwing paper to each other." Yet, he doesn't blame anyone in Canada, just the situation he unwittingly fell into.

November 1991

When I told Ghulam the news that the delegation of Afghan mujahideen had started talks with the Soviet government, his reaction was bleak. He fears that, because Afghan people are not united, this slight glimmer of hope will soon be overshadowed by the beginning of widespread civil war. Apparently, only four of the multiple factions are participating in the talks.

Unfortunately, Afghans have never been united, but things are now somewhat different than in the past. Now, Afghanistan is a huge ammunition dump and littered with mines. Ghulam's fear is that this weaponry will fall into the hands of uneducated and ruthless people intent on their own purposes. I know it is true that even young people have learned how to kill and take revenge. Tragically, he can't see any hope for this generation that has grown up with "wildness" in Afghanistan, and he predicts a dark and uncertain future.

December 1991

I continue to send as much information as I can to Ghulam and his lawyer about the deadly situation, both in the camps and in Kabul. It seems that the Canadian government is getting tough towards Afghan asylum seekers and claims that the situation in Afghanistan is good and poses no danger for anyone. There is even talk of officially recognizing the government of Najibullah[70]!

But the ever-present threat of deportation hangs over these innocent people, haunting their nights and preventing them from making any plans or enjoying the life they had started to build for themselves. Money is tight, Shazia is losing weight, and Ghulam, unable to sleep, is a bundle of nerves and anxiety. Few things can be more frightening than being swallowed up by an impersonal legal system where one's life is put on hold indefinitely and at the mercy of complete strangers —strangers who may not understand the life-threatening circumstances which have brought one to such an impasse in the first place. I must find something more I can do.

[70] . The Soviet-backed president of Afghanistan from 1986 to 1992, previously head of KHAD, the Afghan secret police.

Ghulam finds that, when Westerners first meet him, they always ask him what tribe he belongs to. Sadly, his region has one of the highest poverty and illiteracy levels in the country. Like Shazia, he grew up in a very poor family with numerous brothers and sisters and illiterate parents. He once told me that he couldn't remember ever having breakfast before school because there simply wasn't anything to eat. It was a dream for them to have a hot, full meal.

Eventually, he graduated from medical college, hoping most of all to be able to help his parents and his people. Unfortunately, his hope died when the Russian troops invaded Afghanistan. I learned that, because of his religion and politics, he was hunted all over the country, once imprisoned and, to my horror, even tortured. When he was released, he returned home to practise his profession, but there were so many problems that, despite his efforts, he was compelled to flee to Pakistan. Even there, he had a hard time finding a job until, fortunately, he was invited to join the medical team at the refugee camp clinic where we met.

Unfortunately, this was also where government agents from Afghanistan and some of the fundamentalist Muslims were making life extremely precarious for educated Afghans. Recently, this has escalated, and the number of people being assassinated grows daily. I share Ghulam's outrage on hearing that another hard-working doctor, Dr Rahman Zamani, has been badly injured in a car bombing after spending twelve years helping Afghan refugees in the camps in Pakistan. I met him at his clinic and remember him as a kind, compassionate man who helped me with the children's art project. Fortunately, he's survived, but emigrated abroad. Ghulam laments, "He wasn't a politician, commander, or party leader, and also wasn't handling ammunition. Because he's not follower of fundamentalist, after all of this, he deserved to be hurt?"

October 1992

Ghulam had always thought that the bureaucracy in India and Pakistan was bad enough whereas he now says that Canada is the master. Unbelievably, two long years have passed and still he and Shazia are waiting, whilst the situation in Afghanistan remains unchanged, a dark legacy of nearly thirteen years. During this time, I bought Ghulam a radio, and he listens avidly to the BBC World Service. The first he heard was that the university students were all buying the white cloth that, under Koranic law, is normally used as a burial shroud, but is now worn in defiance of the troops, saying, "Kill me. I am ready for death."

March 1993

The bombshell has exploded, not on the front line, but in a courtroom. Ghulam, at long last, was summoned to the hearing. Despite all our evidence, prayers, and pleas, the immigration adjudicator has ruled that Ghulam and Shazia misrepresented themselves at the Canadian Embassy. They have therefore been issued with a deportation order! My heart leapt into my mouth when I heard.

At the same time, however, they *have* been given the right to appeal and are filling out the application form today. At least there is a slight reprieve and glimmer of hope. Unfortunately, the hearing for the appeal will not take place for several more months. They will have to plead their case before a panel of three judges whose decision will then be irrevocable. My blood runs cold. They must be rescued!

I have begun writing letters, thick and fast, on their behalf with supporting evidence from newspaper articles, Amnesty International Reports, and BBC news to help convince the panel of the grave necessity for this family to remain in Canada. I have contacted their social worker who also has gone to work and is collecting letters of recommendation and circulating a petition. Ghulam will be sending me all the paperwork to show some legal people here. As with Habiba, I must make certain the documents don't fall into the wrong hands. And I must make sure these good people don't give up hope, despite living day by day with such terrible uncertainty and grim prospects.

September 1993

At last came Ghulam's and Shazia's "D-Day"—deportation day. Nervous and fearful, shaking in his brand-new suit, Ghulam was sworn in. He was then asked to explain exactly all that had happened, from beginning to end. Apparently, when speaking about his anxiety over not knowing anything about his mother's fate, one judge told him, "I feel your pain." The fact that both Ghulam and Shazia were employed and never used welfare was pointed out by the government attorney himself. Having spoken with their social worker, I knew that she had been able to produce some thirty letters of reference to their good character, and that the petition for the deportation order to be overturned had been signed by no less than sixty people.

After all the protracted waiting, anguish and uncertainty, the hearing which determined their fate lasted only one hour! The judges pronounced their verdict: "Your deportation order is quashed. Look forward to your future. Court recessed."

Our jubilation couldn't be greater. Of course, it will take several more bureaucratic months before their papers are returned to them confirming their new legal status. It will take an even longer period of time for their fears and anxieties to subside completely, for them to be able to stand up and breathe freely, unbowed by the burden of anguish and dread. But, for the first time in all these terrible years, they can begin to make plans to have a future.

December 1993

With so many new contacts, we've managed to find a retraining programme for Ghulam. He tells me that he is looking forward to being useful again! Shazia has been busy looking for a new house in a better neighbourhood for the children. In the New Year, she will start interviewing for a part-time job in a medical clinic. They can't wait to get their papers so that they can travel abroad for the first time and visit family and friends. No doubt, the greatest source of joy—after their release, that is—is that Ghulam's mother is safe in Peshawar, and we can begin work to reunite the family.

In Ghulam's words, "We're happy, we're free, and we thank God for you. We are proud of your friendship. Shazia, the kids and I will remember you as long as we're alive."

Soraya: The Forgotten "Red-Tape Refugees"

One of Jean's concerns was for the growing number of Afghan refugees who, after escaping to the West, were left living in limbo for unreasonably long periods of time. When visiting Soraya, another adoptive daughter, in what was then West Germany, Jean was dismayed by the physical and psychological impact that the endless waiting and culture shock were having on the exiled Afghan community. As the processing of visas ground slowly on and on, she became the advocate of yet another cause, that of the forgotten "red-tape refugees".

Thatched Cottage, Buckland Newton
January 1981

Not all refugees fit into the generally accepted picture of a crowd of ragged, starving men, women, and children clutching hopelessly at the barbed-wire fence of their refugee camp. At first sight, these others seem to be living in comparative comfort and security. They may have a home of sorts, even a job, however menial.

And yet, they live in a vacuum, in a constant state of frustration, unable to foresee a worthwhile future. Intellectual, cultured, talented, and experienced people are denied the use of the skills they have acquired over many hard-working years because they are strangled by the red tape of politics and bureaucracy.

Their stories must be told to show the world that it is not merely enough to have escaped tyranny and oppression. Promises must be kept. Those who preach compassion must also show it in a practical way. Political expediency must never be allowed to override moral obligations.

I met Soraya several years ago in Kabul through Zahra, my friend who invited me to help teach her English class. Soraya was also an English teacher, and when she came to study on a language programme in the UK, Henry and I saw her frequently. She would stay with us at Thatched Cottage on weekends, or I would visit her and take her out to lunch and on shopping expeditions. She loved my helping her pick out handbags and shoes.

On her return to Kabul, in July of 1979, Soraya saw many changes. At first, she thought that the revolutionary government was taking positive steps towards progress, such as with the land reform programme. But she was also becoming concerned over the increasing number of Russian advisers filling senior positions across all the professions. She was repeatedly told that she should teach Russian, "the language of our friendly and helpful neighbour." It was also worrying that she was being asked to edit English textbooks written by her colleagues but under Russian supervision.

During the following months, Soraya continued to work and help her mother look after the house and her younger siblings. Rumours flew about the city, still under an 8 p.m. curfew after the second Communist coup in September, when the Number Two man in the government, Hafizullah Amin, engineered the overthrow and murder of President Taraki. Soraya gave me to understand that under Amin's brutal regime several relatives and friends had, shockingly, been executed. Every day after work, she and her family would go to the homes of the bereaved and weep. "Looking at people's tearful eyes makes me oh, so sad, but also angry."

She confided to me her growing awareness that she would one day have to leave the country. She feared persecution because of her Western-oriented education and her associations with England. Having relatives who had immigrated many years before to Australia, West Germany, and the States only further jeopardized her job. I dreaded the censor's intervention when she was particularly outspoken, especially as the tribes were spreading their revolt against the Russians. However, nothing seemed to have happened.

All this instability and inability to bring the mass of Afghan people to heel finally resulted in the invasion by Russia just two days before Christmas 1979. Unpopular even with the Soviets, Amin was shot dead and the real power in the Communist Party, Babrak Karmal, who had been considered too pro-Marxist at the beginning for the devout Muslim population, finally surfaced and was instated with all the might and chicanery of Moscow.

Then in the autumn of 1980, Soraya suddenly began to use the simple code we had agreed upon, just in case, before her departure from England. "My lovely mother, will sharing a cup of tea and a chat together ever again be possible? I miss you and Henry very much." She now became especially careful of what she said at her school, as we knew that even some of the pupils had been indoctrinated as spies. As more English courses and textbooks were replaced with Russian ones, she also worried that all her training and experience would be lost and wasted. What made matters worse was that some of the young men in her large extended family had gone to fight with the mujahideen and were wanted by government forces. The army and the police began making surprise raids on their different homes, and the families were threatened with imprisonment if they tried to hide them. It was a terrible time, and they all suffered the loss of those incarcerated or disappeared. Soraya felt that her very soul was being ruined.

At last, she supposedly received an invitation to visit her relatives in America. She had taken a leave of absence and would be applying for a passport. As I read between the lines, I understood that she was planning to escape illegally, for I knew she could not get a passport or a visa. Neither could she obtain a certificate from the UNHCR to validate her status as a bona fide refugee. Fretting and full of anxiety for her, I heard nothing more until after the New Year.

February 1981

For almost a month, even though Soraya was so grateful to be able to speak and write freely, she was still too afraid to tell me about her daring

266

escape and what went wrong. She kept apologizing for her poor English, saying it was the result of the constant threats she had had to endure for studying in the UK, which was "the enemy".

The hardest part was saying goodbye to her mother and father, not knowing if she would ever see them again. They had found and bribed a guide to take her with two other families over the mountainous Khyber Pass. Like others before them, they hid in caves during the day, listening to the explosions from the planes and helicopters. At night, they ventured out, guided by starlight on the fresh snow. What if the guide betrayed them or asked for even more money? A frightening, dreadful time during which eating, sleeping, even washing was forgotten.

Finally, exhausted, half-starved and half-frozen, Soraya arrived in Peshawar and stayed with a friend of her mother's. Other friends helped her with the difficult and dangerous purchase of fake documents on the black market to get her safely out of Pakistan. She was fortunate to have enough money for airfare as well, especially as she would not be using the return part of her ticket, which, nonetheless, was crucial to have for appearance's sake. At every step, she was terrified lest she be caught and sent back to Kabul!

Unfortunately, her plan went awry. Her flight was so delayed that, by the time she arrived in her transit city, she had missed her connection. The next connecting flight to her final destination wasn't until the following day. Without a visa, even for such a short time, she had to agree to leave on the next departing plane to wherever she could get an onward connection, or she would "be parcelled back" to Peshawar. Suddenly, she found herself bundled onto a plane to Frankfurt in West Germany! There, she was stopped by the transit authorities and had to reveal that she was seeking political asylum.

To my utter dismay, although she knew that *no* refugees were being considered by the British government on those grounds, she had been planning to come to London, throw herself on the mercy of the airport authorities, and somehow be allowed to seek political asylum at the US Embassy. In her anguished state of mind she believed it was the right place, a safe haven! She was hoping that she would be given a US visa and could then come with me on one of my trips there and simply not return. Being a refugee from a third-world county makes one look towards the big three most powerful nations as being capable of doing absolutely anything to help those in distress. It is impossible to explain that these countries are less than charitable and that they are more concerned with political and economic manoeuvrings than with the welfare of those they profess to be concerned about.

Stranded and, as she told me, with her heart beating even faster than it had in the Khyber caves, another nightmare began. She found herself almost swept along by a jostling, noisy crowd of refugees from Sudan, Ethiopia, Vietnam, and other war-torn countries. In the confusion, a few scuffles broke out as the police tried to keep people moving along. Some of the young men, having been mujahideen, or freedom fighters, felt threatened at the sight of the police weapons and had to be restrained as they tried to fight back. I've heard that this sometimes leads to unfortunate assaults and arrests.

When Soraya's turn came, to her immense relief, the West German officers were very kind. She was taken to a centre where there were many Afghan families and given a room to share with three other women. Vouchers for food and clothing were also provided. But she was very confused and fearful of the future. By requesting political asylum, she had not just been assigned a place to live, but had also been given a list of rules which stipulated no visa, no travel beyond the city, no language school, and no work.

When we finally spoke, she said, her voice trembling, "My life seems like a broken ship in a big ocean." The one thing she pinned her hopes on was eventually immigrating to the US. The "long wait of the 'red-tape refugees'" had begun.

I must add here that, although Frankfurt is one of the few European cities processing Afghan refugees, not even its Immigration and Naturalization Service (INS) at the US Consulate deals with initial applications. It is through two churches so designated. One is Catholic and one is Protestant, and both are overwhelmed by the volume of applicants. It is critical to show that, as a refugee, you have been persecuted and left your country because your life was in jeopardy. If you add that you have been tortured, beaten, or physically abused, your chances for being granted refugee status increase.

Naturally, the grapevine operates here as in all crowded and oppressed places, and many refugees lie and make up the most horrendous stories and usually get away with it because then the records of the agencies can show how many refugees are being looked after—and funding continues. So, often it is the people who are less deserving who slip through the net, leaving those who know that their own conditions are far worse to wonder how such decisions can be made.

Language is the greatest complication, but in cultures where the preciseness of filling in endless forms is unknown, many mistakes are made through ignorance, and the confusion that arises leads to fear and frustration and a sense of hopelessness bordering on complete despair. How would you react if you were thrown upon alien shores, unable to communicate, subjected to sights and sounds totally foreign, and without familiar family ties, utterly uprooted? Small wonder there are cases of suicide, none of which, incidentally, are reported.

March 1981

In the following weeks, I explained to Soraya the two ways open to her now to be eligible for going to the States. One was to get a sponsor and go at her own expense; the other, to get a sponsor from one of the churches. Either way, it could take more than ten months because so many refugees were applying. She decided to fill in the application with the church, and I began the hugely difficult task of finding her a sponsor, as I have done for others. It requires divulging details of a most private nature, which puts many people off. Of course, it is obvious that such stringent questioning reduces the number of sponsors who qualify, and so, in turn, the number of refugees lucky enough to locate a successful candidate.

Yet, Soraya was certain that she had finally found the key that would open the door for us to lead her to the States. Her hopes were reinforced by the kind, elderly pastor who was head of the church where she had her interview. This sympathetic and dedicated gentleman, Rev. Kopf, pointed out to her that the American NGO programme, for which she had done some work in Kabul, could be of valuable use. He encouraged her to write to the head of the team for a letter in support of her application, which she immediately did.

Her spirits fairly soared when I told her I would visit her as soon as possible.

What a happy reunion! The first of many that were to come over the next several years. I don't believe I've been hugged so fiercely in all my life. I met with Rev. Kopf, and together we arranged for Soraya to move to a house with several Afghan refugee families where she was given a kind of bedsit, at least a room of her own with a little kitchenette. She insisted on cooking for me, and I helped her find her way around the neighbourhood and become familiar with public transport. She especially loved going shopping together. "Not for to buy," she explained, "but like in the olden days, when I stayed with you and Henry."

Of course, whilst there, I made frequent visits to the US Consulate to ask about the status of her application and whether or not the all-important letter had arrived. Each time the answer was the same: "We will notify you when your interview appointment is set."

Eventually, we were able to track down one of her relatives, a cousin by the name of Sahel, who had lived in West Germany since a boy and whose parents had just moved to the States. He was still living in the family home in another city whilst finishing his last year of engineering studies. He was greatly surprised but said he would of course help and go to see Soraya as soon as he could. Knowing that she wouldn't be completely alone now helped her when it came time for us to say goodbye.

I also left her with a radio so that she could listen to music and the BBC World Service. The first broadcast, however, was distressing: "The whole country of Afghanistan is demonstrating to celebrate the anniversary of the success of this government." It was a horrible joke to the Afghan refugees in exile.

May 1981

True to his word, Sahel visited Soraya and introduced her to his Indian friend, Ravi, and his wife, Meena, who lived in Frankfurt. They were about the same age, warm, friendly and very sympathetic people. They began to get together frequently. They would cook each other traditional meals from their respective countries and, on Sundays, the couple would take her out for drives in their car. Soraya got on well, too, with Sahel when he came from time to time, apparently a quiet, well-educated man who helped her with her German. "Oh, dear Jean, there are many good people in the world."

I couldn't wait to phone Soraya: I had finally been able to persuade a friend of mine to become her sponsor. Soraya was so effusive that I was embarrassed. She kept repeating, "My lovely, lovely sweetheart mother! I wish I could have more than the word *thank*!" We immediately informed the US Consulate so that at least her application would be brought forward, as those with sponsors receive priority status.

Soraya found the West German people to be very kind, but sometimes, when shopping, she made mistakes with the things she was buying and received angry looks from the shopkeepers. I explained to her that there are people who unjustly blame the refugees for taking so much from the social services. It pained her, always willing to work but not allowed to. She kept her spirits up by studying German, going for walks, and reading. One of the women in the house was teaching her how to knit. I sent her some English novels—she liked Jane Austen—and her favourite scent with English lavender soap and toiletries. I included some footless long johns in one package so she shouldn't be cold come the winter.

Soraya faced yet another move and another upheaval. She was taken to live in a hostel where she had an unhappy experience. She was shocked to discover that some of the women in their shared dormitory-like room were prostituting themselves. When she refused to be part of this practise, she had to leave the room and wait in the corridor. However, it was so cold and uncomfortable that eventually she discovered a more pleasant way to pass the time. She would go to the public library where it was warm and she could study her German. On my next visit, I insisted that we complain about this condition to the social services, and they found her accommodation in a house with three Afghan families, but apparently did nothing to curb the prostitution.

February 1982

Unfortunately, the Afghans where Soraya was living did not respond to her efforts to make a friendly atmosphere amongst them. Instead, each family seemed to be pitted against the other! I continued to send her money, especially for her to buy herself treats from time to time. I also sent her some practical things like stockings and bras, which she still couldn't bring herself to buy in a department store. She spent a lot of time alone reading and practising her knitting in front of the coal fire in her little room.

At this point, Soraya was hopeful of getting a West German passport, which would allow her to travel and work. How impossible it was for her as well as other refugees to understand. They have such naivety that, whenever they hear President Reagan or some other head of state promise to help the refugees, they assume it means exactly that. The disillusionment hits hard as they learn the true facts whilst languishing in no man's land, without passport, citizenship, or hope.

"I don't mean to make you feel sorry for telling you the stories of my life," she would say, "but I only want to share this part of my life also with you."

June 1982

I decided to telephone the director of the American NGO team whose letter we so eagerly awaited. He was most apologetic about the delay and promised to get the documents accredited immediately. And so he did. They were duly filed at the US Consulate in Frankfurt where, unfortunately, they had to wait until the summer season ended.

During this time, the refugee queue grinds to a halt owing to the curtailment of staff at the Immigration and Naturalization Service as so many return to the States for R&R.[71] Those who do not go on vacation turn their attention to matters arising with the servicemen and their families at the army base near Frankfurt. The uninformed refugees naturally become

---

[71] . Rest and recreation.

agitated and worried when told there are to be no interviews for three months. How could they know that "their" priority does not even merit the replacement of staff so as to continue processing applications? I still tried to get things going by phoning frequently, but the same information droned out: "You will be notified when it is time for your interview, but it is a very long queue." I must see about getting a rota of volunteers to help at the churches with manning the telephone and typing.

In response to Soraya's lament—"Now life is like that: to wait and to waste it"—I tried to help her feel more useful and urged her to think of something worthwhile she could do whilst waiting. I tried to interest her in my suggestions to the church people about organizing some craft, sports or music projects and competitions; or sight-seeing tours sponsored by local business; or even BBC nature documentaries for television that don't need a language and could be useful to show. We discussed how she could start a team of volunteers to meet new refugees at the airport, or to help them with shopping, cooking and nutrition. I even had a list of charities that might donate toys. But she was very depressed, especially with little motivation to study German, thinking she wouldn't need it when in America.

The news from Afghanistan was equally discouraging. She felt that some of the mujahideen were more interested in retaining their individual power and not in the good of the Afghan people. "Without well-organized leadership, such fightings have too many disadvantages and the wastings are more than the gainings."

July 1982

At long last, Soraya was given a West German passport! She could now find a job and receive a free place at a language school. We were both so excited. For the first time, she felt optimistic about the future and even had good dreams about her family back in Afghanistan. At the school, she made friends with another young Afghan woman, Samira, whose two sisters had lived in West Germany for several years. Pooling their money, the four girls decided to rent a small flat together.

The master stroke was finding Soraya a job as a daytime nanny for an American couple, Ray and Millie Turner, whom Henry knew from Kabul and who were being posted to Frankfurt. Job-seeking for Afghan refugees in exile is extremely difficult as former employers who would normally give references have often either been killed or imprisoned. From the outset, Soraya liked the Turners and their two children, Bobby, age four, and Daisy, age two. The hours and pay seemed quite reasonable to me.

October 1982

"You are my mother, so I can tell you the truth," Soraya kept bursting into tears over the telephone. What I learned next was quite shocking. From time to time, I had heard of cases of Afghan refugee women being physically assaulted by male relatives for becoming too Western. I hoped that Soraya had been spared such violence, but nonetheless, she apparently was being subjected to virulent verbal abuse by relatives of Samira's family, two aunts, who had arrived from Pakistan and were temporarily living with them.

They were threatening to write and "denounce" Soraya to her parents, which, of course, caused her great distress. She didn't want to add to the burden of their problems, especially as she was innocent of any wrongdoing. The shouting and the threats frightened her dreadfully, making her feel desperately ashamed and alone.

Sadly, Samira and her sisters had already been cowed into submission and offered no support whatsoever. Everything had to be done according to these women's wishes—what the girls cooked, where they went, what they bought, to whom they spoke. They even wanted Soraya to stop working and receive welfare!

Out of desperation, Soraya pleaded with me, "Please, save my life, for the sense of your words which you have said 'daughter' to me!" She felt trapped in West Germany, trapped in a horrible life, and would cry herself to sleep far into the night. Again, she proposed various schemes for coming to England, willing to do the most menial of tasks; naively, she said she would even plough! She still could not understand why refugees were simply not being processed at the US Consulate in London.

For more than a week, I tried to calm Soraya down with phone calls, and I wrote her daily letters. I tried to give her explanations about this kind of reaction and how to cope with it. She was being treated as though she were in Kabul, but she was responding with independent and Western-oriented behaviour. In the end, I spoke with the aunts, explaining that, if Soraya was living in the West, she was going to act according to Western customs! They were the ones who should be ashamed of how they were treating her, and Soraya's parents would be proud of her for studying and working so hard. I don't think I was very diplomatic.

I spoke with the social services and, fortunately, they found new accommodation for Soraya in a flat with a young Afghan husband and wife and their two small children. It turned out that their families had known each other in Kabul. The flat had four bedrooms, a living room, and a small kitchen and bath. Soraya was pleased with her new surroundings and, slowly, began to regain her self-confidence. "God is kind who has given you to me."

December 1982

At this point, Soraya renewed her efforts to obtain a visa to go to the States, apologizing as she often did for "bothering" me. She hoped that someday she could serve *me* in some way! She had been told that a letter from a US senator written on behalf of a refugee would be an effective way forward. The letter should explain that it was impossible for her to return to Afghanistan without putting her life at risk because of her family status, her work, and her connections with the West. I had already written to the US Consulate to that effect with no response, so, when I next went to the States to visit family and friends in California, I did a bit of digging and discovered a contact with a senator.

With great cheek, I wrote him a letter of appeal trying briefly to set forth the pertinent points yet giving sufficient information to arouse his interest. I asked for his personal intervention, but I never even received an acknowledgement. I never really expected one, although I had read several articles written by him in which he professed his concern for Afghan refugees.

Thatched Cottage,
Buckland Newton

[Address of recipient undisclosed]

20 December 1982

Dear Senator,

I am an American citizen presently living in England. I have spent many years doing business in Afghanistan, during which time I have made many wonderful friends. I continue to maintain business connections, although, since the coup d'etat of 1978, with increasing difficulty. I have sponsored and helped as many Afghan friends as possible and do as much as I can on their behalf, as they seem to have been forgotten by most of the world; another case of broken promises, broken hearts, and broken families.

I write to you concerning the following situation of a young Afghan girl, Soraya, who was forced to flee her home in Afghanistan because of political persecution and in fear of her life. As an English teacher with qualifications from the UK, she found to her dismay that the revolutionary government of 1979, was substituting Russian for English courses. She was warned that her Western associations were also a black mark on her record, which she would have to work hard to overcome.

To make matters worse, the political views of Soraya's family caused them to be subjected to frequent harassment and house searches. This situation created problems so great that the painful decision to separate was finally taken. Soraya undertook the nightmare of escaping, and then, due to unforeseen circumstances, was forced to seek political asylum in West Germany rather than in the United States as she had hoped to do. Her second nightmare was the bewildering and complicated process of applying for a visa to the US where she believed her language skills and her having worked for an American NGO program (see enclosed documents), would better equip her to start a new life.

Recently, on yet another of her frequent visits to the immigration office in Frankfurt, she was told that a letter from a US senator would greatly facilitate her application. This suggestion, though probably well intentioned, is yet another heartbreakingly difficult obstacle for which I am seeking your help.

Could you possibly see your way clear to assist me in my effort to obtain a visa for Soraya? I would be pleased to supply you with any further information, but in conclusion, I would like to say that I know Soraya would cherish the freedom and opportunities of this country and would be a person of whom one would be very proud indeed.

Thank you for reading this long letter.

Very sincerely yours,
Jean H. Willacy

Even at this stage, no one bothered to tell us that Soraya was actually ineligible for a US visa, as she had been granted political asylum and given a West German passport. At no time had she been advised as to the consequences if she accepted. Quite simply, she was no longer a political refugee! It should have been explained by the church agency and also the INS.

I feel that I should have known better, and I blame myself for the eventual outcome of events. But no one said anything! Despite her recognizing how the web of red tape and bureaucracy was closing in around her and how her chances were becoming increasingly slim, she clung to her cherished hope with unwavering courage, counting the days and nights for the long-awaited letters to arrive.

January 1983

On my return to the UK, I telephoned Rev. Kopf for an up-to-date report and learned the outcome of the letters that had, finally, arrived.

They did prove that Soraya had worked with an American programme in Kabul, but, incredibly, the INS pointed out that, under the terms of the contract, all of the money for the project had been handed over to the Afghan government. In other words, government bureaucrats became the official employers and paymasters! The reason for this was obvious: with so much money flowing through their hands, they could siphon off as much as they liked *and* pay much lower wages than the US government would. This catch-22 totally invalidated the fact that Soraya had worked for the Americans! It was yet another sad trick of fate which the INS was quick to adopt.

I was so angry I wrote to the US Consulate to ask why, not long ago, some seventy-three thousand Cubans had been welcomed by US President Jimmy Carter while perhaps as many as three thousand Afghans languished in West Germany. I wanted to ask how is it that while the politicians *proclaim* a desire to help Afghanistan by boycotting sports events, having meetings of the EEC[72] and UN, etc., there is no evidence of help for these "red-tape refugees".

February 1983

On the next visit, we met with Rev. Kopf, and he and I finally managed to convince Soraya of all the strikes against her US visa application because:

1. The INS no longer regarded her a political refugee now that she held a West German passport;
2. She had not worked for an American programme in Kabul; rather, it was deemed an Afghan one;
3. The senator was not going to intervene on her behalf; and
4. There was presumably no chance of getting any visa other than a tourist one.

The effect of this outcome was quite a blow, and, momentarily, we felt crushed. My disappointment was nearly as great as Soraya's because she believed in me, believed that I could help her, and I'd let her down just as surely as any anonymous government. Unless she entered the US illegally

---

[72] . European Economic Community, precursor of the European Union.

and tried to lose herself, she must remain in West Germany. What sort of life could she make there? What sort of future had she?

For Soraya's sake, we just had to rally quickly. What to do? Rev. Kopf could not have been kinder, and we discussed every detail at length and from every possible angle. Finally, a plan began to take shape. It began on my return to England, starting with my writing a second letter of appeal to the director of the project Soraya had worked on.

Thatched Cottage,
Buckland Newton

[Address of recipient undisclosed]

10 February 1983

Dear Sir,

I am writing to you on behalf of Soraya, whom, you will recall, is having difficulty with her application for a US visa. Perhaps you will remember my contacting you last year when, as a result of our telephone conversation, you sent a letter to the Immigration and Naturalization Service (INS) of the US Consulate in Frankfurt explaining Soraya's connection with the project you led in Afghanistan. You concluded your letter by saying that, if you could be of further help, not to hesitate to call on you. That is what I am about to do.

It was hoped that your letter, officially vouching for Soraya's employment by an American agency, would open the door for her obtaining a visa. But the INS pointed out that her salary was actually paid by the Afghan government; therefore, there was no American employer. This is what I call a grossly unfair situation, but it does not alter the hard and fast US policy. So, unfortunately, your kind letter did not succeed in opening the door for Soraya.

Now we have a new and optimistic approach and this is where you come into the picture.

Soraya is going to re-apply for a US visa under Preference Three which is *not* as a political refugee. Preference Three means that a potential U.S. employer must go to his labour board and explain that, because of special qualifications, he/she wishes to employ a specific person who is qualified to do a certain job which cannot be done by an American living in the US.

In other words, if there are any projects that you control, are involved with, or know about where people are needed to assist with any English-language programmes, please bear in mind that this could lead to Soraya's qualifying for a visa under this Preference Three ruling. There may be projects of this kind being conducted in the US (somewhere in that great big country) or in use in near Eastern countries, (i.e. India, Pakistan, Iraq, Saudi Arabia, or other Middle Eastern countries, or even Asian ones). You might know of such projects, as I believe that is largely the nature of your work.

Wouldn't it be marvellous if you could help in this way? I suppose the employer would make the request for Soraya's employment, and the labour board would then have to approve it and send all documents to the church officials, who, in turn, would submit them to the INS in Frankfurt.

From all that I have learned, it would seem that applying for a visa under the Preference Three ruling is much more effective and even faster than as a political refugee, especially these days when there are floods of people applying, and the already strict quotas have been further reduced for one reason or another. I was told that, often times, people who are quite illiterate find some very obscure job requirement under this ruling (which apparently lists every possible kind of job known to man) and are cleared and given visas long before those applying under political asylum rulings.

In any case, I hope you know of some projects whereby Soraya qualifies, and at least that will be a beginning. She knows that she has a long time to wait, but these first two years have taught her patience.

So, the situation, which appeared so black and hopeless, now has a glimmer of light. I know you must be a very busy person, but please do your utmost to give this problem top priority and let me hear from you as soon as possible. If you have any further questions, I would be most willing to accept a collect telephone call.

Thanks for bearing with me, and just please understand that I am full of compassion for Soraya and others like her who are the victims of dreadful circumstances beyond their control.

I needn't tell you how much hope is carried in this letter.

All best wishes and kindest personal regards,

Yours faithfully,
Jean H. Willacy

May 1983

The biggest surprise yet came like a bolt out of the blue, an event so momentous that Soraya hardly dared tell me: she had got married! She feared I would disapprove, as it was an arranged marriage. The only alternative in order for her to marry was to return to a refugee camp in Pakistan. Of course, I would never have encouraged her to defy her parents. I was actually delighted for her as, back in Kabul, she had known and liked the young man, by the name of Sediq, whom they had chosen for her. He had already been living in West Germany. They were married according to the Islamic ceremony last March in Frankfurt. Sahel, who was now working with a West German engineering firm, helped them organize it, and Ravi and Meena gave them a smashing party with the new friends with whom the couple had begun to enjoy a social life for the first time.

A few weeks after this news, Sediq telephoned me. He felt it his duty to pay his respects to Soraya's "lovely Western mother" and reassure me that he would try his best to make her happy. I was deeply touched. He had a part-time evening job and seemed to be very hard working and conscientious. Soraya continued her work as a nanny.

In the meantime, they were sharing the same flat where Soraya had been living with the Afghan family, who, fortunately, were good and kind people. She and Sediq began saving up to find a place of their own. She shyly confessed to me that she was worried about becoming pregnant before they were more settled. Naturally, she had not been taught the facts of life, but I had to laugh to myself—me, giving contraceptive advice at my age!

By now, both Soraya and Sediq had completed their German-language course, but despite all their efforts to find work in their fields of study and expertise, they were, unfortunately, disappointed time after time. Most highly educated Afghan refugees face this almost insurmountable problem because professional positions must first be given to the nationals of their adoptive countries. In West Germany, hard manual labour jobs, such as cutting wood in the forests, looking after graves in the cemeteries, or sweeping the streets, sometimes become available, but they are primarily for men, and mainly Turkish immigrants are employed. Well-qualified women are usually offered only cleaning jobs with very low wages.

Working hours for women also pose a problem, as cleaning offices usually takes place late at night, the same time as when sex shops and bars are plying their trade. Soraya was willing to supplement her income by taking such a part-time job, but whilst she argued that she could take care of herself—and I secretly admired her spunk—Sediq and I reasoned with her that it was better to be safe than sorry. I proposed that we try to find a training course for either one or both of them.

Many Afghans in exile suffer from homesickness and mental health issues. It is easy to lose any hope of finding a job equivalent to what they would have had at home in Afghanistan before the war. Those who have been mujahideen struggle greatly from being idle and from the huge guilt they feel as survivors, believing as they do, even if wounded, that they have deserted their country and its cause. How inadequate, helpless, and frustrated those talented young men like Samandar and the others would feel if made dependent on handouts, unable to put their education and experience to work. Yet another instance of the damage done to people's lives by mindless bureaucracy.

July 1983

Strangely, or perhaps not so strangely, as time went by, we heard not a dicky-bird in response to my letter. Then, another setback. The friend who was going to sponsor Soraya was diagnosed with shingles and, reluctantly, was unable to help. Even so, Soraya was still hopeful that she would be given an interview at the US Consulate. I simply didn't know how to persuade her otherwise.

As it turned out, a new friend, Soraya's next-door neighbour, kindly mentioned to her that there was a vacancy for a part-time teacher's assistant at her children's nursery school. Soraya went for the interview and, to our great delight, she was given the job. Thank goodness that she took her certificates with her when escaping, and that the Turners had given her a glowing reference. Perhaps, this will help her to start letting go of her dream of going to the States, hard as it is for both of us.

August 1983

From time to time, the couple had unhappy news from Afghanistan. The two Communist parties of Afghanistan, Parcham and Khalaq, were fighting each other as well as the Russians, leading to successive battles for control of the capital. With so much deadly, indiscriminate bombing, trying to reach their families was difficult. We tried many ways of sending letters, resorting to code words, different handwritings, and incorrect return addresses, being always oh so careful to avoid the censor. There were cases of house arrest—even imprisonment—for the slightest slip-up.

November 1983

Through some fortuitous timing and a chain of mutual friends of mine and Henry's in Frankfurt, Soraya and Sediq finally found a pleasant, new flat, one all to themselves. They wanted me to be the first to know. Incidentally, whilst looking on their own, they were caught in yet another catch-22, as landlords prefer tenants with full-time jobs, which of course refugees can't get whilst waiting in limbo for the government agencies to deal with their applications. It is so infuriating. Still, Soraya was so happy that, at long last, perhaps she could really begin to believe that her life was improving. It was a relief for her to be occupied, for a while at least, with such mundane things as interior decorating!

Soraya's next "preoccupation" was not a complete surprise: she and Sediq became the doting parents of a little girl, Nazdana, meaning "one we take care of". Sediq kept assuring me over the phone that both "Mama and baby daughter are beautiful and well! I am such a proud Papa!" I couldn't congratulate them enough. They must have thought me quite mad and extravagant at Interflora.

Sediq did have a surprise for me, though, and revealed that, with life more settled for them now, he had taken my advice and enrolled in a certificate course in business and management and could look forward to an apprenticeship with a large company.

When I was able to speak to Soraya, she gave me the best news of all: at last she had come to terms with living in West Germany: "I have enough. I am happy." And so am I.

PART 5

Memories of Home, Dreams of Homecoming

"Mommy, don't the Russians have a country? Is that why they took ours?" —Zabir, eight years old

An Exhibition in Paris

Jean's initial plan was to raise funds and awareness by exhibiting Afghan refugee children's wartime drawings. Travelling from camp to camp, often through torrential rains over washed-out roads, she distributed hundreds of boxes of crayons and notebooks to the camp schools, making follow-up visits of encouragement and praise as she collected the artwork. She only later realised that this project today would be called art therapy, helping exorcise the children's terrors and recapture some of their innocence.

Her exhibition began as an illustrated talk given with an Afghan student friend at the Dorset County Library in Dorchester on 25 September 1987. Encouraged by the response, Jean expanded it and, through a series of mutual friends, was invited by Médecins du Monde to exhibit in Paris. Shortly before her departure for the opening ceremony, she was interviewed by journalist David Wilson for The Sunday Times.[73] *He entitled her forthcoming exhibition* "The Chilling Record of Afghan Children."

Ladies and gentlemen, good evening and thank you for coming tonight for, in so doing, we both know you are interested in hearing and learning more about the Afghan crisis.

Between 1967 and 1980, I lived in and had a business in Afghanistan. I was captivated by this incredible mountainous country from my first glimpse of it, and steeped myself in its beautiful landscape, culture, history, and people. That is, until the Russian invasion in 1979.

We usually learn about such situations like the Afghan war through our press, radio, or television—the media as it is collectively known. But

---

[73] . 6 October 1987.

the focus of their reports is inevitably on the military conflicts and/or the political machinations, which seem to dominate the output of *all* the media. It seems to me that precious little space is given to explaining the humanitarian problems which are on a monumental scale and which are endured on a daily basis.

For a long time, since the coup of 1978, when Afghan friends quickly became "refugees" and naturally turned to an American for help, I had been concerned with this aspect of the Afghan crisis and had helped in various resettlement programmes. But, by February of this year, I felt terribly drawn to do something more. Without knowing exactly what I could do, I flew to Pakistan. I spent nearly three months living near the border in Peshawar and in several of the refugee camps in nearby Mardan in order to better assess the situation and to decide what my contributing role could be as an independent individual.

As a result of what I saw and experienced, I decided to put my photographic background to use to reveal the plight of these courageous people and, especially, the tragedy of the children. I thought, 'Let the children speak for what is happening.' This led me to work closely with the teachers in the camp schools, who agreed to my idea of having the children draw pictures of their experiences of war, of their life in exile, of what they remembered of their homes in Afghanistan, and of what dreams they had for their future.

The Afghans are merely pawns in the game being played by the super powers. As one little eight-year-old boy said to his mother, "Mommy, don't the Russians have a country? Is that why they took ours?" In the naïve simplicity of their drawings, the children tell us what it is like to be bombed, to have death and destruction all around you, to be frightened and lost in a world you cannot understand. They reveal the daily struggle of life in the camps where their parents strive to stay alive and to maintain their families in constant risk of disease, hunger, and exposure. What is left to them is their abiding Islamic faith, the strength of their family life, and their confidence in the mujahideen engendered by the adults around them.

This exhibition comprises fifty mounted drawings by children from the ages of seven to fifteen, many attending school for the first time. To put the drawings into their proper context, they are exhibited in conjunction with my own contemporary photographs of life in the camps. The most difficult part for me has been selecting the most representative works from amongst the many I brought back. Yet, how rewarding that so many children wanted to take part in my project. Most are drawn by boys, as very few girls go to schools.

What does the future hold for them? I think this remarkable collection of drawings speaks for itself and gives us a clear message. Will we listen in time to save these and other refugee children?

The Artwork of War by Afghan Refugee Children

After Jean's death, it was important that the children's drawings be returned, if not to their rightful owners, then to an Afghan institute where they could be displayed, appreciated, and preserved. The collection, together with an extensive selection of Jean's slides, is now housed at the Louis and Nancy Hatch Dupree Foundation at the Afghanistan Center at Kabul University. This prestigious center is dedicated to preserving and teaching Afghan heritage, history and culture.

The Drawings

Afghanistan's Blood Flood

Home

My Brave Brothers

Get Out!

Keeping Faith Alive in Wartime

Camp Garden

I offer my greetings and hail to the saint Prophet (Mohammad)
Greetings and hails to the beloved Prophet
Greetings and hails to those who recite the Qur'an
Greetings and hails to the family and the children of the Prophet Oh God.

My Father

They Kept Coming

My Home in the Middle

They Are Not Our Leaders – Gorbachev and Najibullah

My Homeland

All I Remeber

The Children

Bridge to Schools in Swat Valley Refugee Camp

Children Greeting Jean with Their Drawings

Refugee Camp School for Boys

Refugee Camp School for Girls

Can We Save Their Innocence?

Denied Their Childhood

Far From Home

Left Behind

PART 6

Battling the Bureaucrats

The Afghan Relief Programme in Pakistan by Nancy Hatch Dupree

When researching for this book, I had the great pleasure and honour of corresponding with the "Grandmother of Afghanistan", the eminent historian Nancy Hatch Dupree (1929-2017). Both Nancy and her husband, the archaeologist Louis Dupree (1925-1989), were highly esteemed American scholars, authors, and authorities in the field of Afghan culture and history.

Forced from their work and adoptive home in Afghanistan after the communist coup of 1978, they settled in Peshawar where they founded and directed the Agency Coordinating Body for Afghan Relief (ACBAR).[74] As a central depository for reports and surveys, one of the aims of the agency was to coordinate and to prevent duplication of humanitarian aid to Afghan refugees, one of Jean's own frustrations.

At the beginning of her work with refugees, Jean received decisive encouragement from Nancy, who, all these years later, generously accepted my invitation to contribute this chapter.

Louis and I were long-time residents in Afghanistan prior to the Soviet invasion. Louis excavated prehistoric sites and I wrote historical guidebooks for the Afghan Tourism Organization. Like so many Westerners, we also left the country after the coup when the leaders of the Saur Revolution refused to renew Louis' work permit. No work permit, no residence permit. Declared *persona non grata* in August 1978, we spent much of our time

---

[74] . Now based in Kabul, ACBAR continues to play a vital role in coordinating NGOs and their relief programmes in Afghanistan.

in Room 22 at the colonial-style Dean's Hotel in Peshawar. Here we had grandstand seats from which to observe the unfolding drama, including the monumental complexities of dealing with both logistical and political issues.

To say the scene was chaotic would be grossly inadequate! First came a few European NGOs. Soon Pakistani manufacturers of canvas tents and other necessities arrived unabashedly scrabbling for large, lucrative contracts. In the gardens of Dean's Hotel, sample tents were subjected to simulated assaults of rain, dust, and wind storms to prove how resistant the various qualities of canvas would be. At times, these antics were positively hilarious. Bargaining was fierce and highly vocal. Competition and suspicion between NGOs was tense.

It was May 1988 before the UN set up Operation Salaam to coordinate emergency humanitarian and economic relief for Afghan refugees. The commitment for 1990 was $650 million. When, therefore, it was announced that the head of Operation Salaam, Sadrudeen Aga Khan, was scheduled to visit Peshawar in August that year, the NGOs prepared to meet him with open hands and visions of cascading dollars. By this time, the number of NGOs had exploded to around sixty, hailing from Europe, Scandinavia, Africa, the Arab world, Australia, Japan, and Pakistan, including Afghan refugees. Each clung to its own ideas of the "right" way to deliver assistance and largely shunned the assistance of the others.

After compliments on the work that the NGO community had achieved, the message they heard from Prince Sadrudeen that morning in Peshawar was, "Thanks. Now we'll take over." Suddenly aware they must work together or be flattened by the UN juggernaut, the NGOs banded together and formed the Agency Coordinating Body for Afghan Relief (ACBAR).

Meanwhile, tribal chieftains in the semiautonomous Federally Administered Tribal Areas (FATA) bordering Afghanistan's eastern provinces were following the injunctions of both the Islam and the Pushtun codes of honour which commanded that it was incumbent upon them to provide succour for their ethno-linguistically related kinsmen. Food and shelter in private homes, in schools, and in mosques were provided by the tribes whilst official rest houses, hospitals, and storage facilities were proffered by the Government of Pakistan (GOP). Waiting to be called upon, the representative for the United Nations High Commissioner for Refugees (UNHCR) patiently took his evening constitutionals in the gardens of another colonial hotel in Rawalpindi, near Pakistan's capital at Islamabad. Finally, as the refugee numbers reached 85,000 in April 1979, the FATA tribal leaders came to him in desperation.

The monumental task of creating a smoothly functioning administration system began. By 1987, three hundred and twenty-eight refugee tented villages (RTVs) existed outside Peshawar in the North-West Frontier Province, now called Khyber Pakhtunkhwa. Some were smallish, extended family units; others were huge settlements of 120,000 inhabitants covering five square miles. The refugees soon found crowded tent living intolerable because it deprived them of the privacy they held dear. But, constructing housing was forbidden by the GOP for fear that this would give the impression the refugees were here to stay, creating political chaos among Pakistanis. The refugees solved this problem by simply constructing houses without foundations, claiming this made them "temporary". Before long, many RTVs all across the country resembled clones of Afghan villages. No fencing enclosed the RTVs, and the refugees were generally able to move freely.

Refugees obtained space and rations in a RTV only after being registered with a political party. Receiving everything from tents to shoes to basic food commodities, depended on being registered. The incentive to be counted in order to receive such disbursements was, therefore, high and gave rise to a multiplicity of ingenious malpractices and multiple registration ploys to bilk the registration system. Unscrupulous wheelers and dealers among the Afghans and their leaders, together with duplicitous Pakistani bureaucrats, blatantly manipulated the misfortunes of the vulnerable for personal gain. Not surprisingly, many of those most taken advantage of were women and children. The situation was compounded by the fact that there were too few trained female Pakistani personnel available to assess conditions in households where men outside the family were denied access. The vulnerable seldom had a voice.

On the other hand, for some women, the refugee experience opened new horizons. Because their men were off fighting the holy war of jihad, women in many households were forced to make decisions they once never dreamed of making. At the same time, they were learning from the NGOs how to organize themselves and how to run small businesses. On repatriation, therefore, these women were ready to become the family income earners whereas their men, who had foregone education in order to fight, returned from the jihad neither intellectually nor emotionally prepared to engage in productive activities. How the family dynamics adjusted as women realized they no longer had to accept diminishment in exchange for security has yet to be explored adequately.

Dialogues with Officialdom

"People die while bureaucrats dither"—Nancy Hatch Dupree

Jean collected and saved everything she could in print about Afghanistan. The following documents are taken from among the wealth of surveys, petitions, newspaper clippings, posters, pamphlets, news bulletins, British and American government reports, magazine articles, notes and letters that fill the boxes of her Afghan-related material.

Whilst helping refugees with the "interminable paperwork" and forms they often could not understand, Jean devised grim but truthful templates that they could use to answer the question of why they were seeking political asylum or sponsorship.

Template 1

To Whom It May Concern;

Many of my business colleagues and friends have been either killed or jailed under the Russian-backed regime beginning in 1978. I, therefore, was forced to flee my country in fear for the lives of my family and self.

Template 2

To Whom It May Concern;

As a Muslim, I could not and would not bow to the Communist regime which has overtaken my country. Some of my relatives and friends have been killed or jailed, so I fled in fear for the lives of my family.

Jean transcribed an interview at the US Consulate on behalf of a young Afghan friend studying in the UK.

Today, Razia and I went to the US consulate to request a temporary visa for four weeks to Washington D.C. for the purpose of visiting her sister. It has been three years since they last saw each other when both were refugees in Pakistan.

Razia filled in the forms and we waited our turn. When called, we went up to the desk where the Immigration Officer checked her passport, a letter from the British Council, and the telegram from her sister in the US inviting Razia to visit there.

Indicating the passport, the officer's first remark was, "You want a US visa on such an old paper? We will never issue you a visa on this."

He then asked questions concerning my stay in Britain and why I had no British travel documents and no Afghan passport. (The reason for this was or should have been obvious.)

Second question was where Razia had stayed before arriving in Britain. Answer: Pakistan from 1982 to 1985.

"You mean you lived in a refugee camp and now you want to go to America?"

Razia explained that she lived in Peshawar but had worked in a camp as a Lady Health Visitor.

The officer then disdainfully replied, "You are just a refugee with no approved document, therefore you have no right to enter the USA."

Razia answered, "Please don't condemn me for being a refugee."

"I won't condemn you, but I am not going to issue you the visa."

At this point he rose from his seat and in an overly loud voice, which clearly carried to all corners of the crowded room, announced, "We will NOT issue you the visa and there is no point arguing with me because you will not win."

He then turned around, picked up her form with her picture and threw it into a reject tray behind him. Staring at me, he dismissed us in the most insulting and humiliating tone saying, "Next please."

Jean prepared meticulously for meetings with lists of questions, forthright criticisms, and, sometimes, her own solutions. Here is an example from one of her many visits to the US Consulate in Frankfurt.

Questions I must ask:

Aid

1. What living facilities are there for refugee families, especially those with children?
2. Need to involve Human Rights Commission? The US *proclaims* a desire to help Afghanistan, but where is the support? Aid money is badly spent.
3. The UN should pay the British Council for English-language courses which are cheaper than US ones.
4. A better introduction to Western culture is desperately needed to combat the culture shock of adjusting.

Red Tape

1. Have families' applications been typed and sent to the US Consulate? If not, why not? (If yes, go to Consulate and ask when interview is scheduled.)
2. If US-sponsored refugees have permanent US visas, how can they petition for other refugees?
3. Get list of names of refugees still accommodated in hotels.

Concerns for Children

1. Children are exposed to the worst aspects of Western Europe.
2. No continuity of schools as refugees are moved from place to place.

The number of letters Jean wrote and received is truly staggering. Her official letters can be divided into her 'please help' letters and letters of thanks for help she herself had given.

Dear Colette;[75]

I have just received an appeal on behalf of the Afghan Children's Hospital in Peshawar from an English friend of mine. She works to save the indigenous Kalash people[76] living in the Rumbur valley in Pakistan, near the refugee camps in Chitral, and also has an interest in Afghan refugees. She thought I might be able to help, and immediately I thought of you and your possible interest.

The hospital is apparently already well established and has a licence to operate as an NGO, but it is short of money and in danger of closing down in the next forty-five days. You and I both know how difficult it is to get that precious licence and to get equipment safely into the country. They are lucky in that respect, but may lose it all for lack of funds, especially as media attention rarely includes the Pakistan-Afghan border area.

Perhaps you might reconsider the policy of sending Afghan children to the US at great expense and with enormous difficulties. Might it not be more humane and efficient, in the long run, to treat these poor children in Peshawar itself? It seems to me that, here, there is a well-put-together hospital/clinic.

---

[75] . One of Jean's friends who ran a prosthesis clinic in California to help maimed and injured Afghan children during the Soviet-Afghan War.

[76] . An ancient indigenous tribe that lives in the remote mountains of Pakistan's northern district of Chitral.

Recently, I have been in contact with a group of Afghan doctors in Wolverhampton who are eager to work in Peshawar at a clinic/hospital on a rotating basis from one to three months at a time. Interested?

Please advise if you want further information. It sounds a good idea to me.

What news of your postponed holiday to England? Hope this finds you well. Let me hear from you soon.

Much love, Jean

Keen to support even the smallest effort against the Soviet invasion, Jean made a donation to a periodical published by Afghan university students and refugees in New Delhi. The manager was probably also the President of the Association for Afghanistan Freedom Struggle in India.

Mirror of Afghanistan
A Monthly Journal Devoted to Afghanistan Liberation Struggle
P.O. Box No. 3311,
New Delhi 110014

17 January 1982

Dear Madam,

Thank you for your kind letter that give us courage. The Soviet action against independent and sovereign State of Afghanistan goes against all cannons of justice and fair play. All the peaceful and justice-loving nations should stand up unitedly *[sic]* to denounce Soviet aggression. This barbarous savagery on the part of the USSR must be put to an end. Otherwise, the peace and tranquillity of the world will be a thing of the past.

Under existing circumstances, we Afghan students and refugees in India made Association for Afghanistan Freedom Struggle. As you know, government of India do not allow for this activity. We asked one of our Indian friends to register his name for editor-ship of our magazine and myself as manager, and we asked some MPs of Indian Parliament to give their names as advice committee. So, we return your international money order for $15 to you back. Because this is in wrong name.

Madam, since you got much sympathy with our genuine cause, we want that you please propagate in UK for furthermore of our work. Please assist us so we do better work for our nation and humanity also. Let us know how many copies do need each month.

We are looking forward with most profound intent to your kind reply. Thanking you,

Yours Sincerely,

M. Kabir
The Manager & President

Jean also was always on the look-out for job opportunities for refugees, as well as finding sponsors and safe havens for them.

International Medical Corps
1080 Wilshire Boulevard., Suite 2008
Los Angeles CA 90024
(213) 4743927

August 17, 1987

Dear Mrs. Heringman,

Thank you for your interest in the International Medical Corps. We are in receipt of your letter written on behalf of your Afghan friend and her resume. We are touched by your interests in helping the people of Afghanistan.

Our policy in recruitment requires one year of medical experience prior to sending staff to Afghanistan; however, if this young person would be interested in going as a volunteer translator with the possibility of being able to do some nursing, we would consider her application. A one-year commitment would be expected, her expenses paid by us.

I am enclosing some information to give you a better understanding of our organization. If your interest still remains, please contact the Los Angeles office and speak with Sandy.

Again, thank you for your interest in the people of Afghanistan.

Sincerely,
Robert R. Simon, MD
Chairman of the Board

Jean had an excellent working relationship with the Afghanaid team and was forever grateful for their help and support whilst she was in Pakistan. She was delighted to reciprocate when asked if the organization could use her photographs for a promotional video of their work.

Afghanaid
18 Charing Cross Road
London WC2H OLT

28 June 1988

Dear Jean,

I would like to thank you properly for lending us your transparencies. Thanks in large part to you, I have managed to collect an impressive selection of pictures for our slide/tape show. I am now researching the sound track and preparing the script. The aim is to have a short documentary-type video for donors, schools, and supporters that tells "'the Afghan story'" and explains AfghanAaid's work.

In the meantime, I would like to reassure you that your pictures are safe and that they will be returned as soon as we have finished with them.

I still think you should approach publishers about doing a book.

I hope you are well and that I will see you soon.

With best wishes,
James

Jean's Challenge to the Aid Agencies

Jean had the highest regard for the Voluntary Agencies (VOLAGs) and admired individual aid workers in the camps. Nonetheless, she preferred to act as a free agent. This independence allowed her to reach out to refugees who were left behind unaided, and distanced her from what she sometimes saw as petty bickering, inefficiency, and political interference.

The summer of 1989 found Jean at her home in the UK. Despite the earlier Soviet withdrawal, she knew that the terrors and privations facing refugees continued unabated. She wrote this article to send to various humanitarian organizations and to present at fund-raising events for Afghanistan at which she was a guest speaker.

Ladies and Gentlemen,

In the past eleven years, the number of voluntary agencies (VOLAGs) assisting Afghan refugees in Pakistan has increased dramatically. There are now upwards of one hundred agencies. Nobody can accurately say how many millions of refugees have received and benefited from their assistance.

At the beginning of the mass exodus of Afghan refugees into Pakistan in 1978, the Pakistani government met many emergency needs, mainly tents and blankets, for it was winter and the rainy season. Even some office equipment was provided for the fledgling refugee administration. But decisions had to made quickly: where to *put* the endless stream of humanity; how to ease the trauma of a nation moving into exile; who

318

should register the refugees; how to separate disparate tribal groups; what to do for water, tools to dig latrines, soap to help keep a semblance of cleanliness; where to find firewood for cooking and cooking utensils; how to care for the wounded and general health of the refugee population; and, critically, how to lighten the tremendous burden on the Pakistani government and on the Pakistani villagers near whom the refugees first settled. The list was endless.

Afghan aid groups quickly sprang up all over the world and their representatives rushed to Peshawar. Among the first to note the demand for office space were some of the Pakistani house and property owners. They quickly supplied accommodation for the swelling number of aid workers and for their clinics and their educational and welfare centres: quite naturally, at an immense profit. Barred from owning property, the refugees countered with the virtual takeover of the transportation business which quickly grew to enormous size as the population doubled, trebled, and quadrupled.

The emergency relief agencies moved, oh so slowly, into high gear. Without a central coordinating committee, inevitably there was a repetition of services. Visiting dignitaries would often come laden with blankets—so much so that many refugees were literally smothered with them. Without a proper distribution system, many refugees would sell their surplus blankets to purchase basic necessities. Aid "gifts" such as medical supplies, food, shelter materials, and vehicle parts found their way onto the flourishing black market. The refugee crisis became *big business* for many Pakistani merchants and for those Afghans unscrupulous enough to capitalize on the misfortunes of their countrymen.

The overburdened administration had also to contend with deliveries of inappropriate foods and outdated drugs with instructions in languages incomprehensible for those dispensing them. Small wonder that the refugee tented villages are still considered the dumping ground of irksome national surpluses.

Finally, the UNHCR was invited in. With the relief programme in full swing, health became the highest priority. It is something of a miracle that, in spite of the overcrowding, lack of sanitation, poor water supplies, and meagre food allowances, there has been no epidemic. Now came the eye and dental clinics; the mother-child obstetrics and gynaecological clinics;

nutritional education; midwifery training; vaccinations; and treatment for tuberculosis and for diarrhoea, a big camp killer due to unsanitary habits. Two psychiatric centres were opened, both for men, alongside workshops for the war-wounded and paraplegics where Afghans have learned how to make prosthetics. Trained Afghans have been encouraged to contribute their skills wherever possible.

Today, even the provision of food has been overtaken by the next worst problem—ignorance is greatest. Educational programmes have proliferated, especially to teach English and to train Afghans to teach, although materials and books are hard to come by. Women and girls, of course, are restricted in the camps from attending school; only health classes are permitted.

In like manner, the VOLAGs have established many income-generating programmes to help improve the economic conditions and to try to preserve the Afghan heritage of crafts and skills. Hand embroidery by the women needs marketing, as does carpet weaving, but quilt making, tailoring, shoemaking, plumbing, carpentry, auto mechanics, electricity, masonry, and so on prove useful here and can carry over in years to come. Never before have so many Afghans been within reach of so many development programmes.

Yet, despite the patient determination of the aid workers of the VOLAGs, a great many refugees remain suspicious of any foreign assistance, which they regard as interference. Exile has forced many refugees to abandon their traditional tribal ways, and consequently they suffer a loss of pride, identity, and self-respect. All are at the mercy of loneliness, despair, uncertainty, and fear. Enforced idleness and demoralizing dependency give rise to anger and frustration. Refugees have no papers, which means that their status is always changing. The men need to find employment, the women are sometimes forced to beg or, worse, sell themselves. In fact, the entire refugee way of life threatens the very essence of Afghan culture.

Moreover, from the beginning, Afghan refugees have been forced into a political decision just in order to survive. To get rations, they *must* join a party! They have to pay the mullahs to register. The International Rescue Committee is the only pure aid organization; the others give with strings. This is against human rights. All help, therefore, should and must be non-political.

All surveys are hated, some for being inaccurate and others for just gathering dust with no action taken. I believe the following questions and proposals, coming from first-hand experience and over a period of time, rather than from a flying visit to a "model camp", are more relevant and could make a significant improvement to the lives of the refugees:

1. Why not make a project out of getting medicine for midwives? Why not build a pharmaceutical plant?
2. How about funding an already existing medical training program for graduate doctors?
3. Exactly what plans are proposed for women's development and assistance? Training programmes for Afghan women are desperately needed. Why are they at a standstill?
4. What orientation training is given to European women going to Muslim Pakistan?
5. How do Pakistani or Afghan women view European volunteer workers? Do they offend? If so, how?
6. How do refugee women view volunteer European male workers?
7. How do they regard the programmes offered? What is missing?
8. What do female refugees think the new government ought to do for women?
9. Why do diplomats and aid workers get sent to safety from Kabul? What about the *people* of Kabul? Are they not also worthy of protection?
10. How have the agencies responded to tribal mixing?
11. Are there any rehabilitation programmes inside Afghanistan for injured victims? How will they be helped to readjust to community life and, if possible, become useful?

It will be interesting to see how or if the skills acquired by the refugees will fit into their lives at the time of repatriation. For repatriation is the goal of all refugees. They face three options, but not one of these options is now fully open. Voluntary repatriation is currently elusive, enmeshed as it is in world politics and floundering in tribal warfare. It also runs counter to the growing power of the Communist Afghan government. A second option is local integration, also not feasible because it would destabilize

Pakistan. The third option is resettlement in a third country, which cannot be entertained because of the size, composition, and desires of the majority of the refugees. Therefore, the special requirements of temporary asylum must be continued by the VOLAGs, even though the Soviet army of invasion and occupation has withdrawn some five months ago.

Afghanistan will never be the same. That cannot be denied. It has suffered devastation and destruction within the country on a scale so colossal that we, who have not witnessed it, cannot possibly begin to comprehend what it entails. Afghan refugees in exile have also had to endure endless bombardment, but of a different kind: the well-intentioned but nonetheless destructive foreign influence of the VOLAGs. All of us who are concerned about and who care for the Afghan people and their country should endeavour to help retain the essence of Afghan culture and seek to rekindle the flickering fire of hope, so that once again, it may flourish.

PART 7

Epilogue

Self-Discovery

Reflecting on her stay in Pakistan in 1987, Jean wrote this candid self-appraisal from one of the refugee camps on the eve of her return home to Dorset. No one would have guessed that, at the beginning of this trip, she herself was struggling to overcome deep-set fears for own future, nor that she was also embarking on her own, ultimately, life-affirming journey. With a clear path ahead, she would continue to labour on behalf of Afghan refugees until a few years before her death.

During the night, I had a good review of what has happened to me in these nearly three months in the refugee camps in Pakistan. It was sparked off by yet another encouraging, supportive, and praising letter from my sister, Peg, whose letters have helped me a lot. She is right: books are not written about people like us. But it doesn't matter, for we know in our very souls what good we have given to others, as did our parents before us. With the perspective one acquires with distance, I can now see things in myself that I like. It's taken a long time and has been a very painful process, but I'm there.

I *have* got my confidence back. I have a zest for living and learning, and I am not afraid to attempt to climb mountains. I know my dear mother and father would be proud of my life as it is—one continuous series of hands held out to help others. I can do many things, and this current project proves it. I *will* have the exhibition, I *will* get Habiba's book published, and there is so much more to come.

With all this flowering about me, I shall never really be alone. I've left too many bits and pieces of me with too many people during my sixty-seven and a half years not to feel I've made a contribution to life.

So, I can rest my case because that experience has truly made me see my strengths and be grateful for them.

Refugee Camp, 1987

APPENDICES

Jean's Afghan Timeline

1967 Jean arrives to live and work in Afghanistan during the final years of the monarchy. Zahir Shah has been king for almost forty years.

1973 The Prime Minister, Mohammed Daoud, overthrows his cousin the king and installs himself as the first president of the Republic of Afghanistan.

1978 Jean witnesses the coup d'etat, known as the Saur Revolution. Led by the communist commander Nur Muhammad Taraki, the revolutionary forces kill President Daoud, and Taraki becomes president of Afghanistan in his place.

1979 In another power struggle, Taraki is murdered and replaced by fellow communist Hafizullah Amin who institutes a brutal, if short-lived, regime.
The Soviet Union invades Afghanistan.
Amin is assassinated by Soviet agents and the Soviet favourite, politician Babrak Karmal, is installed as president.
Jean is caught up in the tragic consequences for many of her Afghan friends.

1980 Jean is forced to leave the country and resolves to help those fleeing for their lives into neighbouring Pakistan where they become stateless refugees.

1986   Karmal is replaced by the ruthless Mohammed Najibullah who had been head of the secret police.

1987   Jean holds a fundraising exhibition in Paris under the auspices of Médecins du Monde with Afghan refugee children's drawings and her own photographs.

1988   The Geneva Accords between Afghanistan and Pakistan are signed with the US and USSR as guarantors to secure the withdrawal of Soviet troops and the voluntary return of Afghan refugees.

1989   The last of the defeated Soviet troops leave Afghanistan. One third of the population has been killed or become refugees. Jean writes of the on-going need for the voluntary agencies to continue their support.

1990   Civil war rages between the factions of mujahideen, setting the stage for the rise of the Taliban.
Jean is seriously injured in an automobile accident.

1991   The Soviet Union collapses. Jean recovers and continues to help her extended family of Afghan refugees.

1992   The Peshawar Accords are signed by some of the leaders of the mujahideen factions and the Islamic State of Afghanistan is created.
The mujahideen take Kabul and Najibullah is deposed.
Violent power struggles lead to the Battle of Kabul that lasts for four years.

1996   The Taliban seize Kabul, hang Najibullah and impose Sharia law on the population. Jean despairs, as do so many refugees, of ever being able to return to Afghanistan.

Glossary

Where Jean uses terms in Pashto, Farsi or Urdu, her spelling and definitions have been respected.

Afghani: Name of Afghan currency.

Ashkana: Outdoor assembly or meeting place with the ground often covered with animal hides.

Baksheesh: a bribe or tip.

Baleh: 'Yes' or 'Okay'.

Burqa: The loose, full-length outer garment worn by Muslim women so that they are respectfully and completely covered when in public. It is draped over their heads and bodies with a small net grille or mesh to hide their eyes but which they can see through.

Buzkashi: The fast and furious national sport of Afghanistan, akin to polo. Two teams of horsemen battle fiercely at full gallop to take possession of a goat's carcass in a test of cunning, courage, and strength.

Chador: The loose, full-length, all-enveloping outer garment worn by Muslim women in public, draped over the head and held closely in front under the chin with only the face showing.

Chadri: Name often used for the Afghan *burqa,* usually a sky-blue colour in Kabul.

Chai: Sugary green or black tea, often made with milk, and flavoured with spices such as cardamom and cinnamon.

Chand: How much?

Chapan: A heavy, embroidered winter coat for men.

Charpoy: A traditional Indian-style, low bed strung with ropes used for seating.

Chelou rice: Persian rice dish, flavoured with saffron and cumin, especially favoured for its crunchy crust.

Chokidar: Gatekeeper or caretaker.

Da'yi: Midwife.

Entero-Viroform: Medication for traveller's diarrhoea.

Inshallah: God-willing.

Jihad: A holy war against the enemies of Islam.

Jumma: Friday or Friday prayers in Islam.

Kalash: An ancient indigenous tribe that lives in the remote mountains of Pakistan's northern district of Chitral.

Karakul: Breed of sheep especially prized for its silky, soft grey wool.

Khad: Afghan secret police.

Khoda hafez: Goodbye.

Lapis lazuli: A semi-precious gemstone, highly prized for its rich, deep blue colour, used since antiquity for jewellery and mined primarily in northern Afghanistan.

Muezzin: The cleric who calls Muslims to prayer from the minaret of a mosque.

Mullah: Islamic religious leader and teacher.

Naan: Soft, flat bread cooked in a clay oven.

Namaq: Sold.

Nanawat: Intermediary.

Naswar: A moist, smokeless, powdered tobacco that is taken like snuff or stuffed into the mouth or cheek for lengthy periods of time.

Ne: No.

Potassium permanganate: Used as a general disinfectant and for purifying water.

Pulao rice: Basmati rice cooked in broth seasoned with herbs and spices until golden brown.

Postincha: Fur-trimmed Afghan winter coat, colourfully embroidered on the suede-like outer side and lined inside with soft karakul lambswool.

Qabli pulao: Rice with raisins and carrots.

Roo b'raah: Straight ahead.

Rubab: One of the national musical instruments of Afghanistan. Similar to a lute, it is short-necked and fretted, and carved in one piece from the trunk of a mulberry tree.

Sad: 100 Afghanis.

Sarod: Classical Indian musical instrument, similar to a sitar, but without frets on the neck and producing a deeper, more resonant sound.

Serai: Palace or great house.

Shalwar kameez: A long, tunic-like shirt with loose-fitting trousers, traditionally worn by women in Afghanistan, India and Pakistan.

Sitar: Classical Indian string instrument with a small, pear-shaped body and a long, fretted neck, played by plucking.

Shikara: Wooden, often canopy-covered, and brightly coloured taxi-boats used on Dal Lake in Srinigar (Kashmir).

Shinwari kebab: Rib of lamb made into kebabs, and named after one of the large Pashtun tribes.

Tashakor: Thank you.

Tashnab: Bathroom.

Veena: Similar to a sitar, but with a short, thick neck, often carved into a dragon's head.

VOLAGS: Voluntary Agencies.

Index

Afghanaid   - xx, 175, 176, 179,
    181, 182, 183, 198, 204, 205,
    213, 215, 234, 257, 317

Afghan Women's Organization   -
    24, 25, 26

Afghanistan Centre at Kabul University
    (ACKU)   - xxi

Agency Coordinating Body for Afghan
    Relief (ACBAR)   - 307, 308
Amin, Hazifullah - 265, 266, 329

Austrian Relief Commission
    - 179, 180, 182, 193, 196, 199,
    200, 207, 208, 212

Baghicha refugee camp   - 206, 217

Bazaar- 3, 14, 15, 24, 25, 27, 28, 29,
    43, 51, 64, 66, 76, 77, 78, 83,
    84, 85, 87, 94, 133, 168, 170,
    172, 173, 176, 178, 193, 196,
    200, 204, 209, 214,

BBC   - 103, 104, 107, 111, 119, 257,
    262, 270, 273
Black market   - 109, 173, 176,
    267, 319

Buckland Newton   - 165, 170,
    242, 251, 264, 276, 279

Bukhara - 13, 15

Burqa - 50, 101, 331, 332

Buzkashi   - 15, 16, 17, 331

Chador - 209, 210, 212, 254, 331

Chadri - 50, 65, 87, 101, 194, 332

Chelou rice   - 18, 332

Children's drawings   - xx, 177,
    179, 197, 200, 209, 330

Commission for Afghan Refugees
    - 212

Communist   - xxiv, 18, 100, 101,
    102, 104, 106, 107, 108, 111,
    112, 113, 116, 117, 118, 122,
    172, 213, 246, 250, 265, 266,
    283, 307, 312, 321, 329

Communist Party- 104, 266

Conference of Non-Aligned Countries
    - 105

Cranborne, Lord Robert   - 213, 215

Daoud, Mohammed   - 26, 100, 101, 102, 103, 105, 106, 107, 109, 110, 117, 329

Dari - 46, 102

Deportation   - 260, 262, 263

Divorce - xxiii, 121, 140

Drought - 43, 81, 87, 101

Dupree, Nancy Hatch   - xiii, xiv, xvi, xix, xx, xxi, 290, 307, 311

Family Planning - 101, 141, 142, 180, 200

Farsi   - xxiv, 4, 8, 25, 26, 46, 47, 48, 49, 51, 54, 55, 56, 60, 61, 63, 64, 66, 77, 86, 88, 91, 106, 108, 206, 331,

Geneva Accords - 330

Geneva Convention   - 175

Hindu Kush   - 4, 29, 31, 42, 74, 99, 102, 103, 104, 113

Immigration - xxv, 167, 196, 257, 258, 259, 262, 268, 272, 277, 279, 312,

Indo-Pakistani War   - 80
International Rescue Committee   - 179, 320

Iran   - xiv, 100, 113, 122

Islam - 106, 112, 116, 117, 118, 122, 156, 168, 308, 332

Islamabad   - 166, 167, 169, 172, 215, 242, 252, 254, 259, 309,
Jihad - xiv, 167, 176, 228, 309, 310, 332

Kabul - xiii, xiv, xvi, xx, xxi, xxiii, xxiv, xxvi, 1, 3, 6, 7, 14, 19, 20, 21, 24, 25, 27, 29, 46, 47, 50, 52, 57, 58, 64, 70, 71, 74, 75, 76, 79, 82, 84, 87, 95, 103, 104, 110, 115, 119, 130, 133, 134, 135, 139, 141, 146, 172, 173, 176, 177, 204, 214, 251, 252, 253, 254, 256, 257, 258, 260, 265, 267, 269, 273, 275, 278, 281, 290, 307, 321, 330, 332,

Kalash People   - 314

Karakul sheep   - xxiv, 2, 9, 24, 29, 31, 32

Karakul Institute - 24, 27

Karmal, Babrak - 101, 112, 122, 266, 329, 330,

Khad - 252, 253, 260, 332

Khanabad   - 43, 44, 45

Khyber, Mir Akbar   - 102, 104

Khyber Pass   - 29, 102, 214, 216, 267

Khalq Party   - 118, 121,

Kopf, Rev.   - 269, 270, 277,
     278, 279

Kuchi People   - 11, 154, 158

Kunduz - 3, 7, 8, 9, 14, 15, 18, 19, 20,
     21, 42, 43, 45

Lapis lazuli   - 25, 100, 332

Liquorice root   - xxiv, 1, 2, 115,

Mardan refugee camp   - 182,

Marriage- 134, 138, 145, 151, 152, 194,
     230, 253, 281,

Mazar-i-Sharif   - 45, 118,

Médecins du Monde   - xxv,
     287, 330
Moscow - 10, 29, 101, 102, 266
Mujahideen   - 168, 172, 173, 176,
     178, 181, 183, 184, 205, 209,
     211, 228, 232, 234, 236, 238,
     239, 252, 260, 266, 268, 273,
     282, 288, 330,

Mullah - 100, 112, 122, 159, 195,
     197, 198, 202, 204, 207, 210,
     320, 333,

Naderi Shah   - 100, 101, 108,
     109,114,

Najibullah, Mohammed   - 296, 330
Nasir Bagh refugee camp   - 210,
     212, 214

National Islamic Front for Afghanistan
     (NIFA)   - 168
Operation Salaam- 308,

Parcham - 101, 102, 104, 112, 118,
     120, 121, 122, 283

Pashto- xxiv, 2, 54, 56, 106, 177, 180,
     201, 239, 331,

Pashtun - 11, 54, 67, 100, 174, 334,

People's Democratic Republic of
     Afghanistan   - 111
People's Palace   - 109, 126
Peshawar   - xiii, xxv, xxvii, 167,
     168, 169, 170, 171, 173, 174,
     176, 180, 182, 198, 200, 204,
     205, 207, 214, 220, 240, 242,
     243, 247, 254, 257, 263, 267,
     288, 307, 308, 309, 312, 314,
     315, 319, 330,

Postincha   - xxiv, 1, 24, 40, 333

Potassium permanganate   - 86,
     196, 333

Pulao rice   - 13, 18, 20

Qabli pulao   - 67

Refugee camps   - xiii, xv, xix,

Refugee children - xvi, 256, 287, 289,
     290, 330

Refugee tented village (RTV)   -
     309, 319
Russian invasion of Afghanistan
     - xxiii,

Salang Pass   - 4, 5, 6, 8, 9, 19, 20,
     23, 28

Salang Tunnel   - 7, 21, 102

Sarod - 91, 334
Saur Seven   - 108, 112

Saur Revolution   - xiii, 102, 307, 329

Shalwar kameez   - 171, 178, 334

Sitar   - 27, 90, 91, 334

Soviet-Afghan War   - 314

Soviet Invasion of Afghanistan   -
     xv, xxiv, 307, 315

Ratebzad, Anahita   - 121
Rubab - 90, 333
Segal, Margaret   - 179
Steiner, Gabi   - 179, 180
Taraki, Nur Mohammed   - 101, 102,
     107, 111, 116, 117, 119, 265, 329,

Thatched Cottage - 165, 170, 234, 242,
     250, 264,

United Nations High
     Commission for Refugees
     (UNHCR) - 198, 203, 210, 236,
     266, 309, 319

Veena - 90, 334
Volags - 179, 180, 181, 202, 318, 320,
     322, 334,

Wakkhan Corridor   - 100, 113,

Zamani, Dr. Rahman   - 200, 202,
     203, 261,

41482948R00222

Made in the USA
Middletown, DE
06 April 2019